Rights and the Common Good

THE COMMUNITARIAN PERSPECTIVE

Amitai Etzioni

St. Martin's Press
New York

Executive editor: Don Reisman
Managing editor: Patricia Mansfield-Phelan
Project editor: Amy Horowitz
Production supervisor: Alan Fischer
Art director: Sheree Goodman
Cover design: Rod Hernandez

9 8 7 6 5
f e d c b a

For information, write:
St. Martin's Press, Inc.
175 Fifth Avenue
New York, NY 10010

ISBN: 0-312-08968-6 (paperback)
      0-312-10272-0 (hardcover)

Acknowledgments

It is a violation of the law to reproduce these selections by any means whatsoever without the written permission of the copyright holder. Selections that are not included in the following list were written specifically for this volume.

Mary Ann Glendon. "Rights in Twentieth Century Constitutions." Adapted with permission from the *University of Chicago Law Review* 59 (1992): 519.
Christopher Lasch. "Communitarianism or Populism?" Copyright © 1992 *New Oxford Review.* Reprinted with permission from the *New Oxford Review* (1069 Kains Ave., Berkeley, CA 94706).
Juan Williams. "Japan: The Price of Safe Streets." Copyright © 1991 *The Washington Post.* Reprinted with permission.
Ronald Bayer and Kathleen E. Toomey. "Preventing HIV: Rights, Duties, and Partner Notification." Adapted from the *American Journal of Public Health* 82(8): 1158–64. Copyright © 1992 American Public Health Association. Reprinted with permission.

Acknowledgments and copyrights are continued at the back of the book on page 293, which constitutes an extension of the copyright page.

Preface: We, the Communitarians

Communitarians seek to rebuild community. However, we do not believe that a return to villages or small-town America is necessary. What is needed, rather, is a strengthening of the bonds that tie people to one another, enabling them to overcome isolation and alienation. Above all, it is necessary to reestablish in communities the moral voice that leads people to encourage one another to behave more virtuously than they would otherwise. Communities need to foster civility—a sense of social order and mutual consideration. If they do not, we will be reduced to relying on hordes of inspectors, auditors, police, IRS and INS and FBI agents, of which there are never enough in a society whose moral foundations have crumbled.

Communitarian ideas and ideals have been around at least since the Old Testament. Many of the issues that we explore are discussed in the works of the Ancient Greeks. Early sociologists, such as Émile Durkheim, struggled with them. The editor was trained by a master communitarian, Martin Buber. More recently, the term has been associated with the works of Charles Taylor, Hans Joas, Jonathan Boswell, Adam Swift, Michael Sandel, Michael Walzer, and Philip Selznick, among others. There are several collections of communitarian essays and a major review work (Robert Booth Fowler, *The Dance with Community*, Lawrence: University of Kansas Press, 1991). Here, in *Rights and the Common Good*, rather than retrace these origins or provide one more overview, we focus mainly on the two core communitarian issues: the balance between individual rights and social responsibilities, and the roles of social institutions that foster moral values within communities.

Recently, communitarian thinking has broadened from an intellectual trend into a growing movement in which the editor takes an active part. In 1990 a group of fifteen ethicists, social philosophers, and social scientists met in Washington, D.C., at the invitation of the editor and his colleague, William Galston. As we explored matters that afflict our society, we expressed our distaste for the effects of tele-democracy—the polarization of debate and public life dominated by "sound bites." We were troubled by pressures to be labeled either conservative or liberal, Pro-Life or Pro-Choice, for or against the death penalty. We were disturbed that a person is under duress to be for free trade or be labeled a Japan-basher; to be for immigration (presumably unlimited) or be called a racist (because some of those who seek to restrict immigration seek to apply limits to certain kinds of people); and so on. (I refer to this malaise as "the curse of either/or.") Many issues, we suggested, could not be properly discussed using such simplistic, stark, oppositional terms. And we saw the reaction "If you are not for us, you must be against us," as unnecessarily divisive, as antagonistic to the spirit of community.

More deeply, we were troubled that many Americans are rather reluctant to accept responsibilities. We were distressed that many Americans are eager to spell out what they are entitled to, but are slow to give something back to others and to the community. We adopted the name "communitarian" to emphasize that the time had come to attend to our responsibilities to our communities.

Communitarians recognize a need for a new conceptual, social, and philosophical map. The designation of camps as liberal or conservative, as Left or Right, often no longer serves. At one extreme we see authoritarians (such as the Moral Majority and Liberty Bell) who urge the imposition of their moral positions on all others. They insist on prayer in schools and would force women to "stay in the kitchen." At the other end of the spectrum we see radical individualists (libertarians, such as the intellectuals at the Cato Institute; civil libertarians, especially the American Civil Liberties Union; and laissez-faire conservatives) who believe that if individuals are left on their own to pursue their choices, rights, and self-interests, all will be well. For our part, we suggest that free individuals require a community that protects them from encroachment by the state and sustains morality by drawing on the gentle prodding of kin, friends, neighbors, and other community members. As a source for guiding behavior, this moral encouragement is preferable to government controls or fear of authorities.

The communitarian movement seeks to shore up the moral, social, and political foundations of society. It builds on the elementary social science observation that people are born without any moral or social values. If they are to become civil, they must acquire values. Later, they may rebel against these values or seek to modify them, but first they must have them. Historically, the family was the societal entity entrusted with laying the foundation for moral education. Schools were the second line of defense. Community bonds— whether centered around religious institutions, schools, town meetings, or other establishments—served to reinforce values that had been previously acquired. These social institutions were the seedbeds of virtue in which values were planted and cultivated.

We find that in contemporary society, to a significant extent, these seedbeds have been allowed to whither. We should not be surprised, then, that the young ignore our entreaties to "just say no" to the numerous temptations society puts in their way, or that children kill children without showing remorse.

We need to restore the seedbeds of virtue if society is to regain civility. Such restoration does not entail a simple return to the traditional past, a past that had its own defects—a society that discriminated against women and minorities and was at least a bit authoritarian. Specifically, we need first to expect that both mothers and fathers dedicate themselves to their children and that as a community we again value children. We must enable parents to be parents by providing for more flexible work hours, opportunities to work at home, paid leave when children are born (as is the case in Europe), and a reduction of the marriage penalty in the tax code.

Schools must put character education at the top of their agendas and not permit the pressure to increase academic achievements to crowd it out. Educators must be aware that everything that happens in schools sends a message to students. Are school corridors, parking areas, and cafeterias disorderly danger zones or places where people learn to respect one another? Are sports used to teach that winning is the only thing or that playing by the rules is essential? Are grades handed out on the basis of hard work or some other social criteria? Schools need to engage in self-evaluation and should recognize and prioritize their goals so that they reinforce rather than undermine the educational message they are supposed to carry.

Communities happen, to a large extent, in public spaces. When our parks, sidewalks, squares, and other public spaces are threatened by crime, communities are thwarted. Community policing, neighborhood crime watches, drug checkpoints, and domestic disarmament are among the new devices that may help communities recapture them. Above all, we need to increase the certitude that those who commit a crime will be punished. This guarantee of a consequence is more important than an increase in the size of a penalty. And needless to say, if families and schools do a better job of transmitting values, the communities' public safety burdens will grow lighter.

Finally, civility requires that the vigilant protection of rights not evolve into extremism in which new rights are manufactured at will (such as the "right" to rent a car or the right of women to use the men's room) and in which each right is treated as an absolute. The Constitution opens by directing the federal government to attend to the general welfare, the common good. The courts have long balanced individual rights with social responsibilities. They have authorized sobriety checkpoints, screening gates at airports, and drug testing for those who have the lives of others directly in their hands. A civil society requires careful nurturing of both rights and responsibilities—not the dominance of one at the expense of the other.

To further develop communitarian ideas and to share our thinking with our fellow community members, in January 1991 we started a communitarian quarterly, *The Responsive Community: Rights and Responsibilities.*

On November 18, 1991, at a 1960s-style Teach-In, we issued a communitarian platform, summarizing our approach and listing our basic positions (included in this book). Seventy community leaders, from many walks of life, joined us in signing the platform. As active citizens, we shared the communitarian platform with those already in office as well as with those running for office, and with those to whom they are accountable—our fellow citizens. At the Teach-In, we saw the first signs of interest not only in the public at large but also among our elected officials, as four senators—two Democrats (Al Gore and Daniel Patrick Moynihan) and two Republicans (Dave Durenberger and Alan Simpson)—joined us in our discussions. Strong letters of support followed from Senator Bill Bradley of New Jersey and then Secretary of Housing and Urban Development Jack Kemp. In 1993 we took the next step by launching a communitarian membership association, the Communitarian Network, to serve as the organized core of the communitarian movement.

Rights and the Common Good is about the intellectual framework of the communitarian approach, about communitarian ideas and concepts, the questions that challenge communitarian thinking, and the answers it is groping with.

ACKNOWLEDGMENTS

I would like to acknowledge the work of W. Bradford Wilcox, my research assistant, who proved invaluable in helping to put this volume together. By lending a hand with editorial comments and the process of compiling articles and nudging authors along, he helped ensure that the book came to press. Bill Thomas put the volume to bed.

Finally, I want to thank the reviewers at St. Martin's Press, who provided useful guidance in bringing this volume to completion: Richard Flacks, University of California—Santa Barbara; David M. O'Brien, University of Virginia; Larry D. Spence, Pennsylvania State University; Clyde Wilcox, Georgetown University; and Leonard Williams, Manchester College.

This book has a complementary volume entitled *Communitarian Thinking: New Essays* (University of Virginia Press, 1994). Communitarians of all stripes were invited to contribute to one of these two volumes. We hope in future editions of these books to include the work of those who were unable to participate at this time and to include communitarian writings from earlier generations.

Amitai Etzioni

Contents

Introduction

AMITAI ETZIONI

Societies, like bicycles, teeter and need continuously to be pulled back to the center lest they lean too far toward anarchy or tyranny. The current legal and moral commitment to guaranteeing individual rights grew out of a concern about protecting persons from government excesses. The current commitment to advancing social responsibilities, on the other hand, reflects a concern that social institutions be properly nourished rather than abandoned. Because no society is ever perfectly balanced, communitarians seek to discern the direction a society is leaning at any one point in history and to cast their weight on the other side. Thus, in Albania, China, or even the former Soviet Union, a communitarian would fight for expanding and enshrining individual rights. In the United States, at the onset of the 1990s, communitarians felt that social responsibilities particularly needed shoring up.[1] Note that we do not suggest that responsibilities should replace rights or vice versa. On the contrary, they require one another. Strong rights presume strong responsibilities.

A finding from a poll illustrates the issue. The poll, reported by Morris Janowitz, found that young Americans believed that they had a right to trial by jury but were rather reluctant to serve on one.[2] This position is, first of all, illogical. It ignores the fact that if one's peers will not serve there will be no jury of one's peers. On a deeper level, it fails to recognize that rights and responsibilities are corollaries, two sides of the same coin: one person's right is a claim on another's responsibility. Finally, it is a morally defective viewpoint: people are seeking to take and not to give. No society can survive if people only want rights and are unwilling to assume responsibilities.

Where is the point of balance, the elusive center? How do we decide that in a particular area an imbalance needs to be corrected? Following are four criteria that must be applied together in making such a decision.

1

1. ESTABLISHING A CLEAR AND PRESENT DANGER

No adjustments should be implemented unless there is a clear and present danger—a real, readily verifiable, sizable social problem or need. Unfortunately, in a media-centered society, prophets of alarm rapidly gain wide audiences. There are frequent calls on policymakers and citizens alike to tighten their belts and modify their life-styles, as well as demands for laws and constitutional protection to combat some imagined or anticipated scourge. For example, in the mid-1970s Americans were told that they must be forced out of cars and into mass transit because the United States was running out of oil. More recently, they were told that America must introduce central planning in the workplace in order to compete with the Japanese. And so on.

If policymakers and citizens were to respond to every cry of "wolf," society would frequently be run through the ringer, shaken, and rearranged at great cost. Unfortunately, on most issues it is nearly impossible to discern well in advance which dangers are real and which are wildly exaggerated, if not outrightly false. Hence, we reluctantly conclude that it is best to try not to predict too far into the future. Instead, we should embrace the humbler posture of not acting (especially in a grand way that involves major economic and human costs and diminutions of liberties) until a clear and present danger exists. Because the evidence that they endanger large numbers of lives, if not the very fabric of society is incontestable, we believe that nuclear weapons, handguns, AIDS, and drugs are clear and present dangers. Killer bees, on the other hand, are not clear and present dangers, and global warming may not justify the kind of draconian measures that have been advocated recently.

Clear and present danger can also be determined when there is a direct link between a cause and an effect. If a man points a machine gun at another person's head, for example, we have the right to take away the man's property—that is, the gun—and to wrestle him to the ground. The danger is clear and present. At the same time we would not condone, indeed we would penalize, the same conduct if we only suspected that the gun owner might so use his weapon.

An actual case illustrates the issue at hand. After several train wrecks involving engineers impaired by drugs or alcohol, the U.S. Department of Transportation maintained that random testing of train engineers for drugs and alcohol was warranted. Radical individualists opposed the policy for the usual reasons: only individualized case-by-case evidence of "probable cause" was proper ground, they said. They also claimed that it would even be improper to test an engineer stumbling away after a wreck unless there was evidence that he or she was drinking or was taking drugs. In February 1988, a federal appeals court in California agreed with these individualists, ruling that it was unconstitutional to administer drug tests to those who drive trains.

However, the following evidence suggests that there may be a direct link between the drug and alcohol abuse of train engineers and train wrecks. A 1979 study found that 23 percent of railroad operating employees were "problem drinkers," many of whom had gotten drunk on the job. Of all the train accidents between 1975 and 1984, drugs or alcohol were "directly effecting" causes in 48 of them, accounting for 37 fatalities and 80 injuries. Since then, the danger seems only to have become worse. Out of 179 railroad accidents in 1987, the engineers in 39 of the cases tested positive for drugs, 34 percent more than in 1986. In a January 1987 crash, 16 people died and 174 were injured when an Amtrak train was struck by a Conrail train. Both the engineer and brakeman on the train were under the influence of marijuana.

When 23 percent of railway employees—that is, nearly one out of four—is affected by this problem, and when railway employees directly deal with life and death, we would hold that *not* testing train engineers and other high-risk groups, such as airline pilots, for drugs and alcohol presents a clear and present danger to society.

2. EXAMINING OPTIONS TO CONSTITUTIONAL REINTERPRETATIONS

Each year over 300,000 people in the United States die from smoking. Assume we agree as a community that because the human toll is so great, we should discourage smoking, especially among the young (over 87 percent of present-day smokers began before they were 21). Moreover, assume we agree that the link between smoking and ill health is sufficiently strong for smoking to be considered a direct cause, thereby justifying a publicly initiated effort to change behavior. Even if we accept the radical individualist notion that people ought to be free to choose their own purchases, even if self-injurious, we can argue that smoking harms others. Passive smoking accounts for approximately 2,400 cases of lung cancer per year, and in 1986 approximately 1,600 people died as a result of fires caused by smoking. And finally, people overwhelmingly show that their real preference is to stop; that 90 percent of smokers have tried to quit is a signal that they want help.

Now assume further that these findings, if they hold under continued scrutiny, indicate a clear and present danger; it does not yet follow that we need to reinterpret the Constitution. First, we ought to look for ways that do not require any tampering with the Constitution. Armed with this criterion, we might conclude that raising taxes on cigarettes is more justifiable than prohibiting cigarette ads. First, the result is more efficient; a 10 percent increase in price is reported to correlate with a 12 percent decrease in demand. Other studies corroborate this correlation by demonstrating that young people's taste for cigarettes is highly controlled by price. On the other hand, although advertising may persuade some young people to pick up the smoking habit, it is widely agreed that its main effect is to shift smokers from one brand to another.

Second, and more to our point, we should note that curbing ads raises constitutional issues of freedom of speech, whereas raising taxes does not. Hence, even if prohibiting ads proved to be more efficient, raising taxes would still be preferable as long as we could show that cigarette ads were not significantly more influential than prices.

3. LIMITING ADJUSTMENTS AS MUCH AS POSSIBLE

If there is no effective alternative to adjusting the constitutional balance between individual rights and social responsibilities, we must look for options that will make the most minimal intrusion possible, rather than proceeding with a policy sledgehammer.

The debate over *Miranda* rights provides a good example of how we might find ways to trim rather than pound. In recent years, *Miranda* has been criticized for excessively favoring criminals. The extent to which the ruling actually hobbles the police and prosecutors is a much debated, much scrutinized topic. Whether recent court rulings have sharply or only moderately affected the reach of *Miranda* it is difficult to tell. However, over the last ten years, the balance has tilted somewhat away from rights for criminals and toward greater public safety. Our concern here is to illustrate what a reasonable intermediary position on *Miranda* would be rather than to examine the intricacies of these issues.

At one extreme of this discussion is the radical individualist position that no changes to *Miranda* should be made whatsoever, as if this rather recent legal tradition, one that did not go into effect until 1966, had the standing of the Bill of Rights and the sanction of the Founding Fathers. At the other extreme, authoritarians argue that many *Miranda* rights accord criminals more constitutional protection than is afforded their victims. Former Attorney General Edwin Meese wanted to do away with *Miranda* altogether because, he said, "it provides incentives for criminals not to talk" and "only helps guilty defendants." The Office of Legal Policy of the U.S. Attorney General under the Reagan administration even issued a position paper that called for a wholesale overturning of *Miranda*.

A reasonable intermediary position seems to be to let evidence stand, even if a technical error was made in its collection, as long as (1) there is no indication of bad faith and (2) the error is recorded in the relevant personnel file at the appropriate law enforcement agency to avoid any repetition of such error. This position was found acceptable in a 1985 Supreme Court case when a suspect had confessed to a crime before he was read his Miranda rights, was later informed of his rights, and then confessed again. The Court unanimously agreed that the first confession could not be used as evidence even if given voluntarily and without coercion, but it ruled 6 to 3 that the unsolicited admission of guilt did not taint the second confession. In a similar decision in 1987, the Supreme Court ruled that the police are not required to tell a suspect about each crime for which he or she may be questioned.

Another example of a carefully honed adjustment is the introduction of some restrictions on the inadmissibility of evidence uncovered by the police during a discovery procedure that was technically flawed. In *United States v. Leon*, the police believed they had a search warrant for a house in which they had gathered incriminating evidence. Later, they discovered that the clerk had written the address incorrectly on the warrant. In 1984 the Supreme Court ruled that the evidence gathered should not be excluded on the basis of the technical mistake.

The debate over the rights of students provides still another example of a reasonable intermediary position on the issue of limiting adjustments. Many observers agree that both the substantive rights of public school students and their due process rights have reached a level that has made it difficult for public schools to function. Linda Bruin, legal counsel for the Michigan Association of School Boards, writes, "Following the split decision in *Goss v. Lopez*, 419 US 565 (1975), which struck down an Ohio statute permitting student suspensions from school without a hearing, educators expressed fears that they no longer would be able to discipline students efficiently."[3] The subject is complicated by the fact that procedures for disciplining students vary from state to state.

What is an intermediary position between according students full-fledged Fourth Amendment rights when they are threatened with disciplinary action, and declaring students fair game to any capricious school authority? It seems reasonable that students who are subject to expulsion should be granted due process; that is, they should be notified of the nature of their misconduct and given an opportunity to respond before expulsion takes place. Still, the threat of expulsion need not guarantee students the right to counsel or the right to call for cross-examination and the testimony of witnesses; this would unduly encumber the ability of schools to maintain an educational environment. Moreover, schools should be allowed to maintain additional restrictions and simplified procedures because they are meant to be small, cohesive communities rather than adversarial environments. Far from this being a novel approach, several state courts have already modified school policies in the directions we suggest.

To reduce the danger of slipping down the slope toward excessive duties, it is important to draw additional moral and legal "notches" along the way. Thus, students need not be provided with the right to due process when they want to protest a grade, but that right must be upheld for those students threatened with expulsion. Stemming drug abuse is another area where a limited adjustment of due process could be considered. Radical individualists strongly oppose any modification of due process, searches, seizures, and tests without compelling case-by-case evidence that modification is justified. Authoritarians, on the other hand, would suspend such constitutional protections to "win the war on drugs." Some communitarians, like the author, seek intermediate principled "notches" and find, for example, that a strong case can be made for random searches of automobiles on public highways, but not for random searches of homes. Autos are an optional means of transportation, convey passengers on public territory, and travel in places where behavior under the influence of drugs may affect others; in contrast, homes are true castles, truly private, and what we do in them is much less likely to harm others.

Another reasonable measure would be to require people who drive into open-air drug markets to show their driver's license and car registration. This situation actually arose in Inkster, Michigan, a small community just outside Detroit (see Chapter 7), where the drug trade was so rampant that the local residents could rarely go into the streets and lived in constant fear for their lives and the corruption of their children. The county sheriff set up roadblocks from midnight to six A.M. each night, checking drivers' licenses and registrations. The tactic broke up the open drug market but had to be stopped when the ACLU intervened in local court.

One more option that may help abate open-air drug trafficking is the proposal by the mayor of Alexandria, Virginia, to arrest those who are "loitering for purposes of engaging in an unlawful drug transaction." Unlike old loitering laws that the police historically used to harass minorities, the new "loitering plus" statutes are designed to prevent discriminatory arrests by defining eight conditions that must be met before an arrest can be made. For example, the person must be present in a drug-trafficking area for more than fifteen minutes, during which time he or she must have face-to-face contact with more than one person involving actions indicating that they are concealing an object to be exchanged.

New measures designed to reduce the constitutional impact of these adjustments have been enacted, and others may follow. In June 1990, the Supreme Court approved roadside sobriety checkpoints, which the ACLU had successfully opposed in several states. A court majority argued that the checkpoints, which last less than 90 seconds, are minimally intrusive. The intrusion of the checkpoints can be diminished even further if the authorities systematically and repeatedly inform drivers that such checkpoints are being operated, without disclosing their precise locations. This hardly detracts from their efficiency, but it makes them less threatening to legal traditions; once the potential of a search on a given road is posted, travel thereon can be construed as implied consent. (True, the courts have ruled that a person's agreement to be subject to unreasonable procedures is not valid, even if given before the fact; however, these checkpoints are reasonable.) Similarly, several courts have ruled that job requirements for all train engineers, air traffic controllers, police officers, and other workers whose professions entail high risk to the public may include consent to be subject to drug and alcohol tests. (Workers may be given a year's time to relocate if they refuse to accept the requirement.)

Aside from legal considerations, matters concerning practical burdens are involved. For example, the courts may correctly object to sobriety test points that create major traffic jams. They can insist that safe places be provided for drivers to pull off the road, that drivers have adequate warning that they must stop, and so on. Indeed, the fact that these tests last less than two minutes is in their favor. The argument that random urine tests are highly intrusive is quite compelling, but so is the fact that the roadblocks and highway sobriety checks in Michigan are less invasive.

Although it is convenient to distinguish between legal and practical considerations of an adjustment, it should be noted that they are intertwined. To wit, burdens imposed by the government on a practice could rise to a point where they would become a form of undue government harassment—one of the main abuses against which the Bill of Rights is meant to protect us.

In short, far from yielding to demands that the authorities gun down any private airplane or speedboat that approaches a U.S. border unidentified, break down the doors of people's homes at midnight, quarantine all HIV-positive persons, and so on, to combat drugs and AIDS, we see justifications for introducing many measures that are minimally intrusive, in either legal or practical terms. Thus, sobriety checkpoints; searches of cars on public roads; roadblocks on roads leading to open-air drug markets; testing of train engineers, pilots, air traffic controllers, and other individuals whose jobs entail high risk to others; and a requirement that people with AIDS disclose the identity of their sexual partners, if the precautions indicated are taken, are both overdue and legitimate.

4. MAKING SPECIAL EFFORTS TO MINIMIZE OR AVOID SIDE EFFECTS

We should also take pains to reduce the deleterious impacts of a given policy. For example, if confidentiality is not maintained, AIDS testing and contact-tracing can lead to a person losing his or her job and health insurance. Hence, such a program should be accompanied by a thorough review of the controls limiting access to lists of the names of those tested; professional education programs on the need for confidentiality; and penalties for unauthorized disclosure of HIV status and for discrimination against people with AIDS or HIV carriers. These measures may seem cumbersome, but are clearly appropriate in view of the great danger AIDS poses for individuals and the high cost to society.

A good example of a limited crime-prevention program that has kept negative side effects to a minimum, and as a result has enhanced its own acceptability, are airport X rays and metal detectors. These devices allow for the confiscation of weapons that could otherwise be brought on board, and thus help prevent hijacking. The searches are deliberately not used to stop drug trafficking and other crimes.

Taken together, these criteria may guide policymakers, legislatures, judges, and fellow citizens as they ask which new social responsibilities they should add, which old ones they should honor, which individual rights are fundamental, and which ones must be trimmed to make room for new mores and policies, all in the name of enabling society—in which all rights ultimately are anchored—to be sustained. Much of this book is dedicated to exploring the variety of ways in which we can redress the balance of rights and responsibilities.

THE ROLE OF VIRTUE

Another way to approach the same subject is to realize the deeper context of the issue before us. At stake is the question "What constitutes the good society, the virtuous society?" Not everybody agrees that this question should be asked, let alone answered. Radical individualists argue that once a certain conduct is defined as virtuous, then an essential foundation of our society is undermined. They fear that those members of society who fail to display the characteristics considered virtuous will be treated as inferior, if they are not discriminated against outright.

Communitarians argue that a society without some shared virtues cannot exist. A society cannot tolerate a condition in which all behavior is considered of equal merit. We must condemn not merely murder, rape, robbery, and other behaviors we call crimes (that is, counter to virtue), but also the destruction of the environment, discrimination against others, and many behaviors that endanger the sustainability of our communities and the values we hold dear. Moreover, the ultimate defense against intolerance is not to regard all behavior as equally meritorious but to consider mutual respect a key societal strength. It is within a healthy social context that social responsibilities and individual rights find their ultimate home. Struggling to ensure that both are well attended to goes a long way to make a society virtuous.[4]

NOTES

1. See Amitai Etzioni, "What Fascists?" *The Responsive Community* (Winter 1990–1991), 1(1), pp. 12–13 and the Communitarian Platform.
2. Morris Janowitz, *The Reconstruction of Patriotism: Education for Civic Consciousness* (Chicago: University of Chicago Press, 1983), p. 8.
3. Linda L. Bruin, "School Discipline: Recent Developments in Student Due Process Rights," *Michigan Bar Journal*, November 1989, p. 1066.
4. For additional discussion, see Amitai Etzioni, *The Spirit of Community* (New York: Crown Publishers, 1993); Robert Bellah et al., *The Good Society* (New York: Alfred A. Knopf, 1991); and William Galston, *Liberal Purposes* (New York: Cambridge University Press, 1991).

The Responsive Communitarian Platform: Rights and Responsibilities

PREAMBLE

American men, women, and children are members of many communities—families; neighborhoods; innumerable social, religious, ethnic, work place, and professional associations; and the body politic itself. Neither human existence nor individual liberty can be sustained for long outside the interdependent and overlapping communities to which all of us belong. Nor can any community long survive unless its members dedicate some of their attention, energy, and resources to shared projects. The exclusive pursuit of private interest erodes the network of social environments on which we all depend, and is destructive to our shared experiment in democratic self-government. For these reasons, we hold that the rights of individuals cannot long be preserved without a communitarian perspective.

A communitarian perspective recognizes both individual human dignity and the social dimension of human existence.

A communitarian perspective recognizes that the preservation of individual liberty depends on the active maintenance of the institutions of civil society where citizens learn respect for others as well as self-respect; where we acquire a lively sense of our personal and civic responsibilities, along with an appreciation of our own rights and the rights of others; where we develop the skills of self-government as well as the habit of governing ourselves, and learn to serve others—not just self.

A communitarian perspective recognizes that communities and polities, too, have obligations—including the duty to be responsive to their members and to foster participation and deliberation in social and political life.

A communitarian perspective does not dictate particular policies; rather, it mandates attention to what is often ignored in contemporary policy debates: the social side of human nature; the responsibilities that must be borne by citizens, individually and collectively, in a regime of rights; the fragile ecology of families and their supporting communities; the ripple effects and long-term consequences of present decisions. The political views of the signers of this statement differ widely. We are united, however, in our conviction that a communitarian perspective must be brought to bear on the great moral, legal, and social issues of our time.

Moral Voices

America's diverse communities of memory and mutual aid are rich resources of moral voices—voices that ought to be heeded in a society that increasingly threatens to become normless, self-centered, and driven by greed, special interests, and an unabashed quest for power.

Moral voices achieve their effect mainly through education and persuasion rather than through coercion. Originating in communities, and sometimes embodied in law, they exhort, admonish, and appeal to what Lincoln called the better angels of our nature. They speak to our capacity for reasoned judgment and virtuous action. It is precisely because this important moral realm, which is neither one of random individual choice nor of government control, has been much neglected that we see an urgent need for a communitarian social movement to accord these voices their essential place.

Within History

The basic communitarian quest for balances between individuals and groups, rights and responsibilities, and among the institutions of state, market, and civil society is a constant, ongoing enterprise. Because this quest takes place within history and within varying social contexts, however, the evaluation of what is a proper moral stance will vary according to circumstances of time and place. If we were in China today, we would argue vigorously for more individual rights; in contemporary America, we emphasize individual and social responsibilities.

Not Majoritarian but Strongly Democratic

Communitarians are not majoritarians. The success of the democratic experiment in ordered liberty (rather than unlimited license) depends not on fiat or force, but on building shared values, habits, and practices that assure respect for one another's rights and regular fulfillment of personal, civic, and collective responsibilities. Successful policies are accepted because they are recognized to be legitimate, rather than imposed. We say to those who would impose civic or moral virtues by suppressing dissent (in the name of religion, patriotism, or any other cause), or censoring books, that their cure is ineffective, harmful, and morally untenable. At the same time divergent moral positions need not lead to cacophony. Out of genuine dialogue clear voices can arise, and shared aspirations can be identified and advanced.

Communitarians favor strong democracy. That is, we seek to make government more representative, more participatory, and more responsive to all members of the community. We seek to find ways to accord citizens more information, and more say, more often. We seek to curb the role of private money, special interests, and corruption in government. Similarly, we ask how "private governments," whether corporations, labor unions, or voluntary associations, can become more responsive to their members and to the needs of the community.

Communitarians do not exalt the group as such, nor do they hold that any set of group values is ipso facto good merely because such values originate in a community. Indeed, some communities (say, neo-Nazis) may foster reprehensible values. Moreover, communities that glorify their own members by vilifying those who do not belong are at best imperfect. Communitarians recognize—indeed, insist—that communal values must be judged by external and overriding criteria, based on shared human experience.

A responsive community is one whose moral standards reflect the basic human needs of all its members. To the extent that these needs compete with one another, the community's standards reflect the relative priority accorded by members to some needs over others. Although individuals differ in their needs, human nature is not totally malleable. Although individuals are deeply influenced by their communities, they have a capacity for independent judgment. The persistence of humane and democratic culture, as well as individual dissent, in Eastern Europe and the Soviet Union demonstrate the limits of social indoctrination.

For a community to be truly responsive—not only to an elite group, a minority or even the majority, but to all its members and all their basic human needs—it will have to develop moral values that meet the following criteria: they must be nondiscriminatory and applied equally to all members; they must be generalizable, justified in terms that are accessible and understandable: for example, instead of claims based on individual or group desires, citizens would draw on a common definition of justice; and they must incorporate the full range of legitimate needs and values rather than focusing on any one category, be it individualism, autonomy, interpersonal caring, or social justice.

RESTORING THE MORAL VOICE

History has taught that it is a grave mistake to look to a charismatic leader to define and provide a moral voice for the polity. Nor can political institutions effectively embody moral voices unless they are sustained and criticized by an active citizenry concerned about the moral direction of the community. To rebuild America's moral foundations, to bring our regard for individuals and their rights into a better relationship with our sense of personal and collective responsibility, we must therefore begin with the institutions of civil society.

Start with the Family

The best place to start is where each new generation acquires its moral anchoring: at home, in the family. We must insist once again that bringing children into the world entails a moral responsibility to provide not only material necessities, but also moral education and character formation.

Moral education is not a task that can be delegated to babysitters, or even professional child-care centers. It requires close bonding of the kind that typically is formed only with parents, if it is formed at all.

Fathers and mothers, consumed by "making it" and consumerism, or preoccupied with personal advancement, who come home too late and too tired to attend to the needs of their children, cannot discharge their most elementary duty to their children and their fellow citizens.

It follows, that *work places* should provide maximum flexible opportunities to parents to preserve an important part of their time and energy, of their life, to attend to their educational-moral duties, for the sake of the next generation, its civic and moral character, and its capacity to contribute economically and socially to the commonweal. Experiments such as those with unpaid and paid parental leave, flextime, shared jobs, opportunities to work at home, and for parents to participate as volunteers and managers in child-care centers should be extended and encouraged.

Above all, what we need is a *change in orientation* by both parents and work places. Child-raising is important, valuable work, work that must be honored rather than denigrated by both parents and the community.

Families headed by single parents experience particular difficulties. Some single parents struggle bravely and succeed in attending to the moral education of their children, while some married couples shamefully neglect their moral duties toward their offspring. However, the weight of the historical, sociological, and psychological evidence suggests that on average *two-parent families are better able to discharge their child-raising duties* if only because there are more hands—and voices—available for the task. Indeed, couples often do better when they are further backed up by a wider circle of relatives. The issue has been wrongly framed when one asks what portion of parental duties grandparents or other helpers can assume. Their assistance is needed in addition to, not as a substitute for, parental care. Child-raising is by nature labor-intensive. There are no labor-saving technologies, and shortcuts in this area produce woefully deficient human beings, to their detriment and ours.

It follows that *widespread divorce*, when there are children involved, especially when they are in their formative years, is indicative of a serious social problem. Though divorces are necessary in some situations, many are avoidable and are *not in the interest of the children*, the community, and probably not of most adults either. Divorce laws should be modified, not to prevent divorce, but to signal society's concern.

Above all, we should cancel the message that divorce puts an end to responsibilities among members of a child-raising family. And the best way to cancel that message is to reform the economic aspects of divorce laws so that the enormous financial burden of marriage dissolution no longer falls primarily on minor children and those parents who are their principal caretakers. Just as we recognized in the 1960s that it was unjust to apply to consumers laws that were fashioned for the dealings of merchants with one another, we must now acknowledge that it is a mistake to handle divorces involving couples with young children with a set of rules that was tailored mainly to the needs and desires of warring husbands and wives alone. The principle of "children first" should be fundamental to property settlements and support awards.

Schools—The Second Line of Defense

Unfortunately, millions of American families have weakened to the point where their capacity to provide moral education is gravely impaired. And the fact is that communities have only a limited say over what families do. At best, it will take years before a change in the moral climate restores parenting to its proper status and function for many Americans.

Thus, by default, schools now play a major role, for better or worse, in character formation and moral education. Personal and communal responsibility come together here, for education requires the commitment of all citizens, not merely those who have children in school.

We strongly urge that all educational institutions, from kindergartens to universities, recognize and take seriously the grave responsibility to provide moral education. Suggestions that schools participate actively in moral education are often opposed. The specter of religious indoctrination is quickly evoked, and the question is posed: "Whose morals are you going to teach?"

Our response is straightforward: *we ought to teach those values Americans share*, for example, that the dignity of all persons ought to be respected, that tolerance is a virtue and discrimination abhorrent, that peaceful resolution of conflicts is superior to violence, that generally truth-telling is morally superior to lying, that democratic government is morally superior to totalitarianism and authoritarianism, that one ought to give a day's work for a day's pay, that saving for one's own and one's country's future is better than squandering one's income and relying on others to attend to one's future needs.

The fear that our children will be "brainwashed" by a few educators is farfetched. On the contrary, to silence the schools in moral matters simply means that the youngsters are left exposed to all other voices and values but those of their educators. For, one way or another, moral education does take place in schools. The only question is whether schools and teachers will passively stand by, or take an active and responsible role.

Let us note that moral education takes place least in classroom lectures (although these have a place) and is only in a limited measure a matter of developing moral reasoning. To a much greater extent, moral education is fostered through personal example and above all through fostering the proper institutional culture—from corridors and cafeteria to the parking lot and sports. In effect, the whole school should be considered as a set of experiences generating situations in which young people either learn the values of civility, sharing, and responsibility to the common good or of cheating, cut-throat competition, and total self-absorption.

Education must be reorganized to achieve a better integration between work and schooling. Educators need to search for ways to connect schooling with activities that make sense to young people; and the many businesses who employ high school students part-time ought to recognize that they are educators too. These early work experiences will either reinforce responsible habits and attitudes, or will serve as lessons in poor civics and deficient work ethics.

WITHIN COMMUNITIES

A Matter of Orientation

The ancient Greeks understood this well: A person who is completely private is lost to civic life. The exclusive pursuit of one's self-interest is not even a good prescription for conduct in the marketplace; for no social, political, economic, or moral order can survive that way. Some measure of caring, sharing, and *being our brother's and sister's keeper* is essential if we are not all to fall back on an ever more expansive government, bureaucratized welfare agencies, and swollen regulations, police, courts, and jails.

Generally, no social task should be assigned to an institution that is larger than necessary to do the job. What can be done by families should not be assigned to an intermediate group—school and so on. What can be done at the local level should not be passed on to the state or federal level, and so on. There are, of course, plenty of urgent tasks—environmental ones—that do require national and even international action. But to remove tasks to higher levels than is necessary weakens the constituent communities. This principle holds for duties of attending to the sick, troubled, delinquent, homeless, and new immigrants; and for public safety, public health, and protection of the environment—from a neighborhood crime watch to CPR to sorting the garbage. The government should step in only to the extent that other social subsystems fail, rather than seek to replace them.

At the same time, vulnerable communities should be able to draw on the more endowed communities when they are truly unable to deal, on their own, with social duties thrust upon them.

Many social goals, moreover, require partnership between public and private groups. Although government should not seek to replace local communities, it may need to empower them by strategies of support, including revenue-sharing and technical assistance. There is a great need for study and experimentation with creative use of the structures of civil society, and public–private cooperation, especially where the delivery of health, educational, and social services is concerned.

Last, but not least, we should not hesitate to speak up and express our moral concerns to others when it comes to issues we care about deeply and share with one another. It might be debatable whether or not we should encourage our neighbors to keep their lawns green (which may well be environmentally unsound), but there should be little doubt that we should expect one another to attend to our children and to vulnerable community members. Those who neglect these duties should be explicitly considered poor members of the community.

National and local service, as well as volunteer work, is desirable to build and express a civil commitment. Such activities, bringing together people from different backgrounds and enabling and encouraging them to work together, build community and foster mutual respect and tolerance.

Americans should *foster a spirit of reconciliation*. When conflicts do arise, we should seek the least destructive means of resolving them. Adversarial litigation is often not the optimal way; mediation and arbitration are often superior. We should favor settlements that are fair and conciliatory even if we have to absorb some losses. Going for the last ounce of flesh is incompatible with community spirit. (It is said that marriage works better when each side is willing to give 75% and expect 25%, rather than each give 50% and expect 50%. The same holds for other close relations.)

We should *treat one another with respect* and recognize our basic equality, not just before the law, but also as moral agents.

Duties to the Polity

Being informed about public affairs is a prerequisite for keeping the polity from being controlled by demagogues, for taking action when needed in one's own interests and that of others, and for achieving justice and the shared future.

Voting is one tool for keeping the polity reflective of its constituent communities. Those who feel that none of the candidates reflect their views ought to seek out other like-minded citizens and seek to field their own candidate rather than retreat from the polity. Still, some persons may discharge their community responsibilities by being involved in nonpolitical activities, say, in volunteer work. Just as the polity is but one facet of interdependent social life, so voting and political activity are not the only ways to be responsible members of society. A good citizen is involved in a community or communities but is not necessarily active in the polity.

Paying one's taxes, encouraging others to pay their fair share, and *serving on juries* are fully obligatory. One of the most telling ills of our time is the expectation of many Americans that they are entitled to ever more public services without paying for them (as reflected in public opinion polls that show demands to slash government and taxes but also to expand practically every conceivable government function). We all take for granted the right to be tried before a jury of our peers, but all too often we are unwilling to serve on juries ourselves.

Cleaning Up the Polity

We need to revitalize public life so that the two-thirds of our citizens who now say they feel alienated or that the polity is not theirs will again be engaged in it.

Campaign contributions to members of Congress and state legislatures, speaking fees, and bribes have become so pervasive that in many areas of public policy and on numerous occasions the public interest is ignored as legislators pay off their debts to special interests. Detailed rationalizations have been spun to justify the system. It is said that giving money to politicians is a form of democratic participation. In fact, the rich can "participate" in this way so much more effectively than the poor that the democratic principle of one-person one-vote is severely compromised. It is said that money buys only access to the politician's ear; but even if money does not buy commitment, access should not be allotted according to the depth of one's pockets. It is said that every group has its pool of money, and hence as they all grease Congress, all Americans are served. But those who cannot grease at all or not as well, lose out, and so do long-run public goals that are not underwritten by any particular interest groups.

To establish conditions under which elected officials will be able to respond to the public interest, to the genuine needs of all citizens, and to their own consciences requires that the role of private money in public life be reduced as much as possible. All candidates should receive some public support, as presidential candidates already do, as well as some access to radio and television.

To achieve this major renewal and revitalization of public life, to reinstitute the prerequisites for attending to the public interest, *requires a major social movement,* akin to the progressive movement at the beginning of the century. For even good causes can become special interests if they are not part of such a movement, keeping their strategies and aims in constant dialogue with larger aims and multiple ends. Citizens who care about the integrity of the polity on either the local, state, or national level should band with their fellows to form a neo-progressive communitarian movement. They should persevere until elected officials are beholden not to special interests—but only to the voters and to their own consciences.

Freedom of Speech

The First Amendment is as dear to communitarians as it is to libertarians and many other Americans. Suggestions that it should be curbed to bar verbal expressions of racism, sexism, and other slurs seem to us to endanger the essence of the First Amendment, which is most needed when what some people say is disconcerting to some others. However, one should not ignore the victims of such abuse. Whenever individuals or members of a group are harassed, many *nonlegal measures* are appropriate to express disapproval of hateful expressions and to promote tolerance among the members of the polity. For example, a college campus faced with a rash of incidents indicating bigotry may conduct a teach-in on intergroup understanding. This, and much more, can be done without compromising the First Amendment.

Rights versus Rightness

The language of rights is morally incomplete. To say that "I have a right to do X" is not to conclude that "X is the right thing for me to do." One may, for example, have a First Amendment right to address others in a morally inappropriate manner. Say one tells a Jew that "Hitler should have finished you all" or a black, "go back to Africa," or worse. Rights give reasons to others not to coercively interfere with the speaker in the performance of protected acts; however, they do not in themselves give me a sufficient reason to perform these acts. There is a gap between rights and rightness that cannot be closed without a richer moral vocabulary—one that invokes principles of decency, duty, responsibility, and the common good, among others.

Social Justice

At the heart of the communitarian understanding of social justice is the idea of reciprocity: each member of the community owes something to all the rest, and the community owes something to each of its members. Justice requires responsible individuals in a responsive community.

Members of the community have a responsibility, to the greatest extent possible, to provide for themselves and their families: honorable work contributes to the commonwealth and to the community's ability to fulfill its essential tasks. Beyond self-support, individuals have a responsibility for the material and moral well-being of others. This does not mean heroic self-sacrifice; it means the constant self-awareness that no one of us is an island unaffected by the fate of others.

For its part, the community is responsible for protecting each of us against catastrophe, natural or man-made; for ensuring the basic needs of all who genuinely cannot provide for themselves; for appropriately recognizing the distinctive contributions of individuals to the community; and for safeguarding a zone within which individuals may define their own lives through free exchange and choice.

Communitarian social justice is alive both to the equal moral dignity of all individuals and to the ways in which they differentiate themselves from one another through their personal decisions.

Public Safety and Public Health

The American moral and legal tradition has always acknowledged the need to balance individual rights with the need to protect the safety and health of the public. The Fourth Amendment, for example, guards against unreasonable searches but allows for reasonable ones.

Thus, although people with AIDS must be vigilantly protected from invasions of their privacy and from job and housing discrimination, the community must be allowed to take effective measures to curb the spread of the disease. Although drug dealers' civil rights must be observed, the community must be provided with constitutional tools that will prevent dealers from dominating streets, parks, indeed, whole neighborhoods. Although high school students must be protected against wanton expulsion, places of learning must be able to maintain the social-moral climate that education requires.

We differ with the ACLU and other radical libertarians who oppose sobriety checkpoints, screening gates at airports, drug and alcohol testing for people who directly affect public safety (pilots, train engineers, etc.). Given the minimal intrusion involved (an average sobriety checkpoint lasts 90 seconds), the importance of the interests at stake (we have lost more lives, many due to drunken drivers, on the road each year than in the war in Vietnam), and the fact that such measures in the past have not led us down a slippery slope, these and similar reasonable measures should receive full public support.

There is little sense in gun registration. What we need to significantly enhance public safety is *domestic disarmament* of the kind that exists in practically all democracies. The National Rifle Association's suggestion that criminals, not guns, kill people ignores the fact that thousands are killed each year, many of them children, from accidental discharge of guns and that people—whether criminal, insane, or temporarily carried away by impulse—kill and are much more likely to do so when armed than when disarmed. The Second Amendment, behind which the NRA hides, is subject to a variety of interpretations, but the Supreme Court has repeatedly ruled, for over a hundred years, that it does not prevent laws that bar guns. *We join with those who read the Second Amendment the way it was written, as a communitarian clause, calling for community militias, not individual gun slingers.*

When it comes to public health, people who carry sexually transmitted diseases, especially when the illness is nearly always fatal, such as AIDS, should be expected to disclose their illness to previous sexual contacts or help health authorities to inform them, to warn all prospective sexual contacts, and to inform all health care personnel with whom they come in contact. It is their contribution to help stem the epidemic. At the same time, the carriers' rights against wanton violation of privacy and discrimination in housing, employment, and insurance should be scrupulously protected.

The Human Community

Our communitarianism is not particularism. We believe that the responsive community is the best form of human organization yet devised for respecting human dignity and safeguarding human decency and the way of life most open to needed self-revision through shared deliberation. We believe that the human species as a whole would be well served by the movement, as circumstances permit, of all polities toward strongly democratic communities. We are acutely aware of the ways in which this movement will be (and ought to be) affected by important material, cultural, and political differences among nations and peoples. And we know that enduring responsive communities cannot be created through fiat or coercion, but only through genuine public conviction.

We are heartened by the widespread invocation of democratic principles by the nations and peoples now emerging from generations of repression; we see the institutionalization of these principles as the best possible bulwark against the excesses of ethnic and national particularism that could well produce new forms of repression.

Although it may seem utopian, we believe that in the multiplication of strongly democratic communities around the world lies our best hope for the emergence of a global community that can deal concertedly with matters of general concern to our species as a whole: with war and strife, with violations of basic rights, with environmental degradation, and with the extreme material deprivation that stunts the bodies, minds, and spirits of children. *Our communitarian concern may begin with ourselves and our families, but it rises inexorably to the long-imagined community of humankind.*

IN CONCLUSION

A Question of Responsibility

Although some of the responsibilities identified in this manifesto are expressed in legal terms, and the law does play a significant role not only in
regulating society, but also in indicating which values it holds dear, our first
and foremost purpose is to *affirm the moral commitments of parents, young
persons, neighbors, and citizens*, to affirm the importance of the communities
within which such commitments take shape and are transmitted from one
generation to the next. This is not primarily a legal matter. On the contrary,
when a community reaches the point at which these responsibilities are
largely enforced by the powers of the state, it is in deep moral crisis. If
communities are to function well, most members most of the time must
discharge their responsibilities because they are committed to do so, not
because they fear lawsuits, penalties, or jails. Nevertheless, the state and its
agencies must take care not to harm the structures of civil society on which we
all depend. *Social environments, like natural environments, cannot be taken
for granted.*

It has been argued by libertarians that responsibilities are a personal
matter, that individuals are to judge which responsibilities they accept as
theirs. As we see it, responsibilities are anchored in community. Reflecting
the diverse moral voices of their citizens, responsive communities define what
is expected of people; they educate their members to accept these values; and
they praise them when they do and frown on them when they do not. Although the ultimate foundation of morality may be commitments of individual
conscience, it is communities that help introduce and sustain these commitments. Hence, the urgent need for communities to articulate the responsibilities they expect their members to discharge, especially in times, such as our
own, in which the understanding of these responsibilities has weakened and
their reach has grown unclear.

Further Work

This is only a beginning. This platform is but a point in dialogue, part of an
ongoing process of deliberation. It should not be viewed as a series of final
conclusions but ideas for additional discussion. We do not claim to have the
answers to all that troubles America these days. However, we are heartened
by the groundswell of support that our initial efforts have brought to the
communitarian perspective. If more and more Americans come forward and
join together to form active communities that seek to reinvigorate the moral
and social order, we will be able to deal better with many of our communities'

problems while reducing our reliance on governmental regulation, controls, and force. We will have a greater opportunity to work our shared public policy based on broad consensus and shared moral and legal traditions. And we will have many more ways to make our society a place in which individual rights are vigilantly maintained, while the seedbeds of civic virtue are patiently nurtured.

PART I

The Communitarian Paradigm

Rights, Mary Ann Glendon warns in her essay, can be extended and expanded so that they undermine their own currency. And if we turn every difference of interest or opinion into a matter of rights, she notes, we undermine the capacity of communities to work out differences. Thus, parties in conflict are more likely to end up bringing their disputes to the courts, where bearers of different rights clash. This is not a call to curtail rights, but a communitarian concern that rights will be undermined by boundless minting.

Dallin Oaks takes us to the next step by asserting that strong rights presume strong responsibilities. To claim a right for one person is to lay a claim of responsibility on another. And if we claim rights but are not willing to assume responsibilities, we undermine the civil order. Studies show that young Americans are, quite properly, keen to maintain their rights to be tried before a jury of their peers if they are charged with committing a crime. However, at the same time many try to dodge jury duty. As we have said, such an attitude is both illogical (if peers will not serve, there will be no jury of peers) and unethical (because jury evaders seek to take and not to give to the commons).

What has caused the recent tendency to stress rights and to neglect personal and social responsibilities, such as the duty to care for oneself and contribute to the common good? Robert Bellah finds the answer in individualism run amok. Individualism is at the foundation of the American republic, a country built by refugees fleeing authoritarianism. However, over the past few decades, the notion that one should maximize oneself and pursue one's psychological wants and proclivities with ever less regard for others has become a major source of our social disorder and discontent.

There is a close link between the themes of rights and responsibilities and that of rebuilding the community, the subject of Christopher Lasch's chapter. Liberals, Lasch points out, have responded to the ravages wreaked by an unrestrained market by relying more and more on the state. However, state regulations and welfare programs have proved worse than the problems they sought to cure, he writes. The recognition of a third realm, that of community, in which people do things for one another is critical. It is often overlooked in the polarizing debate between those who favor the private sector and those who seek to rely on the public one.

The secret lies in balance. We must avoid a society that goes overboard in either direction. While we live in a society in which people shirk responsibilities and neglect the community, Juan Williams provides us with a vivid depiction of a society in which the scale is tipped far in the other direction.

CHAPTER 1

Rights in Twentieth Century Constitutions

MARY ANN GLENDON

In the 1960s and 1970s, when the judicial rights revolution was in full swing, poverty lawyers and allied legal scholars urged the courts to add to the expanding catalog of constitutional rights certain social and economic rights—to housing, education, and a minimum decent subsistence. The advocates of welfare rights were not deterred by the absence of pertinent constitutional language. After all, if the Court could find a right to privacy in the "penumbra" of the Bill of Rights, who knew what else might be discovered there? Those efforts to constitutionalize what were historically matters of legislative discretion had only partial success. The Supreme Court did hold that, once government grants certain statutory entitlements such as welfare and disability benefits, the recipients have a constitutional right not to be deprived of those benefits without procedural due process.[1] The Court declined, however, to find that the entitlements themselves were constitutionally required.[2]

That result is hardly surprising in view of the fact that the welfare state was not even a twinkle in the eye of the Founding Fathers. It is worth speculating, however, about what a contrary holding in the 1960s and 1970s might have meant. The experience of other liberal democracies is illuminating in that connection, for most of their constitutions *do* contain welfare rights or solemn acknowledgments of collective responsibility to provide minimum decent subsistence to needy citizens.[3]

The chief lesson to be learned from examining the way welfare is imagined in foreign legal systems is that, in this area as in so many others, the United States is in a class by itself. The age of our Constitution is just one of many features that sets the United States apart from other liberal democracies. Our regime of constitutional rights was over a century old when the New Deal transformed the liberal nightwatchman state into a liberal regulatory welfare state. In most of the nations with which we ordinarily compare ourselves, the sequence was just the reverse. In Canada, France, and Germany, for example, the foundations of the welfare system were in place well before the appearance there of regimes of judicially enforceable constitutional rights.[4] Another element of American distinctiveness is the refusal of American governments to ratify international human rights instruments containing social and economic rights. And finally there is the unusual structure of our welfare state, which, to a much greater extent than elsewhere, leaves pensions, health, and other benefits to be organized privately, mainly through the work place, rather than directly through the public sector. A brief elaboration of these points will suffice to show how differently rights and responsibilities are understood in American and other North Atlantic contexts.

RIGHTS BEFORE WELFARE

Americans are justly proud of the fact that, prior to 1945, we were one of very few countries where constitutional rights were protected by the institution of judicial review. Our courts seldom exercised their power of reviewing governmental action for conformity to constitutional norms, however, until the turn of the century. Then, American judges began energetically striking down factory laws and other early social legislation, while legislatures in the rest of the industrialized world were laying the foundations of their welfare states with statutes broadly similar in spirit to those our courts were nullifying.

It was not until the active period of constitution-making that followed World War II that bills of rights and institutional mechanisms to enforce them were widely adopted by other nations.[5] At that time, most liberal democracies did not adopt the American method of judicial review, but instead opted for variants of a system that has come to be known as the "European model" of constitutional control. The principal feature that distinguishes the European from the American model is that, under the European, constitutional questions must be referred to a special tribunal that deals only or mainly with such matters. In the United States, and in the handful of countries that have imitated our system, ordinary courts have the power to rule on constitutional issues in regular lawsuits. Even among the nations that have adopted a form of the American model—Canada, Japan, and the Republic of Ireland—the United States remains unique. For no other country's courts have exercised their power to declare executive or legislative action unconstitutional with such frequency and boldness as their American counterparts.

WHAT COUNTS AS A RIGHT?

A renowned European legal historian recently compiled a "basic inventory" of rights that have been accepted by most Western countries at the present time.[6] The list included, first and foremost, human dignity; then personal freedom; fair procedures to protect against arbitrary governmental action; active political rights (especially the right to vote); equality before the law; and society's responsibility for the social and economic conditions of its members. It is hard to say what would strike most American readers of that list as more strange—the omission of property or the inclusion (in a catalog of "rights") of affirmative welfare obligations. Yet the list is an accurate one. Welfare rights (or responsibilities) have been accorded a place beside traditional political and civil liberties in the national constitutions of most liberal democracies.[7] It is the eighteenth-century American Constitution that, with the passage of time, has become anomalous in this respect.

The fact that welfare rights have been accorded constitutional status in so many countries cannot be attributed exclusively to the relatively recent vintage of their constitutions. To a great extent, it is a legal manifestation of attitudes toward the state that are traditionally less suspicious than American attitudes.[8] Continental Europeans today, whether of the Right or the Left, are much more likely than Americans to take for granted that governments have affirmative duties to actively promote the well-being of their citizens. The leading European conservative parties espouse openly and in principle what American conservatives have only accepted grudgingly and *sub silentio:* a mixed economy and a moderately interventionist state. A broad social consensus in Europe supports the subsidization of child-raising families and accepts the funding of health, employment, and old age insurance at levels most Americans find scarcely credible.[9] American politicians of both the Right and the Left, by contrast, find it almost obligatory to profess mistrust of government.

INTERNATIONAL WELFARE RIGHTS

Article 25 of the United Nations Universal Declaration of Human Rights, adopted by the General Assembly in 1948, provides that "everyone has the right to a standard of living adequate for the health and well-being of himself and his family, including food, clothing, housing and medical care and necessary social services, and the right to security in the event of unemployment, sickness, disability, widowhood, old age or other lack of livelihood in circumstances beyond his control." To implement that principle, the U.N. Covenant on Economic, Social, and Cultural Rights was opened for a signature in 1966. The Covenant came into force a decade later after being ratified by nearly ninety countries. The United States is the only one of the liberal democracies that has failed to ratify that instrument or its companion, the U.N. Covenant on Civil and Political Rights.[10]

A large part of the explanation for this reticence, no doubt, resides in our prudent unwillingness to subject ourselves to the jurisdiction of international organizations dominated by critics of the United States. But in some respects, and particularly where economic and social rights are concerned, our reluctance also seems to be attributable to traditional American ideas about which sorts of needs, goods, interests, or values should be characterized as fundamental rights. Another reason, about which I will have more to say presently, is probably a concern that the overburdened American civil litigation system is not well equipped to handle the consequences of characterizing a vast new range of interests as fundamental rights.[11]

WELFARE RIGHTS AND WELFARE STATES

The questions that are apt to come to the minds of most Americans when they become aware of the existence of welfare rights in foreign constitutions are: How have these rights worked out in practice? Does the experience of other nations shed any light on what might have happened here if the Supreme Court had accepted arguments made in the late 1960s and early 1970s that welfare rights could and should be made part of our constitutional regime instead of remaining purely legislative creations?

Interestingly, in practice, the contrast between the United States and countries with constitutional welfare rights is much less sharp than it appears on paper. For no liberal democracy has ever placed social and economic rights on precisely the same legal footing as the familiar civil and political liberties.[12] In some countries, for example, constitutional welfare language is so cryptic as to remain meaningless without extensive legislative specification (e.g., the German republic is a "social" state).[13] More commonly, the various social and economic rights are specifically enumerated, but their special nature is flagged by presenting them as statements of political principles and goals to guide the organs of government as they carry out their respective functions. For example, the Swedish Instrument of Government, in a section titled "The Basic Principles of the Constitution," provides:

> Art. 2. . . . The personal, economic and cultural welfare of the individual shall be fundamental aims of the activities of the community. In particular, it shall be incumbent on the community to secure the right to work, to housing and to education and to promote social care and security as well as a favorable living environment.[14]

Continental lawyers call such rights "programmatic" to emphasize that they do not give rise to directly enforceable individual claims, but await implementation through legislative or executive action and budgetary appropriations. Programmatic rights figure prominently in the constitutions of the Nordic countries, as well as in the French, Greek, Italian, Japanese, and Spanish constitutions. In all those countries, the welfare state has been constructed by legislation through ordinary political processes—just as it has been in the United States.

We cannot conclude, however, that "programmatic" rights and obligations are of no practical significance. One important legal effect is that they endow the statutes enacted to carry out the constitutional "program" with a strong presumption of constitutionality. Nor can we discount the likelihood that these aspirational statements have a modest influence on public, judicial, and legislative deliberation about rights and welfare, especially in countries where constitutional welfare commitments have issued from, or were grafted onto, a well-established welfare tradition.

On the other hand, at the most practical level, there does not appear to be any strong correlation between the presence of, or the degree of emphasis on, welfare rights in the constitutions of affluent democracies and the generosity of welfare states as measured by the proportion of national expenditures devoted to health, housing, social security, and social assistance.[15] For example, the United Kingdom, with no constitutional welfare rights (and no single-document constitution), devotes proportionately more of its resources to social expenditures than its richer "neighbor" Denmark, where rights to work, education, and social assistance are constitutionally guaranteed. And social expenditures consume considerably more of the budget of the Federal Republic of Germany, whose constitution merely announces that it is a "social" state, than they do in Sweden or Italy where welfare rights are spelled out in some detail.[16] (It has always been hard to fit the United States into such comparisons because of the peculiar structure of our welfare state. But most analyses give us a relatively poor showing in many respects, especially where assistance to child-raising families is concerned.)[17]

If there *is* a relation between the constitutional status of welfare rights and the type and strength of welfare commitments in a given society, it seems to be but a loose relationship of consanguinity, with both the constitution and the welfare system influenced by such factors as the homogeneity or diversity of the population; the degree to which mistrust of government has figured in the country's political history; the vitality of political parties; the health of the legislative process; and the degree of individualism in the culture. This kind of inconclusive speculation seems to lead only to the sort of conclusions that make sociology so unsatisfying to many people. It is difficult to become excited about the idea that a host of mutually conditioning factors, of which the constitutional status of welfare rights may be both cause and consequence, are involved in determining the shape of a given country's welfare state—its basic commitments, the priorities among those commitments, the spirit in which it is administered, the degree of support and approval it wins from taxpayers, and the extent to which it disables or empowers those who resort to it.

WHAT IF . . . ?

That very inconclusiveness, however, is taken by some rights enthusiasts as a basis for arguing that social and economic rights should be constitutionalized.

If the experience of other liberal democracies is any guide, the argument runs, there is unlikely to be any harm in granting constitutional status to such rights and some beneficial effects might well ensue. Those are risky inferences to draw from cross-national comparisons, for reasons that reside, not in the foreign experience, but in our own distinctive American culture of rights. We Americans, for better or worse, take rights very seriously. Not only the term, but the very idea of "programmatic" rights is unfamiliar and uncongenial to us. It is almost inconceivable that constitutional welfare rights, had they appeared in the United States, would have been regarded by the public or treated by the legal community as purely aspirational. Americans are accustomed to the notion that if we have a constitutional right to something, we can go to court to enforce that right and that, standing behind the court's order are sheriffs, marshals, and the National Guard, if necessary.

As soon as we begin to imagine constitutional welfare rights that are other than programmatic guides for legislative action, however, we are headed down a road that no other country, including the socialist states, has traveled. That does not mean that we cannot make an educated guess about the destination of such a trip. The most directly foreseeable consequence of according constitutional status to social and economic rights in the United States would be a litigation explosion of heroic proportions. Would the benefits of that litigation outweigh the disadvantages? It is sometimes said that such lawsuits will prod government agencies into being more responsive and responsible. But the costs of legal defense (in dollars and morale) as well as the occasional high damage award could prod financially strapped local providers in the other direction, toward service cutbacks or the elimination of some programs altogether.

UTILITY OF CROSS-NATIONAL COMPARISONS

No other country has had any experience that can guide us here. The fact is that we Americans place a unique degree of reliance on the system of damage awards (both in ordinary personal litigation and in constitutional tort litigation) to perform certain social tasks that other advanced industrial nations handle with a more diverse range of techniques including, notably, direct health and safety regulation and more comprehensive systems of social insurance.[18]

Nevertheless, the experiences of other countries may help us to find our own path by heightening our awareness of indigenous resources that we ourselves are inclined to overlook or underrate. In recent years, policymakers in other welfare states have begun to gaze wistfully at the American capacity for cooperation between governmental and nongovernmental organizations in the areas of health, education, and welfare, and at the ability our sort of federalism gives us to innovate and experiment creatively with diverse approaches to stubborn social problems. The United States represents a rare working example, albeit an incomplete and imperfect one, of the principle of *subsidiarity:*

the notion that no social task should be allocated to a body larger than the smallest one that can effectively do the job.

The reason why these American novelties are attracting increased interest in more highly centralized welfare states is that every country within the democratic world in its own way is grappling with a common set of problems: how to provide humanitarian aid without undermining personal responsibility; how to achieve the optimal mix in a mixed economy; how to preserve a just balance among individual freedom, equality, and social solidarity. The basic problem is nothing less than the great dilemma of how to hold together the two halves of the divided soul of liberalism—our love of individual liberty and our sense of a community for which we accept a common responsibility.

Below the surface of that dilemma lies a long-neglected political problem. It is that neither a strong commitment to individual and minority rights, nor even a modest welfare commitment like the American one can long be sustained without the active support of a citizenry that is willing to respect the rights of others (not just in the abstract but often at some cost to themselves); that is prepared to accept some responsibility for the poorest and most vulnerable members of society; and that is ready to take significant responsibility for themselves and their dependents. Liberal democratic welfare states around the world are now demanding certain kinds of excellence in their citizens to a nearly unprecedented degree. They are asking men and women to possess and practice certain virtues that, even under the best of conditions, are not easy to acquire—respect for the dignity and worth of one's fellow human beings, self-restraint, self-reliance, and compassion.

The question that seldom gets asked, however, is this: Where do such qualities come from? Where do people acquire an internalized willingness to view others with genuine regard for their dignity and concern for their well-being, rather than as objects, means, or obstacles? These qualities cannot be generated by governments or instilled by fear and force. The fact is that both our welfare state and our experiment in democratic government rest to a great extent on habits and practices formed within fragile social structures—families, neighborhoods, religious and workplace associations, and other communities of memory and mutual aid—structures that are being asked to bear great weight just at a time when they themselves do not seem to be in peak condition.

The question then becomes: What, if anything, can be done to create and maintain—or at least to avoid undermining or destroying—social conditions that foster the peculiar combination of qualities that are required to sustain our commitments to the rule of law, individual freedom, and a compassionate welfare state? In a large, heterogeneous nation like the United States, the question is particularly urgent. America is especially well endowed with social resources, but we have tended to take that social wealth for granted, consuming our inherited capital at a faster rate than we are replenishing it. Like an athlete who develops the muscles in his upper body but lets his legs grow weak, we have nurtured our strong rights tradition while neglecting the social foundation on which that tradition rests.

Communitarianism, which can be understood as democracy's environmental movement, is helping to heighten awareness of the political importance and the endangered condition of the seedbeds of civic virtue. Toward that end, it will be necessary to take a fresh look at our constitutional framework and to recall that individual rights are but one set of elements in a larger constitutional structure. As it happens, those parts of the constitutional design that have been neglected by constitutional lawyers in recent years—federalism, the legislative branch, and the ideal of government by the people—have an important bearing on the maintenance of the social capital on which all rights ultimately depend.

And so, by a circuitous route, a cross-national approach to rights and the welfare state points back toward the American Constitution and toward the "Madisonian understanding that individual liberty and strong local institutions need not be at cross-purposes with one another."[19] If the United States' endangered social environments do indeed hold the key to simultaneously maintaining a liberal regime of rights and a compassionate welfare state, then we need to start thinking about the effect of both rights and welfare, as currently conceived, on the settings where we first learn to respect the rights of and care for the needs of others. Reflection on our own tradition, moreover, should give us pause concerning the disdain for politics that underlies so much current American thinking about legal and social policy. For one of the most important lessons of 1789 is the same one the world learned anew in 1989: that politics is a way not only of advancing self-interest, but also of transcending it. That transformative potential of the art through which we order our lives together represents our best hope for living up to our rights ideals and our welfare aspirations in the coming years.

NOTES

1. *Goldberg v. Kelly*, 397 U.S. 254 (1970) (welfare entitlements); *Matthews v. Eldridge*, 424 U.S. 319 (1976) (social security disability payments).
2. For example, *Lindsey v. Normet*, 405 U.S. 56 (1972) (no constitutional right to housing); *San Antonio Independent School District v. Rodriguez*, 411 U.S. 1 (1973) (no constitutional right to education).
3. Louis Favoreu, "La protection des droits économiques et sociaux dans les constitutions," in *Conflict and Integration: Comparative Law in the World Today* (Tokyo: Chuo University Press, 1988), pp. 691–92.
4. France adopted a limited form of constitutional control only in 1958, and Canada established judicial review only in 1982. In Germany, although some courts in the Weimar Republic had claimed the power to rule on the constitutionality of laws, constitutional review did not become a significant feature of the legal order until 1951 when the Federal Constitutional Court was established in what was then West Germany. Donald Kommers, *The Constitutional Jurisprudence of the Federal Republic of Germany* (Durham, N.C.: Duke University Press, 1989), pp. 6–11.

5. For a concise survey, see Louis Favoreu, "American and European Models of Constitutional Justice," in David Clark, ed., *Comparative and Private International Law: Essays in Honor of John Henry Merryman* (Berlin: Duncker & Humblot, 1990), p. 105.

6. Franz Wieacker, "Foundations of European Legal Culture," *American Journal of Comparative Law* 37 (1990): 1, 29.

7. The formulations vary from the bare recitation in the German Basic Law of 1949 that the Federal Republic of Germany is a "social" state (*Basic Law*, Article 20), to detailed lists of specific social and economic rights such as those contained in the constitutions of France, Italy, Japan, Spain, and the Nordic countries.

8. Gerhard Casper, "European Convergence," *University of Chicago Law Review* 58 (1991): 441, 445.

9. See William Pfaff, *Barbarian Sentiments: How the American Century Ends* (New York: Hill & Wang, 1989), p. 25.

10. Richard Lillich, "United States Ratification of the United Nations Covenants," *Georgia Journal of International and Comparative Law* 20 (1990): 279.

11. The United States did, however, sign the Universal Declaration and the Helsinki Final Act of 1975 which (like the Universal Declaration) calls for a nonbinding commitment to stated international norms of human rights.

12. Favoreu, "La protection," puts it this way: "[T]here are two categories of fundamental rights: immutable and absolute rights that exist whatever the epoch or the reigning ideology; and other rights, known as economic and social rights, that 'carry a certain coefficient of contingency and relativity' and whose recognition is a function of the state of society and its evolution" (p. 701).

13. German Basic Law of 1949, Article 20.

14. Gisbert H. Flanz, "Sweden," in Albert P. Blaustein and Gisbert H. Flanz, eds., *Constitutions of the World* (Dobbs Ferry, N.Y.: Oceana Publications, 1985), pp. 9–11.

15. The percentages of central government expenditure devoted in 1988 to health, housing, social security, and welfare in selected countries with "high-income economies" are as follows.

Federal Republic of Germany	67.6
Sweden	55.3
Norway	46.8
Italy	45.8
United Kingdom	44.5
United States	44.0
Canada	43.2
Ireland	42.7
Denmark	42.4

Source: Table 11 (Central Government Expenditure), *World Development Report 1990* (1990), pp. 198–99.

16. German Basic Law of 1949, Article 20.

17. See Sheila Kammerman and Alfred Kahn, *Income Transfers for Families with*

Children: An Eight-Country Study (Philadelphia: Temple University Press, 1983); Samuel Preston, "Children and the Elderly in the U.S.," *Scientific American* (December 1984), pp. 44–49; and Timothy Smeeding and Barbara Torrey, "Poor Children in Rich Countries," *Science* (November 1988), p. 873.
18. Basil S. Markesinis, "Litigation-Mania in England, Germany, and the USA: Are We So Very Different?" *Cambridge Law Journal* 49 (1990): 233, 242–43, 263.
19. Akhil Amar, "The Bill of Rights as a Constitution," *Yale Law Journal* 100 (1991): 1131, 1136.

CHAPTER 2

Rights and Responsibilities[1]

DALLIN H. OAKS

I propose to discuss rights and responsibilities and their relation to law and the legal profession. I will suggest that we have tried to promote too many societal goals through rights and have given too little attention to responsibilities. After discussing some of the strengths and weaknesses of the rights approach and the responsibilities approach, I will suggest some ways that law and the legal profession can promote the voluntary fulfillment of responsibilities.

In the vocabulary of the law, a right signifies a claim enforceable by law. This kind of right cannot exist without law. In this sense, a person with a right can always compel action or inaction by someone. Lawyers thrive on rights. The enforcement of rights provides employment for the legal profession. In relation to rights, a lawyer functions as a popular champion—a gladiator or an enforcer. No wonder lawyers like rights.

Responsibility connotes duty or obligation. In one sense, responsibility is simply the duty side of someone else's right; that kind of responsibility is enforceable. I speak of a different kind. I refer to an obligation or duty that, as a practical matter, is not enforceable by legal processes. Such responsibilities include those that are owed to one's conscience and to one's God, and many that are owed to one's fellow beings, community, and a host of other groups. These kinds of responsibilities are the rent we pay for the privilege of living in a civilized society. They include such familiar virtues as tolerance, trustfulness, benevolence, patriotism, respect for human and civil rights, participation in the democratic process, and devotion to the common good.

There are important differences between rights and responsibilities. "Rights" is a lofty term, enshrined in the consciousness of Americans. The best known and most highly revered portion of our Constitution is the Bill of Rights. A person who can put needs or desires in terms of rights captures the high ground of moral discourse.

Responsibilities are necessities we respect, but we rarely stand up and cheer for them. In contrast to rights, which can be enforced, responsibilities can only be encouraged. Not many members of the legal profession like to preach or listen to a sermon on responsibilities. The best such sermon I have encountered is Elliot L. Richardson's speech at an American Bar Association meeting just after the Watergate tragedy, published in the *Buffalo Law Review*. He commented that "the drumbeat accompanying the steady forward march of rights during the past decade" has been so insistent "that the voice of obligations has scarcely been heard." He then gave this brilliant summary of the relationship between rights and responsibilities—or obligations, as he calls them:

> Obligations in any case, transcend rights: the full extent of my obligation to respect my neighbor's right to worship as he pleases cannot be spelled out in any court decree. Obligations embody a moral, and not merely a legal, command. And yet, it seems to me, we increasingly tend to behave as if the minimum required by the law were the maximum required of us. . . . In the case of civil rights, the law can enforce their observance but not their respect. Indeed, where there is true respect for other people—the awareness that each is a unique, sacrosanct individual equal in dignity to every other human being—there is an awareness of obligation which is higher and more sensitive than any requirement of the law.

The English legal philosopher A.J.M. Milne makes a strong case for the primacy of responsibilities as a rational matter. Indeed, he asserts in *Freedom and Rights* "that in any joint activity or enterprise, responsibility takes priority over justice." This is because justice is highly individual and takes no account of the common enterprise and the problems of a group as a whole. Because no group enterprise can prosper unless it is advanced by its participants, a member of a group "can never be entitled to insist on doing or having done anything which weakens or undermines the common enterprise." Consequently, Milne concludes that "while it is rational to be just, it is more rational to be responsible and to interpret justice from the wider perspective of responsibility. It is the higher of the two standards of rationality at the level of social morality." He later concedes that this test of rationality is an appropriate guide to policy only when a group is homogeneous and fundamentally united on values.

Milne's insistence on the superior rationality of responsibility provides a corrective for the current overemphasis on the enforcement of rights as a means of promoting worthy social goals. I am trying to contribute to that corrective in this essay. Such an effort is needed, for with the definition of new rights, we have tended to ignore old responsibilities. As a result, the responsibilities approach is now neglected and the rights approach is overburdened.

For example, modern legal discourse has much to say about the rights of children and little to say about the responsibilities of parents. I am dubious about how much we can really help children by defining and enforcing their rights. I think we may do more for children by trying to reinforce the responsibilities of parents, natural and adoptive, even when those responsibilities are not legally enforceable. We might start by reducing our enthusiasm for "nofault" divorces in the case of marriage partners who are parents. In many such cases, we should encourage the parents to keep their marriage together for the sake of interests larger than their own rights, convenience, and desires.

There is a social interest as well as an individual interest in marriage. Professor Bruce C. Hafen expounds the constitutional implications of that fact in his brilliant article in the *Michigan Law Review:*

> [T]he individual and the social interests are so intertwined in family cases that meaningful analysis of the competing interests is rendered impossible by current civil liberties approaches that always give the individual interest a procedurally exalted priority over the social interest. Great need exists for a method of constitutional analysis that will allow for explicit consideration of the social interest in domestic relations.

Another example concerns current laws against discrimination. I wonder whether we can realistically expect to accomplish much more effective enforcement by more extensive use of legal process. Instead of exploring new ways to enforce nondiscrimination rights, we might be more effective by searching for new ways to win hearts to the proposition that each of us has a responsibility to treat persons on their own merits as children of God, whatever their race, creed, color, sex, or national origin.

I seek to promote responsibilities as a worthy alternative to efforts that strive to promote social goals exclusively through the enforcement of rights. By this means, I hope to contribute to a better balance between what John A. Howard, in his address "Education and Freedom," has called "the human impulse to pursue one's own course" and what he calls "the necessity to modify one's conduct according to the needs of the group."

An example will illustrate the legal profession's relative concern with rights and responsibilities. About twenty-five years ago, a group of distinguished lawyers under the leadership of Dean Jefferson B. Fordham of the University of Pennsylvania Law School proposed that the American Bar Association [ABA] establish a Section of Individual Rights. While the ABA was studying the proposal, the proponents added the word "responsibilities" as a political concession in the interest of balance. No one had any objection to this addition, but, according to Dean Fordham, the proponents devoted very little thought to what the Section could do under the heading of individual responsibilities because they were preoccupied with individual rights.

Even after the name was changed, the formal proposal was devoted exclusively to explaining the importance of individual rights. The only mention of responsibilities pertained to how rights would be secured, as in the statement, "[W]e of the organized Bar have a tremendous responsibility as such in the field of individual rights." The other submissions to the Board of Governors and the discussion that led to approval in the House of Delegates reflect the same emphasis. The new Section's statement of purpose is almost exclusively devoted to the promotion of individual rights. There are passing references to the "correlative nature of both rights and duties" and to the "recognition and enforcement of individual rights and duties," but no explanation is given of responsibilities as a free-standing concern of the Section.

I have been a member of the Section of Individual Rights and Responsibilities since its founding. I am proud of its impressive list of achievements in respect to rights, but I am sorry that it has done little or nothing about responsibility. To cite another measure, the *Index to Legal Periodicals* does not index anything under the heading "responsibility" and this heading is merely a cross-reference in the *Current Law Index* and the *Legal Resource Index*.

One legal educator has suggested why the legal profession does well with rights and poorly with responsibilities. I refer to Cornell Law School Dean Roger C. Cramton's provocative essay, "The Ordinary Religion of the Law School Classroom," which discusses the fundamental value assumptions of legal education. One value assumption is what Dean Cramton calls the law school's "instrumental approach to law and lawyering." Under this approach, law is nothing more than "an instrument for achieving social goals." The goals are, of course, those of the client. The lawyer need not be concerned with selecting goals or with the value questions associated with them because the lawyer is simply the skilled craftsman who works out the means by which predetermined goals are to be achieved. This kind of focus on means gives primacy to a law student's recognizing and enforcing rights and strips away his or her concern for values and responsibilities. The result reminds me of the doctor who told an educator that medical science would soon perfect a means to sever the human mind from the rest of the body and, with appropriate support systems, "keep the brain alive indefinitely with no connection to the heart." As Cullen Murphy recounts it in his article in *Change*, the educator replied, "That's really not new, we've been doing that in our college for years."

Although lawyers unquestionably relate more readily to rights than to responsibilities, there are at least two compelling reasons why the American Bar Association needs a Section that is actively involved with both. First, the enjoyment of rights cannot endure without the voluntary fulfillment of responsibilities. Morris Janowitz, in *The Reconstruction of Patriotism—Education for Civil Consciousness*, reminds us that a democracy needs patriotic citizens who are alive to their duties as well as to their rights. We need reminding. Our generation values the right to vote over the duty to vote and the right to a trial by jury over the obligation to serve as a juror. No society is so secure that it can withstand continued demands for increases in citizen rights and decreases in citizen obligations.

Civic responsibilities, such as honesty, self-reliance, participation in the democratic process, and devotion to the common good, are basic to the governance and preservation of our country. Any person who is concerned with preserving the force of law and the enforceability of individual rights should be profoundly concerned about the civic responsibilities on which the legal order is based. "It is widely recognized," Janowitz declares, "that effective citizenship rests on a rigorous and viable system of civic education which informs the individual of his civil rights and obligations."

Another reason why lawyers are concerned with responsibilities is that some of the goals we seek to achieve by the enforcement of rights may be achieved more effectively and at lower cost by the encouragement of responsibilities. Rights necessarily entail public enforcement. Responsibilities as defined here require only private persuasion and initiative. As a private remedy, responsibilities are subject to all the limitations of voluntary action. But rights are also limited. The enforcement of rights is limited by the resources of government and by the will of government officials. The effectiveness of a rights approach therefore will ebb and flow with the fashions of different administrations and with the fortunes of the economy and its impact on public budgets.

The rights approach also has some side effects that should be counted among its costs. The subject of side effects reminds us of what has been called the first rule of modern packaging: One bag of groceries, when consumed, will produce two bags of trash. One side effect of the rights approach concerns the person who must act to achieve the goal. This approach uses compulsion, whereas the responsibilities approach uses persuasion. Using coercion to enforce rights may embitter the person who is compelled to act. In contrast, the use of persuasion to fulfill responsibilities may ennoble the actor, who sees himself as having responded to a higher impulse.

In a 1978 article in *The Public Interest*, Nathan Glazer has noted other effects of the judicial enforcement of rights, such as those in welfare programs and in educational, penal, and mental institutions. A rights approach reduces the power and authority and, correspondingly, the responsibilities of administrators. It gives primacy to the theoretical knowledge of the lawyer–enforcers over the practical or clinical knowledge of the defendant–administrators.

To cite another cost, the rights approach is subject to internal contradictions that may impair its utility. Individual rights and individual freedom are both worthy goals. Unfortunately, the more government seeks to enforce rights, the more it interferes with freedom. The more it assures one individual's freedom, the less it is able to enforce another individual's rights. This tendency is all too apparent in the long-standing controversy over prayer in the public schools and in a multitude of circumstances involving laws against discrimination. The achievement of one goal for one person often impairs the goal of another. The responsibilities approach has no such contradiction because it subjects freedom to persuasion rather than coercion. Though less effective for achieving a goal in an individual case, the responsibilities approach inevitably imposes less cost on competing goals. The irony that one worthy goal can be attained only at the expense of another worthy goal reminds us of the aphorism, as it appears in P. Dickson's *The Official Rules,* that "[P]roblems worthy of attack prove their worth by hitting back."

What can the legal profession and the law do to encourage the voluntary fulfillment of responsibilities? How can we strengthen the common sense of obligation, so that voluntary action will become a more effective means of attaining worthy goals? The most powerful instrument of conversion to any proposition is the power of example. The legal profession's most powerful sermon on responsibilities is its voluntary compliance with obligations that are unenforceable, especially when a lawyer's fulfillment of public responsibility is done at the expense of his or her private interest. So it is with professional obligations to work *pro bono publico* on matters such as legal services for the indigent, the improvement of the profession, or the administration of justice. Many lawyers fulfill such responsibilities admirably, but their example goes unheeded because it is unnoticed. In an article published in *The California Law Review,* Notre Dame Dean Thomas L. Shaffer said of another effort to improve the profession, "Too many candles are under too many bushels." The profession should increase the power of its positive examples by making them more visible. We should also recognize and work to overcome the fact that too many lawyers devote little or no time to their professional responsibilities. On this subject, too many lawyers fall back on the old maxim that "nothing is impossible if you don't have to do it yourself."

I believe that the public influence and standing of lawyers would also be enhanced if they were seen as professionals who would prevent or mediate controversies rather than concentrate on enforcing rights. In his 1984 annual message to the American Bar, Chief Justice Warren Burger suggested that the entire legal profession "has become so mesmerized with the stimulation of the courtroom contest that we tend to forget that we ought to be healers—healers of conflicts." This plea—that lawyers be healers as well as warriors—is, in substance, a plea for lawyers to be concerned with their own and their client's responsibilities as well as their rights.

We can also encourage the responsibilities approach by strengthening the position of institutions that promote moral development, including the content and observance of responsibilities. I refer to family, to church, to educational institutions, to community organizations, and to educational media programs that are concerned with moral development. If we can improve the performance of these institutions, we will increase the extent to which worthy social goals can be attained through voluntary action.

I illustrate this point by reference to the role of the family. Recent legal and social developments have cast doubt on the value our society places on the family. At the same time, the family is generally conceded to be our most effective instrument for the development of moral values. In view of that fact, our laws and social priorities should be seeking to strengthen families instead of contributing to or acquiescing in their decline. . . .

Any forces that weaken the family or the practice of individual responsibility in family relations diminish the sense of responsibility and the vital work ethic in our society as a whole. Conversely, by strengthening the family and its role as a teacher of moral values, we encourage the fulfillment of responsibilities in society as a whole. The legal profession should be enlisted, and the laws should be shaped to strengthen the family. We should do the same for other institutions and efforts that strengthen our common sense or responsibility, such as the teaching of civic virtues in schools, community organizations, and the media.

The content of the law can also encourage the fulfillment of responsibilities, even without making them legally enforceable. I cite two examples from United States Supreme Court opinions recognizing the constitutional rights of parents in respect to their offspring. The first, *Pierce v. Society of Sisters*, gives voice to the familiar concept that rights are accompanied by responsibilities: "[T]hose who nurture [a child] and direct his destiny have the right, coupled with the high duty, to recognize and prepare him for additional obligations." In this formation, the rights and responsibilities of parents seem to be equivalent, as if they existed together or not at all. More recently, in *Lehr v. Robertson*, the Supreme Court expressed a different idea, suggesting that, at least concerning the father of an illegitimate child, the existence of the right depends on the prior fulfillment of the responsibility. In rejecting an unwed father's claim to a constitutional parental right to a two-year-old child whom he had not reared or supported, the Court declared that "the rights of the parents are a counterpart of the responsibilities they have assumed." Making the existence of a right dependent on the prior fulfillment of a responsibility in some instances would surely help restore the status of responsibilities in our way of thinking.

We have tried throwing money at problems and throwing regulations at problems. I suggest we should now try throwing preachments at some problems. It may even be desirable to afflict responsible parties with the power of a good example. I suggest that it is time our leaders and our teachers turned down the volume on what we deserve and tried to tune us in to how we can serve. As President John F. Kennedy said in a famous line that is honored in memory but ignored in practice: "Ask not what your country can do for you. Ask what you can do for your country."

One of the glories of our free society is the way it protects the interests and worth of the individual against the overbearing preferences of the majority. None of us would have it otherwise. Yet there is truth in John Howard's observation that the "fixation in our thinking about the importance of rights, however well intentioned," is probably one of the reasons for the unsatisfactory performance of some organizations. Why? As Howard observes, "[T]he very concept of rights inclines people to focus on their own well-being and to demand their due, instead of focusing on the well-being of all humanity."

Dr. Ben C. Fisher, in his lecture "The Challenge of Secularism to Christian Education," is surely right in reminding us that our hope for a "unifying principle by which men might dwell together in peace" lies not in acts that affirm the autonomy of the individual but in acts that glorify the brotherhood of man. We cannot raise ourselves by adding to our inventory of individual rights. The fulfillment of individual rights depends on the fulfillment of individual and group responsibilities. If we are to raise ourselves and all humankind, we must strengthen our common commitment and service in the cause of responsibility for the welfare of others and the good of society at large.

NOTE

1. This article is adapted from *The Mercer Law Review*, Vol. 36, 1985.

CHAPTER 3

The Quest for Self

ROBERT N. BELLAH

The discussion of individualism in Tocqueville's *Democracy in America* is illuminating with respect to contemporary American social life.[1] My work is in many ways a continuing conversation with Tocqueville as well as with our fellow citizens. In this paper I would like to bring Emerson into the conversation too, and suggest how close attention to these nineteenth-century texts is helpful in elucidating current social reality.

TOCQUEVILLE AND EMERSON ON INDIVIDUALISM

In a famous chapter entitled "Of Individualism in Democracies," Tocqueville points out that " 'Individualism' is a word recently coined to express a new idea. Our fathers only knew about egoism." Individualism is more moderate and orderly than egoism, but in the end its results are much the same: "Individualism is a calm and considered feeling which disposes each citizen to isolate himself from the mass of his fellows and withdraw into the circle of family and friends; with this little society formed to his taste, he gladly leaves the greater society to look out after itself."[2] As this tendency grows, he wrote, "there are more and more people who, though neither rich nor powerful enough to have much hold over others, have gained or kept enough wealth and enough understanding to look after their own needs. Such folk owe no man anything and hardly expect anything from anybody. They form the habit of thinking of themselves in isolation and imagine that their whole destiny is in their hands." Finally, such persons come to "forget their ancestors," but also their contemporaries. "Each man is forever thrown back on himself alone, and there is danger that he may be shut up in the solitude of his own heart."[3]

Tocqueville saw the isolation to which Americans are prone as ominous for the future of our freedom. It is just such isolation that is always encouraged by

·despotism. And so Tocqueville is particularly interested in all those coun-
tervailing tendencies that pulled people back from their isolation into social
communion. Immersion in private economic pursuits undermines the person
as citizen. On the other hand, involvement in public affairs is the best antidote
for the pernicious effects of individualistic isolation: "Citizens who are bound
to take part in public affairs must turn from the private interests and occasionally take a look at something other than themselves."[4] It is precisely in these
respects that the mores become important. The habits and practices of religion and democratic participation educate citizens to a larger view than their
purely private world would allow. These habits and practices rely to some
extent on self-interest in their educational work, but it is only when self-
interest has been to some degree transcended that they will have succeeded.
Tocqueville even saw the family as playing an important role in tempering
individualism, particularly through the role of women who, under the influence of religion, counter the economic self-interest of their husbands and
communicate to children a morality transcending the interests of the self.[5]

Tocqueville is at his most brilliant in his analysis of the social consequences of American individualism, although his observations about its personal consequences are not without interest. He comments on the competitiveness of Americans and their "restlessness in the midst of prosperity." "In
America," he says, "I have seen the freest and best educated of men in circumstances the happiest to be found in the world; yet it seemed to me that a cloud
habitually hung on their brow, and they seemed serious and almost sad even
in their pleasures," because they "never stop thinking of the good things they
have not got." This restlessness and sadness in pursuit of the good life makes it
difficult to form "strong attachments between man and man." The efforts and
enjoyments of Americans are livelier than those in traditional societies, but
the disappointments of their hopes and desires are keener, and their "minds
are more anxious and on edge." Of such restless, competitive, and anxious
people Tocqueville says, "they clutch everything and hold nothing fast."[6]

Ralph Waldo Emerson, writing at much the same time, gives a remarkably similar picture of American individualism except for his more positive,
even celebratory tone. That more positive tone is perhaps related to an effort
to give individualism a moral meaning that for Tocqueville it did not have.
Toward the end of his Phi Beta Kappa address of 1837, "The American
Scholar," Emerson also describes something that he sees as new in his time:

> Another sign of our times, also marked by an analogous political movement, is,
> the new importance given to the single person. Everything that tends to insulate
> the individual,—to surround him with barriers of natural respect, so that each
> man shall feel the world is his, and man shall treat with man as a sovereign state
> with a sovereign state;—tends to true union as well as greatness. "I learned,"
> said the melancholy Pestalozzi, "that no man in God's wide earth is either willing
> or able to help any other man." Help must come from the bosom alone.[7]

Emerson's devotion to what he calls "the capital virtue of self-trust" makes him leery of the dependence of the self on others but also of others on the self: "A sympathetic person is placed in the dilemma of a swimmer among drowning men, who all catch at him, and if he gives so much as a leg or a finger, they will drown him."[8] The conclusion of these views for social ethics is clear enough, confirming Tocqueville's analysis. In the famous essay on "Self-Reliance" Emerson wrote: "Then, again, do not tell me, as a good man did today, of my obligation to put all poor men in good situations. Are they my poor? I tell thee, thou foolish philanthropist, that I grudge the dollar, the dime, the cent, I give to such men as do not belong to me and to whom I do not belong."[9] Here we see tangible evidence of Emerson's rejection of the normative authority of the New Testament and his intention to deliver a comparable revelation for his own day.

What is surprising about this quick look at the teachings of Tocqueville and Emerson on individualism is how accurately they describe our condition today, whether we like it or not. Ordinary Americans may be completely unconscious of their link to an earlier America, but the individualism that Tocqueville described and Emerson exemplified is more vigorous than ever among middle-class Americans.[10]

THE QUEST FOR THE SELF

Many Americans share Emerson's emphasis on self-reliance and his belief that help comes only from our own bosom. As one therapist put it, "In the end you're really alone and you really have to answer to yourself." Many Americans also tend to share Emerson's view that society is inimical to the individual and that the quest for the self involves freeing ourselves from society. As Emerson put it, "Society is everywhere in conspiracy against the manhood of every one of its members."[11] Thus, the quest for the self is a quest for autonomy, for leaving the past and the social structures that have previously enveloped us, for stripping off the obligations and constraints imposed by others, until at last we find our true self, which is unique and individual.

One of the strongest imperatives of our culture is that we must leave home. Unlike many peasant societies where it is common to live with parents until their death and where one worships parents and ancestors all one's life, for us leaving home is the normal expectation and childhood is in many ways a preparation for it. For some the process is quite smooth; for others there is considerable conflict. The presence of conflict does not mean that the cultural pattern of leaving home is in doubt. Indeed, a degree of conflict over this issue is to some extent expected. However painful the process of leaving home, for parents or for children, the really frightening thing would be the prospect of the child never leaving home.

An equally important aspect of self-reliance is taking responsibility for our own views. Very often this means not only leaving home but leaving church as well, though perhaps not literally. We may continue to belong to the church of our parents. But the expectation is that at some point we will decide on our own that that is the church to belong to. We cannot defend our views by saying that they are simply those of our parents or of the church in which we were raised. On the contrary, they must be particularly and peculiarly our own. A 1978 Gallup poll found that 80 percent of Americans agreed with the statement, "An individual should arrive at his or her own religious beliefs independent of any churches or synagogues."[12]

Finding the right occupation is certainly an important part of the quest for the true self. But for middle-class Americans today work is less of a calling and more of a career, less something one deeply identifies with and more a means toward self-fulfillment. Getting locked into a particular slot or organization is often seen as constricting to the autonomy of the self, and midlife job changes or even career changes are widely advocated.

Where work is frustrating and confining and contains few intrinsic satisfactions, as it is for many Americans at all status levels, the quest for the true self may be pursued most urgently in the sphere of leisure and private life. In urban middle-class America, the choice of private "lifestyle" is probably freer than ever before in our history. Most of the constraints of traditional marriage have been called into question. (The expectation that it is normal to get married at all has dropped sharply over the past thirty years.[13]) One young mother of two decided that it was immoral to go on living with her husband when sex had lost its excitement, so the couple separated, each had therapy, and only after a year and the resolution of the problem did they resume living together. Many others involved in long and apparently satisfying marriages indicated that their commitment to the marriage was contingent on the continued satisfactions that it offered. We need not believe they will actually act on their ideology to notice how powerfully the ideology of self-fulfillment undercuts all sustained commitments in our society.

The quest for the self then, pursued under the predominant ideology of individualism, involves separating out from family, religion, and calling as sources of authority, duty, and moral example. It means autonomously pursuing happiness and satisfying one's own wants. American individualism seems determined more than ever to press ahead with the task of letting go of all criteria other than a radically private validation.

REACHING OUT

However Americans extol the autonomy and self-reliance of the individual, they do not imagine that a good life can be lived alone. Those we interviewed would almost all agree that connectedness to others in work, love, and community is essential to happiness, self-esteem, and moral worth. We must now consider how they, as autonomous individuals, reach out to others and how they conceive of the community that results.

Radical American individualism seems to contain two conceptions of human relations—contractual bargaining and expressive identity—which at first glance may appear incompatible but which were firmly asserted by Emerson and are accepted by many Americans today. Looking at individuals as "sovereign states," we might imagine the only relations possible between them to be by treaty, that is, by contract. The contractarian model has long been popular in America and takes new, psychologically nuanced forms today. But Emerson also noted that "sovereign" individuals, when they have freed themselves from convention and tradition, are identical to "nature," which is the same for all. The idea that deep within our unique and individual selves there is an expressive identity with all other selves is an idea that is widespread among many Americans. But these two notions of relatedness apply to radically different spheres. Expressive identity applies most of all to situations of love and intimacy, which are usually intense but of short duration. Contractual bargaining is the norm of everyday relationships, even the everyday aspects of marriage and friendship. What links the two seemingly disparate types together is the fact that both depend on the absolutely autonomous wills of the individuals involved. What both types avoid is the notion that there is any objective normative order governing the relationship, any transcendent loyalty above the wishes of the individuals involved, any community that is really there independent of the wills of the individuals that compose it. Naturally, relationships that are dependent entirely on spontaneous feeling or contractual bargaining alone are fragile, frustrating, and difficult to sustain.

Because "conventional roles" no longer have authority for many middle-class Americans and because spontaneous feeling, though highly valued, is often untrustworthy and transient, the contractual model, long familiar in our economic life, has more and more entered the sphere of private relationships, often under the aegis of popular psychology. It is, however, not always an easy model to live with, and it exacts a high price in terms of the stability of relationships. "Commitments take work, and we're tired of working," sighs Alec, a young therapist, "and we come home from work, the last thing I want to do, you know, is for people to sit down and say, 'Well, let's sit and work on our relationship. Let's talk about it.' Yes, but I worked eight and a half hours today, you know. Let's just sit down and watch the boob tube." His protest ends in a confession: "It's like you periodically ask yourself, like, 'Is this worth my effort? Is this worth that?' " Faced with ongoing demands to work on their relationships as well as their jobs, separate and equal selves are led to question the contractual terms of their commitments to each other: Are they getting what they want? Are they getting as much as they are giving? As much as they could get elsewhere? If not, they are tempted to withdraw and look elsewhere for fulfillment. Therapeutic experts may counsel them that lasting commitments are necessary for self-fulfillment. But within this "giving–getting" model each person must test such claims against his or her experience, case by case, and judge them in the light of his or her own "values." Because each person's feelings and values are subjective, the difficulties in figuring out the bottom line and interacting appropriately with others are daunting enough to make "long-term relationships" almost as unstable in their actual prospects as they are formidable in their therapeutic demands.

Yet many of those who seem to be committed to a radically individualistic ideology do not really seem to live in accordance with their belief, or better, they find their usual individualistic language inadequate to explain how they actually live. A successful California lawyer who has been married for a long time and who is accustomed to explaining all his actions in cost/benefit terms, was finally pressed in an interview to see that no interest-maximizing calculus could really account for what was in those terms an irrational commitment. At last he affirms that his happiness with his wife comes from "proceeding through all these stages together. It makes life meaningful and gives me the opportunity to share with somebody, have an anchor, if you will, and understand where I am. That for me is a real relationship." Here he is groping for words that would express his marriage as a community of memory and hope, a context that actually defines who he is, not a forum in which an empty self maximizes satisfactions.

In another case, a woman who had renewed her commitment to Judaism at first explained her action to us in individualistic terms. Judaism provides "structure" in a chaotic world, she said. In the religious community she has found help with day-care as well as a place where the joys and sufferings of everyday life can be shared. In her highly educated mentality, it is as though communal ties and religious commitments can be recommended only for the benefits they yield to the individual, for the social, emotional, and cultural functions they perform. But there was a moment in our conversation with her when she transcended these presuppositions. She said, "The woman who took care of my daughter when she was little was a Greek Jew. She was very young, nine, ten, eleven, when the war broke out, and was lying at the crematorium door when the American troops came through. So that she has a number tattooed on her arm. And it was always like being hit in the stomach with a brick when she would take my baby and sit and circle her with her arm, and there was the number." In that moment she was no longer in the "giving–getting" mode. She knew herself as a member of a people, which includes the living and the dead, parents and children, inheritors of a history and a culture that tells her who she is and that she must nurture through memory and hope.

Many of those to whom we talked seemed caught in the tensions created by radical American individualism. We strongly assert the value of our self-reliance and autonomy. We deeply feel the emptiness of a life without sustaining social commitments. Yet we are afraid to articulate our sense that we need each other as much as we need to stand alone, for fear that if we did we would lose our independence altogether. The tensions of our lives would be even greater if we did not in fact engage in practices that constantly limit the effects of an isolating individualism, even though we cannot articulate these practices nearly as well as we can the quest for autonomy.

POLITICS AND THE PUBLIC SPHERE

If the ideology of American individualism creates problems in sustaining intimate relationships, it causes even greater difficulty for involvement in the public sphere. Just as, in spite of our individualism, Americans do sustain long-term relationships, so do they also frequently become publicly involved. But our individualism skews and limits the kinds of public undertaking we are likely to engage in as well as our understanding of them.

Middle-class Americans view success in the occupational sphere as an essential prerequisite for a fulfilled life. But many of them do not think that personal success is enough. Only if one makes a personal, voluntary effort to "get involved" in helping others, they say, will one's life be complete. Americans in larger numbers than in many societies do join voluntary associations, service clubs, and church societies whose main purpose is to help the unfortunate or better the community. Such activities bring great personal satisfaction. The happiness and joy of giving are earned by making a free individual decision to join such an organization, to accept its discipline, and to participate in its charitable work. For these Americans, the self-interest demanded by the individualistic pursuit of success needs to be balanced by the sympathy of the voluntary act of concern for others. Without the joyful experience of support from such a community, an individual would find it difficult to make the effort to be a success, and success achieved would likely turn to ashes in one's mouth. Without some individually deserved success, an individual would have little voluntarily to contribute to his or her chosen community.

It is, of course, no easy task to strike a balance between the kind of self-interest implicit in the individualistic search for success and the kind of concern required to gain the joys of community and public involvement. A fundamental problem is that the ideas Americans have traditionally used to give shape and direction to their most generous impulses no longer suffice to give guidance in controlling the destructive consequences caused by the pursuit of economic success. It is not, as many recent social critics have claimed, that Americans have become less generous today than in the past. Many Americans are convinced, at least in theory, that a selfish seeker after purely individual success could not live a good, happy, joyful life. But when they think of the kind of generosity that could redeem the individualistic pursuit of economic success, they often imagine voluntary involvements in local, small-scale activities resembling a family, a club, or an idealized community in which individuals' initiatives interrelate to improve the life of all. They have difficulty relating this ideal image to the large-scale forces and institutions shaping their lives. This is what provides the pathos underlying many of our conversations about work, family, community, and politics. Many convey the feeling that sometimes their very best efforts to pursue their finest ideals seem senseless.

It is rarely the process of "getting involved" as a moral act that is thought to be senseless. Instead, the difficulty has to do with the realm of politics. For a good number of people, the very notion of politics connotes something morally unsavory, as though voluntary involvement is commendable and even fulfilling up to the point at which it enters the realm of officeholding, campaigning, and organized negotiating. Thus, their judgments about the goodness of citizenship in the wide sense of public involvement and responsibility turn negative in peculiar ways when they extend beyond the bounds of their local concerns and into the activities and institutions Americans term *politics*.

In one sense, politics is making operative the moral consensus of the community, where that consensus is thought to flow from agreement among individuals reached through free face-to-face discussion. The process of reaching such a consensus is one of the central meanings of the word *democratic* in America. It idealizes an individualism without rancor. For this understanding, citizenship is virtually coextensive with "getting involved" with one's neighbors for the good of the community. Many times Americans do not think of this process as "politics" at all. But where this understanding is seen as a form of politics it is the New England township of legend, the self-governing small town singled out by Tocqueville, that remains as the ideal exemplar.

In sharp contrast to the image of consensual community stands another understanding, for which politics means the pursuit of differing interests according to agreed-upon, neutral rules. This is the realm of coalitions among groups with similar interests, of conflicts between groups with opposing interests, and of mediators and brokers of interests, the professional politicians. The *politics of interest*, which is what we call this second type, is what Americans frequently mean by the term *politics*. It is sometimes celebrated by political scientists as *pluralism*, but for ordinary Americans the connotation is often negative. The politics of interest is frequently seen as a kind of necessary evil in a large diverse society, as a reluctantly agreed-to second best to consensual democracy.

Instead of a realm of spontaneous involvement with others to whom people feel akin, they enter the politics of interest for reasons of utility, to get what they or their group needs or wants. To the extent that many of those we talked to saw *politics* as meaning the politics of interest, they regarded it as not entirely legitimate morally—hence, the generally low opinion of "the politician" as a figure in American life. Politics suffers in comparison with the market. The legitimacy of the market rests in large part on the belief that it rewards individuals impartially on the basis of fair competition, a legitimacy helped by the fact that economic transactions are widely dispersed and often invisible. By contrast, the politics of negotiation at local, state, and federal levels, though it shares the utilitarian attitudes of the market, often exposes a competition among groups in which inequalities of power, influence, and moral probity become highly visible as determinants of the outcome. At the same time, the politics of interest provides no framework for the discussion of issues other than the conflict and compromises of interests themselves. Thus, the routine activities of interest politics, visibly conducted by professionals and apparently rewarding all kinds of inside connections while favoring the strong at the expense of the weak, must appear as an affront to true individualism and fairness alike.

Citizenship is more difficult and discordant for the individual in this second understanding of politics than in the ideal of community consensus. It means entering the complicated, professional, yet highly personal business of adversarial struggles, alliance building, and interest bargaining. It requires dealing with others from quite different consensual communities. For most people, it lacks the immediacy of everyday involvement unless urgent interests are at stake. Thus, supporting candidates by voting is the typical expression of this understanding of politics for most people, keeping politics at arm's length.

Thus, the culture of individualism does not prevent Americans from entering the public sphere, but it does limit and distort their understanding of it. If human action is always either the spontaneous expression of sympathy or the rational calculation of self-interest, then when the spontaneous form fails only the rational is left. The public realm is not considered exclusively as a realm of Hobbesian conflict because most Americans see the national community, at moments at least, as a local community writ large. Thus, millions of Americans could identify with the individual American athletes competing in the Los Angeles Olympic Games and root for "U.S.A., U.S.A." as they would for the local high school football team. But where it is a question not of our similarities but of our differences, then most Americans see only conflict and power. Objective political norms that speak not only of individual rights and fair procedures, but also of substantive justice, are hard to comprehend within an individualist vocabulary. Therefore, national politics, when the veneer of local rhetoric, of "family, neighborhood, and work," is removed, makes little sense to most Americans. It is not narcissism or hedonism that prevents Americans, who continue in many ways to be a generous and compassionate people, from understanding those different from themselves. It is the limitations of their cultural resources.

INDIVIDUALISM AND AMERICAN MORES

We have described American individualism from Emerson to the present and have considered some of its consequences for private and public life, for morality, and for politics. It is time to return to Tocqueville to consider whether the restraints which he saw the American mores of his day placing on individualism are still operative, or whether the destructive consequences which he feared an unchecked individualism would have are beginning to materialize.

By way of summary of what has been said so far, we may reformulate Tocqueville's argument in a way that is somewhat more explicit than he ever does himself. We have characterized individualism, following Tocqueville and with the help of Emerson, as a way of thinking about human action which can conceive of human relatedness only as the result of spontaneous feeling or calculated interest. Tocqueville is fully aware of both of these aspects of an individualistic culture. He stresses repeatedly the "natural compassion" or "sympathy" that citizens in a democracy feel for one another: "It often happens in the most civilized countries of the world that a man in misfortune is almost as isolated in the crowd as a savage in the woods. That is hardly ever seen in the United States. The Americans, always cold in manner and often coarse, are hardly ever insensitive, and though they may be in no hurry to volunteer services, yet they do not refuse them."[14] Tocqueville, who is fully aware of the importance of self-interest in the motivation of Americans, often sees sympathy and interest working together to promote public-spirited actions. At times, Tocqueville even seems to feel that a combination of sympathy and an educated self-interest, a "self-interest properly understood," would be enough to sustain free institutions in America.

There is an ambiguity in the way Tocqueville uses the term *mores*. On the one hand, it is a purely descriptive term. American mores are simply the way Americans do things, the pattern of American life, close to what we would mean when we speak of "American culture." On the other hand, *mores* has a normative meaning. It includes the notion of duty, obligation, or moral rightness, and it refers particularly to social obligations. Here *mores* is close to the German *Sittlichkeit*, the institutionalized pattern of social obligations. From this understanding of mores individualism is ambiguous. It is certainly part of a cultural pattern. It even has a normative component, one we can understand better perhaps with the help of Emerson than Tocqueville: the obligation to remain true to the self regardless of all other considerations. Yet from individualism a *social* ethic does not flow. Social relatedness depends entirely on the spontaneous feeling or rational calculation of individual wills. The social order has no normative validity in itself. It is merely the instrument or the expression of individual selves. From this point of view, individualism cannot be part of the mores but is antithetical to them.

Clearly, however subtly Tocqueville analyzes the possibility that individualism in America can be turned to the service of the common good and the preservation of free institutions, in the end he does believe that only an objective moral order, with obligations that transcend individual feelings and interests, will be equal to that task. In the narrower sense, therefore, the term *mores* refers to that objective moral order. As we have said, there are two spheres where Tocqueville finds mores in this second sense significant: political participation and religion.

In both of these spheres in America, an objective moral order is problematic because both of them are so heavily invaded by self-interest. In the important chapter "How the Americans Combat the Effects of Individualism by Free Institutions," Tocqueville points out that it is self-interest, often quite petty self-interest, that frequently motivates Americans to participate in the public sphere. But in the end, he says, "The free institutions of the United States and the political rights enjoyed there provide a thousand continual reminders to every citizen that he lives in society. At every moment they bring his mind back to this idea, that it is the duty as well as the interest of men to be useful to their fellow."[15] It is precisely the element of duty that cannot be derived from the interests and feelings of individuals alone.

In the chapter "How the Americans Apply the Doctrine of Self-Interest Properly Understood to Religion," Tocqueville comments on the American tendency to propagate religion on the basis of its earthly or at least heavenly rewards. "Nevertheless," he says, "I refuse to believe that all who practice virtue from religious motives do so only in hope of reward."[16] And a few pages later on, in one of the most earnestly admonitory chapters in the whole book, Tocqueville says, "By their practice Americans show that they feel the urgent necessity to instill Morality into democracy by means of religion. What they think of themselves in this respect enshrines a truth which should penetrate deep into the consciousness of every democratic nation."[17] Tocqueville had already pointed out in Volume I that religion provided for Americans a morality that was objective, certain and stable, which the unimpeded pursuit of interest in the economic and political spheres could never do.

And so we may ask whether today there exist in America, in the midst of our triumphant individualism, mores in the sense of *Sittlichkeit*, which would resist our proclivity to become a collection of atomized individuals who would be easy prey to administrative despotism.

We have already indicated that the ideology of individualism does not describe adequately the lives even of those who espouse it. A completely empty self that operates out of purely arbitrary choice is theoretically imaginable but performatively impossible. The family, the church, the local community, which the middle-class person seeks to shuffle off in the effort to rise in the social hierarchy free of encumbrances, cannot be wholly denied, for we are indelibly constituted by them. On the other hand, for those many Americans for whom objective moral communities still exist, most frequently in the form of churches or other religious associations, but often also in political associations, the insistent language of individualism constantly threatens to make commitment contingent on psychological or material reward.

This is not the place to review our findings on the present state of American mores. At best, what we found are signs of the times, which are far from allowing a prediction of future trends. For many Americans, an objective moral order embodied in living communities clearly does exist. Indeed, throughout America we can find a number of people whom we could call genuine heroes and heroines of everyday life, dedicated to the common good and joyful in their dedication. There is also a great deal of nostalgia for a more coherent America, for "traditional values" and stable communities. The image of the small town we found to be deeply attractive to Americans regardless of their political or ethical views. Yet it would be hard to deny that the individualism that Tocqueville described and Emerson embodied is stronger than ever today. For many Americans the world is indeed divided into the two realms of rational calculation and spontaneous feeling, even though the emptiness of a life that alternates between those realms alone is increasingly recognized.

Perhaps not surprisingly, the alternatives to radical individualism among present-day Americans are not different from those pointed out by Tocqueville: republican politics and biblical religion. Reappropriating those traditions and reviving the communities that carry them seem to be our best hope. Only they can overcome the chasm between person and society that individualism creates. Only they show us that we can be true to our selves, individualists in the best sense, only when we are true to our ethical commitments and collective loyalties in private and public life. Indeed, it is only such commitments and loyalties that constitute a real self, that tell us who we are. Biblical religion and republican politics involve us in communities of memory and hope within which we can sustain the moral ecology that makes a good life possible.

NOTES

1. Robert N. Bellah, Richard Madsen, William M. Sullivan, Ann Swidler, and Steven M. Tipton, *Habits of the Heart: Individualism and Commitment in American Life* (Berkeley: University of California Press, 1985). Much of this paper derives from our joint authorship. Unless otherwise noted, all interviewees mentioned in this paper were subjects of studies conducted for *Habits of the Heart*.
2. Alexis de Tocqueville, *Democracy in America*, tr. George Lawrence, ed. J. P. Mayer (Garden City, N.Y.: Doubleday Anchor, 1969), p. 506.
3. Ibid., p. 508.
4. Ibid., p. 510.
5. Ibid., p. 291.
6. Ibid., pp. 535–538, 565.
7. Ralph Waldo Emerson, *Essays and Lectures* (New York: The Library of America, 1983), p. 70.
8. From "Experience" in ibid., p. 490.
9. Ibid., p. 262.
10. "Habits of the heart" is a phrase Tocqueville uses to describe the mores. See *Democracy in America*, p. 287.

11. From "Self-Reliance," in Emerson, *Essays and Lectures,* p. 261.
12. Reported in Dean R. Hoge, *Converts, Dropouts, Returnees: Religious Change Among Catholics* (Washington, D.C.: United States Catholic Conference; New York: Pilgrim Press, 1981), p. 167.
13. Joseph Veroff, Elizabeth Douvan, and Richard A. Kulka, *The Inner American: A Self-Portrait from 1957 to 1976* (New York: Basic Books, 1981), p. 147.
14. Tocqueville, *Democracy in America,* p. 571.
15. Ibid., p. 512.
16. Ibid., p. 528.
17. Ibid., p. 542.

CHAPTER 4

Communitarianism or Populism?

CHRISTOPHER LASCH

My title is meant to refer to a difference of emphasis, not to an irreconcilable opposition between two positions having nothing in common. The populist and communitarian traditions are distinguishable but historically intertwined; any account of those traditions and their contemporary significance has to do justice both to what unites them and to what sets them apart from each other. Populism is rooted in the defense of small proprietorship, which was widely regarded, in the eighteenth and early nineteenth centuries, as the necessary basis of civic virtue. Communitarianism has its intellectual antecedents in a sociological tradition, initially a conservative tradition, that found the sources of social cohesion in shared assumptions so deeply ingrained in everyday life that they don't have to be articulated—in folkways, customs, prejudices, habits of the heart. Because both traditions shared certain common reservations about the Enlightenment, however, it has not always been easy to tell them apart. Nor has there seemed to be much point in this exercise. Both fell outside the dominant celebration of progress, and their agreement on an issue of such importance has made their differences seem trivial.

If terms like *populism* and *community* figure prominently in political discourse today, it is because the ideology of the Enlightenment is visibly crumbling. The claims of universal reason are universally suspect. Hopes for a system of values that would transcend the particularism of class, nationality, religion, and race no longer carry much conviction. The Enlightenment's reason and morality are increasingly seen as a cover for power, and the prospect that the world can be governed by reason seems more remote than at any time since the eighteenth century. The citizen of the world—the prototype of humankind in the future, according to the Enlightenment philosophers—is not much in evidence. We have a universal market, but it does not carry with it the civilizing effects that were so confidently expected by Hume and Voltaire. Instead of generating a new appreciation of common interests and inclinations—of the essential sameness of human beings everywhere—the global market seems to intensify the awareness of ethnic and national differences. The unification of the market goes hand in hand with the fragmentation of culture.

The collapse of the Enlightenment manifests itself politically in the collapse of liberalism, which in many ways is the most attractive product of the Enlightenment and the carrier of its best hopes. Throughout the twentieth century liberalism has been pulled in two directions at once—toward the market and (notwithstanding its initial misgivings about government) toward the state. On the one hand, the market appears to be the ideal embodiment of the principle—the cardinal principle of liberalism—that individuals are the best judges of their own interests and that they must therefore be allowed to speak for themselves in matters that concern their happiness and well-being. But individuals cannot learn to speak for themselves at all, much less come to an intelligent understanding of their happiness and well-being, in a world in which there are no values except those of the market. Even liberal individuals require the character-forming discipline of the family, the neighborhood, the school, and the church—all of which (not just the family) have been weakened by the encroachments of the market. The market notoriously tends to universalize itself. It does not easily coexist with institutions that operate according to principles antithetical to itself—schools and universities, newspapers and magazines, charities, families. Sooner or later the market tends to absorb them all. It puts an almost irresistible pressure on every activity to justify itself in the only terms it recognizes—to become a business proposition, to pay its own way, to show black print on the bottom line. It turns news into entertainment, scholarship into professional careerism, social work into the scientific management of poverty. Inexorably, it remodels every institution in its own image.

In the attempt to restrict the scope of the market, liberals have therefore turned to the state. But the remedy often proves to be worse than the disease. The replacement of informal types of association by formal systems of socialization and control weakens social trust; undermines the willingness both to assume responsibility for oneself and to hold others accountable for their actions; destroys respect for authority; and thus turns out to be self-defeating. Consider the fate of neighborhoods that serve so effectively, at their best, as intermediaries between the family and the larger world. Neighborhoods have been destroyed not only by the market—by crime and drugs or less dramatically by suburban shopping malls—but also by enlightened social engineering. The main thrust of social policy, ever since the first crusades against child labor, has been to transfer the care of children from informal settings to institutions designed specifically for pedagogical and custodial purposes. Today this trend continues in the movement for day-care, which is often justified on the undeniable grounds that working mothers need it but also on the grounds that day-care centers can take advantage of the latest innovations in pedagogy and child psychology. This policy of segregating children in age-graded institutions under professional supervision has been a massive failure, for reasons suggested some time ago by Jane Jacobs in *The Death and Life of Great American Cities*—an attack on city planning that applies to social planning in general, right across the board: "The myth that playgrounds and grass and hired guards or supervisors are innately wholesome for children and that city streets, filled with ordinary people, are innately evil for children, boils down to a deep contempt for ordinary people."[1] In their contempt, planners lose sight of the way in which city streets, if they are working as they should, teach children a lesson that cannot be taught by educators or professional caretakers—that "people must take a modicum of public responsibility for each other even if they have no ties to each other." When the corner grocer or the locksmith scolds a child for running into the street, the child learns something that can't be learned simply by formal instruction. What the child learns is that adults unrelated to each other except by the accident of propinquity uphold certain standards and assume responsibility for the neighborhood. With good reason, Jacobs calls this the "first fundamental of successful city life"—one that "people hired to look after children cannot teach because the essence of this responsibility is that you do it without being hired."

Neighborhoods encourage "casual public trust," according to Jacobs. In its absence, the everyday maintenance of life has to be turned over to professional bureaucrats. The atrophy of informal controls leads irresistibly to the expansion of bureaucratic controls. This development threatens to extinguish the very privacy liberals have always set such store by. It also loads the organizational sector with burdens it cannot support. The crisis of public funding is only one indication of the intrinsic weakness of organizations that can no longer count on informal, everyday mechanisms of social trust and control. The taxpayers' revolt, though itself informed by an ideology of privatism resistant to any kind of civic appeals, at the same time grows out of a well-founded suspicion that tax money merely sustains bureaucratic self-aggrandizement. The state is clearly overburdened, and nobody has much confidence in its ability to solve the problems that need to be solved.

As formal organizations break down, people will have to improvise ways of meeting their immediate needs: patrolling their own neighborhoods, withdrawing their children from public schools in order to educate them at home. The default of the state will thus contribute in its own right to the restoration of informal mechanisms of self-help. But it is hard to see how the foundations of civic life can be restored unless this work becomes an overriding goal of public policy. We have heard a good deal of talk about the repair of our material infrastructure, but our cultural infrastructure needs attention too, and more than just the rhetorical attention of politicians who praise "family values" while pursuing economic policies that undermine them. It is either naive or cynical to lead the public to think that dismantling the welfare state is enough to ensure a revival of informal cooperation—"a thousand points of light." People who have lost the habit of self-help, who live in cities and suburbs where shopping malls have replaced neighborhoods, and who prefer the company of close friends (or simply the company of television) to the informal sociability of the street, the coffee shop, and the tavern are not likely to reinvent communities just because the state has proved such an unsatisfactory substitute. Market mechanisms will not repair the fabric of public trust. On the contrary, the market's effect on the cultural infrastructure is just as corrosive as that of the state.

We can now begin to appreciate the appeal of populism and communitarianism. They reject both the market and the welfare state in pursuit of a third way. This is why they are so difficult to classify on the conventional spectrum of political opinion. Their opposition to free market ideologies seems to align them with the Left, but their criticism of the welfare state (whenever this criticism becomes open and explicit) makes them sound right-wing. In fact, these positions belong neither to the Left nor the Right, and for that very reason they seem to many people to hold out the best hope of breaking the deadlock of current debate—which has been institutionalized in the two major parties and their divided control of the federal government. At a time when political debate consists largely of ideological slogans endlessly repeated to audiences composed mainly of the party faithful, fresh thinking is desperately needed. It is not likely to emerge, however, from those with a vested interest in the old orthodoxies. We need a "third way of thinking about moral obligation," as Alan Wolfe puts it—one that locates moral obligation neither in the state nor in the market but in "common sense, ordinary emotions, and everyday life." Wolfe's plea for a political program designed to strengthen civil society, which closely resembles the ideas advanced in *The Good Society* by Robert Bellah and his collaborators, should be welcomed by the growing numbers of people who find themselves dissatisfied with the alternatives defined by conventional debate.

These authors illustrate the strengths of the communitarian position along with some of its characteristic weaknesses. They make it clear that both the market and the state presuppose the strength of "noneconomic ties of trust and solidarity," as Wolfe puts it. Yet the expansion of these institutions weakens ties of trust and thus undermines the preconditions for their own success. The market and the "job culture," Bellah writes, are "invading our private lives," eroding our "moral infrastructure" of "social trust." Nor does the welfare state repair the damage. "The example of more successful welfare states . . . suggests that money and bureaucratic assistance alone do not halt the decline of the family" or strengthen any of the other "sustaining institutions that make interdependence morally significant."

Wolfe's recent book, *Whose Keeper?*, contains a useful analysis of the ideological as well as the social and cultural consequences of the developments that have enhanced the influence of the market and the state at the expense of civil society.[2] Early admirers of the market, for example, Adam Smith, believed that selfishness was a virtue only if it was confined to the realm of exchange. They did not advocate or even envision conditions in which every phase of life would be organized according to the principles of the market. Now that private life has been largely absorbed by the market, however, a new school of economic thought offers what amounts to a "new moral vision"—a society wholly dominated by the market, in which "economic relations are no longer softened by ties of trust and solidarity." In the work of Milton Friedman and other spokesmen for what is misleadingly called neoclassical economic theory, "no area remains outside . . . the market," says Wolfe. "There is only one compartment in social life: the one defined by self-interested action." The social democratic reply to free market economics and its extension in the work of philosophers like Robert Nozick is equally unsatisfactory, as Wolfe shows. Like Michael Sandel, Wolfe takes John Rawls as the prime exponent of a social democratic liberalism that conceives of human beings as rootless abstractions wholly absorbed in maximizing their own advantage. Rawls claims that a proper understanding of their own interests leads individuals to appreciate principles of justice that justify a vast expansion of the welfare state; but his view of social relations, as Wolfe explains, is quite similar to the view that elsewhere justifies an expansion of the market. Rawls's theory has no room for trust or conscience, qualities he finds "oppressive." It has no room for affective ties except in their most abstract form. "People in the Rawlsian republic do not love other men and women: they love humankind instead." His theory "teaches people to distrust what will help them most—their personal attachments to those they know—and value what will help them least—abstract principles," which invariably prove a "poor guide to the moral dilemmas of everyday life."

The trouble with the welfare state, as Wolfe sees it, is that it has lost sight of its original purpose, the redistribution of income. Today the welfare state, at least in Scandinavia, is "much more directly involved in the regulation of moral obligations." Wolfe cites the expansion of publicly supported day-care as a case in point. "As the state grows and families weaken, it becomes more difficult to remain hopeful that state intervention will not significantly alter the character of the institutions in civil society." This raises a troubling question: "When government is relied on to furnish rules of moral obligation, will it weaken the very social ties that make government possible in the first place?" Unfortunately, Wolfe does not pursue the question very far. He reserves most of his criticism for the market. Whereas he condemns the market, he is merely "ambivalent" about the state. He is aware of the mounting criticism of the welfare state in Sweden, and he acknowledges the force of what is being said—for example, that "individual responsibility" (in the words of Gunnar Heckscher) is undermined by the notion that "society is to blame" for poverty, delinquency, and many other ills. Wolfe quotes portions of the disparaging account of Swedish society written by Hans Magnus Enzensberger in the early 1980s: "The state's power has grown unopposed, creeping into all the cracks of daily life, regulating people's doings in a way without precedent in free societies." Enzensberger's point, Wolfe concedes, "cannot be dismissed." A few pages farther on, however, he insists that Enzensberger is "incorrect" when he claims that "Scandinavians are in danger of losing their moral autonomy to government."

In any case, the welfare state in our own country is so pathetically weak that it poses no threat to anyone. It may not be "completely satisfactory," but it is clearly preferable to the market. If we had to choose between the Scandinavian systems and our own, we would have to conclude that "the needs of the future generations would . . . be better served" by the former. Wolfe's book does not live up to its promise. What began as a case for a "third way" ends with a qualified endorsement of the welfare state and a ringing endorsement of sociology—an anticlimax, to say the least.

The Good Society, like Whose Keeper?, is much more an attack on the market than on the welfare state. Communitarianism in this form is difficult to distinguish from social democracy. At one point the authors of The Good Society explicitly call for a "global New Deal," notwithstanding their reservations about the "administered society." They have a great deal to say about responsibility, but it is "social responsibility," not the responsibility of individuals, that mainly concerns them. In their plea for "responsible attention" there are overtones of "compassion," the slogan of social democracy—a slogan that has always been used to justify welfare programs, the expansion of the state's custodial and tutelary functions, and bureaucratic rescue of women, children, and other victims of mistreatment. The ideology of compassion, however agreeable to our ears, is one of the principal influences, it its own right, on the subversion of civic life, which depends not so much on compassion as on mutual respect. A misplaced compassion degrades both the victims, who are reduced to objects of pity, and their would-be benefactors, who find it easier to pity their fellow citizens than to hold them up to impersonal standards, the attainment of which would entitle them to respect. We pity those who suffer, and we pity most of all those who suffer conspicuously; but we reserve respect for those who refuse to exploit their suffering for the purposes of pity. We respect those who are willing to be held accountable for their actions, who submit to exacting and impersonal standards impartially applied. Today it is widely believed, at least by members of the caring class, that standards are inherently oppressive, that far from being impersonal they discriminate against women, blacks, and minorities in general. Standards, we are told, reflect the cultural hegemony of dead white European males. Compassion compels us to recognize the injustice of imposing them on everybody else.

When the ideology of compassion leads to this kind of absurdity, it is time to call it into question. Compassion has become the human face of contempt. Democracy once implied opposition to every form of double standard. Today we accept double standards—as always, a recipe for second-class citizenship— in the name of humanitarian concern. Having given up the effort to raise the general level of competence (the old meaning of democracy), we are content to institutionalize competence in the caring class, which arrogates to itself the job of looking out for everybody else.

Populism, as I understand it, is unambiguously committed to the principle of respect. It is for this reason, among others, that it is to be preferred to communitarianism, which is too quick to compromise with the welfare state and to endorse its ideology of compassion. Populism has always rejected both the politics of deference and the politics of pity. It stands for plain manners and plain straightforward speech. It is unimpressed by titles and other symbols of exalted social rank, but it is equally unimpressed by claims of moral superiority advanced in the name of the oppressed. It rejects a "preferential option for the poor," if that means treating the poor as helpless victims of circumstance, absolving them of accountability, or excusing their derelictions on the grounds that poverty carries with it a presumption of innocence. Populism is the authentic voice of democracy. It assumes that individuals are entitled to respect until they prove themselves unworthy of it, but it insists that they take responsibility for themselves. It is reluctant to make allowances or to withhold judgment on the grounds that "society is to blame." Populism is "judgmental," to invoke a current adjective, the pejorative use of which shows how far the capacity for discriminating judgment has been weakened by the moral climate of humanitarian "concern."

Communitarians regret the collapse of social trust but often fail to see that, in a democracy, trust can only be grounded in mutual respect. They properly insist that rights have to be balanced by responsibility, but they seem to be more interested in the responsibility of the community as a whole—its responsibility, say, to its least fortunate members—than in the responsibility of individuals. When the authors of *The Good Society* say that "democracy means paying attention," they seek to recall us to a sense of the common good and to combat the selfish individualism that blinds us to the needs of others. But it is our reluctance to make demands on each other, much more than our reluctance to help those in need, that is sapping the strength of democracy today. We have become far too accommodating and tolerant for our own good. In the name of sympathetic understanding, we tolerate second-rate workmanship, second-rate habits of thought, and second-rate standards of personal conduct. We put up with bad manners and with many kinds of bad language, ranging from the commonplace scatology that is now ubiquitous to elaborate academic evasion. We seldom bother to correct a mistake or to argue with opponents in the hope of changing their minds. Instead, we either shout them down or agree to disagree, saying that all of us have a right to our opinions. Democracy in our time is more likely to die of indifference than of intolerance. Tolerance and understanding are important virtues, but they must not become an excuse for apathy.

The differences between populism and communitarianism, as I argued at the outset, are differences of emphasis, but they have important political consequences. My strongest objection to the communitarian point of view is that it has too little to say about controversial issues like affirmative action, abortion, and family policy. The authors of *The Good Society* assure their readers that they "do not want to advocate any single form of family life." It is the "quality of family life" that matters, in their view, not its structure. But quality and structure are not so easily separable. Common sense tells us that children need both fathers and mothers, that they are devastated by divorce, and that they do not flourish in day-care centers. Without minimizing the difficulty of solving the problems that confront the family, at least we ought to be able to hold up a standard by which to measure the success or failure of our efforts. We need guidelines, not a general statement of good intentions. If communitarians are serious about what Bellah calls a "politics of generativity," they need to address the conditions that are widely believed to make it more difficult than it used to be to raise children. Parents are deeply troubled by the moral climate of permissiveness, by the sex and violence to which children are prematurely exposed, by the moral relativism they encounter in school, and by the devaluation of authority that makes children impatient with any restraints. Much of the opposition to abortion reflects the same kind of concerns, which cannot be addressed simply by taking the position that abortion, like the structure of the family, ought to be a matter of private choice. The privatization of morality is one more indication of the collapse of the community; and a communitarianism that acquiesces in this development, at the same time calling for a public philosophy, cannot expect to be taken very seriously.

NOTES

1. Jane Jacobs, *The Death and Life of Great American Cities* (New York: Random House, 1961).
2. See Alan Wolfe, *Whose Keeper? Social Science and Moral Obligation* (Berkeley: University of California Press, 1989).

CHAPTER 5

Japan: The Price of Safe Streets

JUAN WILLIAMS

Last summer I traveled to Japan on a Japan Society Leadership Fellowship. After two months I had a strange, niggling feeling that there was something missing in my everyday life. My wife called one day from the United States with the answer. She said a woman had been driving her children to the babysitter (near my home in Washington, D.C.) when she inadvertently drove into a lethal crossfire of gunshots being exchanged by rival drug dealers. The woman was shot in the head and died in front of her children.

That is when the revelation hit me. What was missing in my daily routine in Japan was a normal American awareness of the constant threat of crime. On any night of the week, the monster city of Tokyo—population 12 million—is alive, the streets packed with people on dates, in restaurants, walking all over town. On weekends the downtown streets are filled morning to night with shoppers. There are people in the parks after dark. Bikes are unchained; front doors are often left unlocked. The fanciest stores display expensive items, such as Bally shoes, out front and unguarded. Five-year-old children ride the subways alone.

Yet, strange as it may seem to Americans, the nightly news across Japan rarely features a crime story. Japan's cities may be choked with people and cars, but that is because Japan's cities are popular places for living, working, and playing. Crime has not corroded urban life, as it has in many American cities.

"As a woman I feel safest here in all the world," said Wakako Hironaka, 58, who lived in the United States and France before being elected a member of the upper house of the Japanese Diet.

"In Japan, you can take a walk in the park any time," said Robert Whiting, an American author of several books on Japanese baseball who has lived here for twenty-three years. "You can take the subway at midnight, and you don't have to look over your shoulder to see if you're going to get mugged."

Three black American sailors standing on a subway platform and dressed to party on a Saturday night raved about Japan and said they planned to sign up for another tour because "Nobody's going to knock you upside the head here."

But safety has a price.

The underlying reason for the absence of crime in Japan is the group-think that dominates every aspect of life here, which allows the Japanese to surrender concerns over privacy and individual rights to near-complete trust in an all-powerful national police force.

The independence of the police is startling—and somewhat unsettling—to an American. For example, Tokyo police do not answer to the mayor or to any politician. Instead, bureaucrats in the National Police Agency appoint police across the country, set their wages, and determine the size and budget of the local force. The effect is to insulate police from local and national politicians' complaints, as well as any community reaction to their actions. The absolute trust vested in Japanese police is grounded in a conviction rate of more than 99 percent for people charged with crimes (to be precise, 99.83 percent). International human rights groups criticize the Japanese police for such practices as jailing people for as many as twenty-three days without lodging a complaint and for conducting interrogations without allowing suspects access to a lawyer.

"We are of the opinion that free and prompt access to a lawyer is a fundamental safeguard," said Makoto Iwai, the manager of Amnesty International in Japan. According to an Amnesty report issued in January, former Japanese prisoners alleged that they had been beaten, had had their heads banged against the wall, and had been denied food and use of the toilet. But such criticism has sparked no broad public demand for curtailing the police's powers. Even in death penalty cases, the Japanese delegate total authority to the police. The police never announce executions in capital cases (death is by hanging in Japan), and therefore, the media do not report executions; they only come to light in year-end statistics.

Why do the Japanese give the police such power?

Some say it is a cultural artifact of the 400-year period before Japan's modernization, which began in 1868, when samurai had the shogun's authority to enforce justice at will by using their swords to cut of hands and even behead people they judged to be criminal.

But a high-ranking Tokyo policeman who has studied international relations at Johns Hopkins offered a more recent anecdote to explain the difference in the crime picture between Japan and the United States. When the policeman was a little boy, he said, he once spoke rudely to his father, who promptly told him, "We don't need such a bad boy." His father then pushed him out the front door and locked it.

"I knocked on the door and begged him, 'Please, Daddy, I'm sorry. Let me back in; I should be inside,' " the 45-year-old policeman told me, frowning at the old memory.

"Belonging to the family and the organization is our safest haven in Japan," he said. "If you do something wrong, commit a crime, you embarrass your family, your group . . . you risk being put out of your company, your club. In the United States when a child does some mischief, you tell him to go to his room, stay in the house, and that it's okay as long as he is good to go outside [again] where he is independent, an individual, and can act like an adult."

Katsuei Hirasawa, the director of the crime prevention bureau of the Tokyo police, agreed. But he added that Tokyo—and Japan—have been lucky too.

"The luck factor is that we have no arguments over strict gun control," he said, noting that the most common weapon in Japan is a knife, "and we are not so affected by drugs." (Amphetamines are the most popular drug, but their per capita use is far lower than the U.S. rate. While the availability of cocaine is increasing, crack cocaine is unknown.)

"We have no racial problems," he added. "The economy is good and . . . we still get the very best graduates from the best universities competing to join the police force."

Japan does have crime syndicates (called *yakuza*), such as the mobsters who were recently revealed to have bought millions of dollars' worth of Nomura Securities Company stock with the promise that the brokerage would cover any losses. The company has been disciplined, but for the most part there has been little outcry over police practices that generally allow the *yakuza* to engage in criminal activity as long as they do not become too violent or cause too many complaints from the public.

The cozy relationship between the cops and the mob recently led to a scandal when two Thai women, who were used as sexual entertainment in bars owned by the Suzuka syndicate, escaped and sought police protection. The cops gave the women back to the mobsters when the gang threatened to reveal that the cops had beaten up a bar customer. When the story broke, the police claimed that the women had gone back to the mob themselves. Only after an internal police investigation did the two officers involved admit returning the women to the mobsters. After the lie was exposed, the National Police Agency fired one officer, suspended the other for two months, and demoted the local police chief.

As for any public relations problem, the agency issued a brief statement warning its own officers, according to press accounts, that "police contact with *yakuza* can contribute to public distrust." In Japan, that was the end of the story.

On the tiny, bustling streets here, this combination of culture and sociology makes Tokyo a paragon of safety. It has the lowest rates for murder, robbery, rape, and theft of any major city in the world. In 1988 the U.S. homicide rate was seven times greater than Japan's, and the robbery rate 200 times greater; the rate for rape in the same year was 30 times greater.

One key to the low crime rate is the extraordinary contact between police and community. Once or twice a year the police knock on every door in Japan to talk with the residents or businesses about what is happening in the apartment buildings and neighborhood. There are also small police booths—called *kobans*—throughout Tokyo's neighborhoods that are constantly manned by two police officers each. The 1,250 boxes report to the city's ninety-two police stations, which in turn report to nine district headquarters.

Tokyo police report to the National Police Agency, as do all of Japan's 257,375 police. In law-abiding Japan, there is one police officer per 557 people, compared to one police officer for every 357 Americans.

Police in every city and town wear the same uniforms since they all belong to the National Police Agency. The functions of the FBI, the Drug Enforcement Administration, the Bureau of Alcohol, Tobacco, and Firearms, and even the Secret Service and the Securities and Exchange Commission are all performed by the unified national police system, eliminating arguments over coordination and jurisdiction.

"Because we are all one police department, we don't have to stop chasing a criminal at the edge of Tokyo," said Katsuhiko Ikeda, the public relations director of the Tokyo police. "In our surveys we find that 90 percent of the Japanese people say they want to cooperate with the police and give information to the police," said a high-ranking officer. "We do not have this situation that you have in America where people will see a crime and don't call the police. Here, people will call 911 and hold the criminal for the police."

In keeping with the Japanese proclivity for group action, each police station organizes its own neighborhood crime prevention association. There are crime prevention associations in each building, and each of these associations belongs to a citywide crime prevention association. There is also a separate traffic safety association. The success of these associations makes the police into arbiters of standards for social mores in an intrusive way unimaginable in the United States.

For example, the Tokyo Metropolitan Police are now locked in a debate over standards for pornographic publications. The police are not simply enforcement agents in this social argument; it is police officials who review all books, magazines, and comic books to determine if they cross the standard of obscenity—the showing of pubic hair—and whether charges will be brought against the publishers.

In June 1991 the police department's crime prevention bureau ordered the publishers of two magazines to come to its headquarters. The two magazines had published color pictures of nude women with their pubic hair showing; between them, the magazines had sold 270,000 copies.

The publishers were warned that they could face obscenity charges if they broke the police standard again, but no charges were filed against them. The police issued a statement explaining that the public is now more accepting of such photographs if they have some artistic value.

"People don't want the police to be strict," said Katsuei Hirasawa. "The idea of pornography is changing rapidly these days in Japan, so we now are having a headache. We have to set new rules for what is obscene."

"There are regulations for pornography, but what is interesting to me is there is no moral viewpoint to these rules," said Wakako Hironaka, a member of the Japanese Diet. "The rules are there only to avoid discussion of morality or immorality. What seems to matter is that it [pornography] is popular and government and businessmen want to provide it without having disagreements. The police negotiate that relationship."

"We work with people to perform the role of setting the rules of morality," said a Japanese police official, "whereas in the United States, police officers are technicians who apply the law." The police work to maintain their special status by employing a strategy that focuses on intense contact with every neighborhood in Japan. The *kobans* stand at the heart of the effort.

"You can't do anything in this community—everything is known by the police already," said Dr. Michio Nagai, the chairman of the International House of Japan. "That is not taken in a negative sense in Japan. It is taken in a very positive sense. The police are really watching us every day. That is why the community and streets are so safe."

In his 1976 book *Forces of Order: Police Behavior in Japan and the United States*, David H. Bayley, an American professor of political science, noted that the most important function of the *kobans* was "providing information to people about location and addresses," in the crowded, unnumbered maze of houses and businesses in Japan. In addition, Bayley, who spent several months observing the *kobans*, found that in Japan "most people who need police help seek it in person at a *koban*. . . . At least one *koban* plays a musical chime early in the morning to serve as a time check for a neighborhood composed largely of apartment houses. . . . *Koban* officers are the first line of police response."

The *kobans* are supplemented by foot patrolmen, both in uniform and undercover, who walk Tokyo's narrow streets. One result is that Tokyo's low crime rate is complemented by a high rate for solving the few crimes that do occur. For example, there were 1,255 homicides in Japan in 1989, and 1,208 of them were solved; of 1,586 robberies, 1,204 were successfully investigated by police; and of 1,556 rapes, 1,301 were solved. In 1988 Japanese police solved 97 percent of the homicides, 86 percent of the rapes, and 78 percent of the robberies. These figures compare to a 70 percent rate for solving murders in the United States, a 52 percent rate for finding rapists, and a 25 percent rate for solving robberies.

But there is a price tag for the wonderful feeling of safety in Japan. Behind its Western, democratic facade, Japan retains some fundamental authoritarian aspects. In reality, it is a publicly approved police state.

PART II

Policy Applications

The communitarian philosophy has direct implications for numerous policy issues that confront society. Each of the following selections can be examined from two perspectives: the guidance communitarian thinking provides for the particular issue at hand, and the knowledge the communitarian approach itself gives us based on the way it treats a specific policy problem.

If someone at high risk for HIV infection were to come forward for testing and were to test positive for the virus, would that person be expected (morally speaking) or required (legally speaking) to inform previous and future contacts? These are the questions Ronald Bayer and Kathleen Toomey address in Chapter 6. Civil libertarians tend to focus on an individual's right to privacy. However, the Constitution protects citizens from unreasonable search and not from all intrusions into their private space. What is reasonable depends in part on the needs of others and the community. But where are we to draw the line between individual rights and community needs?

The same questions can be asked about the crackdown on the illicit drug trade. Roger Conner describes a case in which a sheriff devised an effective way to shut down an open-air drug market practically overnight. But were his means constitutional? Did his methods violate rights, and if so, were the intrusions reasonable?

The policy issues discussed thus far concern matters that arise out of the Fourth Amendment, which is often invoked in matters concerning crimes, drug testing, sobriety checkpoints, screening gates in airports, and such. The balance of rights and responsibilities, however, applies equally to the freedom of speech and the First Amendment, which many treat with particular reverence. For example, one may not shout "Fire!" in a crowded theater because the harm to the public exceeds the right of the person to expresss him- or herself in that particular manner.

Mary Ellen Gale argues that hate speech should be curbed. That is, you may not insult minorities, women, or other protected groups. About 130 colleges have introduced codes to this effect. Other communitarians, including the editor, hold that people should be able to cope with whatever words are hurled in their direction. The best treatment for hate is education, not

73

expulsion. Sharon Pressner's case examines the controversy within the context of a specific subject, not hate in general but hate as expressed in pornography. Is it better to suppress pornography by law or to sensitize its customers to the abuse some women feel when men take to it?

The Fifth Amendment states that there will be no taking of private property without due compensation. This was a powerful antidote to the king's agents and to all governments that sought to usurp our private assets. For decades "taking" was understood to mean the takeover of one's property. However, over the last few years a line of argument has developed that any imposition of rules or regulations on a citizen's assets—whether these concern the environment, occupational safety, or historical preservation—constitutes a partial taking and hence the government would have to provide compensation. Donovan D. Rypkema provides a strong counterargument, emphasizing the needs of the community.

CHAPTER 6

Preventing HIV: Rights, Duties, and Partner Notification

RONALD BAYER and KATHLEEN E. TOOMEY

As public health officials confronted the acquired immunodeficiency syndrome (AIDS) epidemic in the early 1980s, they came to recognize the crucial importance of confidentiality. Only if those at risk for human immunodeficiency virus (HIV) infection could be convinced that their clinical encounters would not be disclosed without their consent could they be encouraged to undergo counseling and testing. Thus, the Centers for Disease Control (CDC),[1] the Surgeon General,[2] the Institute of Medicine and National Academy of Sciences,[3] and the Presidential Commission on the HIV Epidemic[4] all came to stress a common point: that the protection of the public's health was not compromised by the protection of confidentiality. On the contrary, the protection of confidentiality was a precondition for the achievement of public health goals.

Although the protection of confidentiality was supported by public health officials, gay rights organizations, and civil liberties groups, the best strategy for reaching those unknowingly placed at risk for infection or those who might inadvertently place others at risk was the subject of profound disagreement. Thus did deep and sometimes bitter disputes arise over partner notification in the epidemic's first decade.

Disagreements over the scope and limits of the principle of confidentiality, deep distrust over the motives of public health officials, doubts about the relevance and potential efficacy of traditional public health approaches to sexually transmitted diseases in dealing with AIDS, and the enduring suspicions of those who viewed government agencies as a source of endangerment rather than protection were all involved in the controversy. Each of these factors helped to shape the context within which a profound confusion emerged between two very different approaches to informing unsuspecting third parties about their potential exposure to medical risk.

Each approach has its own history, including a unique set of practical problems in its implementation, and each provokes its own ethical dilemmas. The first approach, involving the moral "duty to warn," arose out of the clinical setting in which the physician knew the identity of the person deemed to be at risk. This approach provided a warrant for disclosure to endangered persons without the consent of the patient and could involve the revelation of the identity of the "threatening" party (the index patient). The second approach— that of contact-tracing—emerged from sexually transmitted disease (STD) control programs in which the clinician typically did not know the identity of those who might have been exposed. This approach was formally predicated on the voluntary cooperation of the patient in providing the names of contacts, never involved the disclosure of the identity of the index patient, and entailed the protection of the absolute confidentiality of the entire process of notification.

Confusion between the two approaches has led many to mischaracterize processes that are fundamentally voluntary as mandatory, and processes that respect confidentiality as invasive of privacy. As late as 1988, *The Washington Post* described the "inherent" conflict in contact-tracing between "two fundamental principles rooted in law and ethics: the individual's right to privacy and the duty of health officials to warn those they suspect or know are in danger."[5] Such misapprehensions were, however, not limited to the popular media. They extended to groups and individuals more familiar with public health practices. In writing about the counterproductive consequences of mandatory measures for the control of the HIV epidemic, June Osborn, dean of the School of Public Health at the University of Michigan and currently chair of the National Commission on AIDS, said, "As to mandatory tracing of the sexual partners of persons with AIDS, the justification offered is that it is a tried and true method of controlling STDs, but in fact it has never worked well."[6]

What can account for the misunderstandings that fed the political controversy? In part, the conceptual confusion can be traced to the tendency to use the same terms—*contacting, notifying, protecting, informing*—to describe the goals of both approaches to informing those placed at risk for HIV infection. The confusion may have been inadvertently compounded by the adoption of the term *partner notification* by the United States Public Health Service (PHS), the Association of State and Territorial Health Officials in 1988, and the Global Programme on AIDS of the World Health Organization in 1989 to describe the full scope of outreach efforts. These efforts range from individuals informing their own partners to contact-tracing by public health workers and even disclosure by physicians without the consent of their patients.

In this essay, we describe the complex problems provoked by attempts in the past decade to implement partner notification. We examine the vicissitudes of the two approaches, underscoring the ethical and political context within which policy decisions have been made. Finally, we argue that in a rapidly changing clinical context in which the early identification of those with HIV infection has become important, and in the context of the changing epidemiology of the epidemic, efforts at partner notification—especially those based on the contact-tracing tradition—will play an important public health role.

THE TRADITION OF CONTACT-TRACING

In 1936 Thomas Parran, the architect of the federal antivenereal disease program, told the National Conference on Venereal Disease Control, "Every case must be located, reported, its source ascertained and all contacts then informed about the possibility of infections, provided with a Wasserman test, and if infected treated."[7] Only such an effort, he believed, could break the "chain of disease transmission." In the 1940s, when effective treatments for syphilis were developed, contact-tracing became a central feature of all STD programs.

Clinicians in STD control programs often did not have knowledge of a patient's background or family relationships. To elicit the names of sexual contacts, it was therefore necessary to obtain the cooperation of the index patient. Although considerable pressure might be applied, and indeed there are undocumented reports that on some occasions STD workers threatened to withhold treatment from those who would not provide the names of contacts, typically the patient's willingness to cooperate dictated the ultimate success of the partner-locating effort. To facilitate such cooperation, STD programs promised that the identity of the index patient would never be made available to contacts who were named. The index patient maintained ultimate control over the process, retaining the ability to withhold or provide names. Thus, the tradition of contact-tracing was predicated on the voluntary cooperation of index patients and on a striking commitment to the protection of their anonymity.

Despite the four decades of experience with contact-tracing, all efforts to undertake such public health interventions in the context of AIDS met with fierce resistance in the first years of the epidemic.[8] Opposition by gay leaders and civil liberties groups had a profound impact on the response of public health officials, especially in states with relatively large numbers of AIDS cases. In San Francisco, a proposal that health department staff offer contact-tracing services to bisexual men whose female partners might unknowingly have been placed at risk was denounced as Orwellian because of the prospect of creating lists of bisexual men and their partners.

Underlying this debate was the fact that in the first years of the AIDS epidemic, no therapy could be offered to asymptomatic infected individuals. Thus, the role of contact-tracing in the context of HIV infection differed radically from its role in the context of other STDs. In the latter case, effective treatments could be offered to notified partners. Once cured, such individuals would no longer pose a threat of transmission. In the case of HIV, nothing could be offered other than information about possible exposure to HIV. For public health officials, who saw in such information an opportunity to target efforts to foster behavioral changes among individuals still engaging in high-risk behavior—behavior that could place both the individual contacted and future partners at risk—that was reason enough to undertake the process. For opponents of contact-tracing, the very effort to reach out to such individuals represented a profound intrusion on privacy, with little or no compensating benefit. The task of behavioral change, they asserted, could be achieved more effectively and efficiently through general education.

By the late 1980s the debate over contact-tracing had shifted from one centered on the ethical issues of privacy to one focused on efficacy. The debate was fueled by questions that had begun to surface about the utility of contact-tracing in the control of syphilis in populations where individuals had large numbers of sexual partners, many of whom were anonymous.[9] This transformation reflected a maturing of the discussion. Early misapprehensions about the extent to which public health officials typically relied on overt coercion in the process, and the degree to which confidentiality might be compromised, had by decade's end all but vanished. With such political concerns allayed, many gay leaders had come to recognize that partner notification, in fact, could be a "useful tool" in efforts to control AIDS.[10]

But as opposition to the tradition of contact-tracing on the part of those committed to privacy all but vanished, a quite different source of opposition emerged: this one challenged the two central principles of the contact-tracing tradition—voluntarism and index-patient anonymity.

The failure to reveal the name of the index patient to those who were notified could, some critics asserted, result in an inadequate warning regarding the source of potential ongoing exposure. These claims were embedded in a much broader political challenge to AIDS policies in the United States that viewed the concern for protecting the rights of those with HIV infection as a capitulation by public health officials to those with a libertarian agenda. Conservative critics of AIDS policy in California proposed a state law that would have required those who were infected with HIV to reveal the names of all their partners.[11] With an almost willful disregard for the complexity of efforts to encourage those with STDs in general, and HIV more specifically, to reveal the names of their partners—just how could someone be compelled to reveal names?—the challenge to voluntarism and index-patient anonymity embodied in such legislative efforts entailed a rejection of the lessons of four decades of contact-tracing, lessons that were rooted in the pragmatics of STD control.

Efforts to subvert the processs of contact-tracing by imposing compulsory features, and the debates about the ethical justification and wisdom of such efforts, must be understood in light of the concern over the extent to which clinicians who knew that their HIV-infected patients would not inform their partners were obligated to breach confidentiality to notify those at risk.

THE DUTY TO WARN

As physicians were called upon to treat patients with infectious diseases, it was inevitable that they would be confronted by the question of whether the duty to protect the privileged communications within the clinical relationship took priority over the obligation to protect others from their patients' communicable conditions.

A misreading of a number of early twentieth-century cases has led some commentators to conclude that state courts had established an affirmative duty to break confidentiality to protect known third parties.[12] Indeed, it was such a misreading that permitted the California Supreme Court to claim the authority of precedent when in 1974 it crafted a doctrine that represented the most striking judicial challenge to the professional discretion of physicians when faced with patients who might endanger third parties. The "protective privilege ends where the public peril begins," wrote the majority in *Tarasoff v. Regents of California*.[13] In this 1974 case the court held that a psychotherapist could be held liable for failing to take adequate steps to protect the known intended victim of his patient, in this instance a patient who had threatened to murder his former girlfriend.

The decision drew a great deal of attention and provoked sharp debate. What had been a matter of professional discretion had been transformed by the court into a legal obligation. Thus, it was with *Tarasoff* that the contemporary legal conception of a duty to warn or protect was created. The precise nature of the required action on the part of the physician was dependent on the unique circumstances involved. The court stated that efforts to protect or warn must be undertaken "discretely and in a fashion that would preserve the privacy of the patient to the fullest extent compatible with the prevention of the threatened danger."[14] For the American Psychiatric Association, *Tarasoff* represented a grave threat to the therapeutic relationship founded on patient candor and involved unacceptable assumptions regarding the capacity of psychiatrists to predict dangerous behavior.[15]

At the root of the *Tarasoff* decision was an ethical judgment that, although confidentiality was crucial to the autonomy of individual patients, the protection of third parties vulnerable to potentially serious harm must be given priority. As a matter of moral principle, that determination provoked widespread support. What remained a matter of great controversy, however, was the question of whether such a determination represented wise public policy. Would the recognition of a legal duty to warn or protect so subvert the trust necessary to the therapeutic relationship that patients with violent fantasies would be constrained from talking about them with their therapists? Would the reduction in candor ultimately harm the public good by limiting the capacity of therapists to help their patients control their dangerous impulses?

The *Tarasoff* doctrine and its ethical underpinnings provided the backdrop to the disputes that would surface as physicians confronted the dilemma of how to respond to HIV-infected patients who refused to inform their needle-sharing or sexual partners of their exposure[16] when the clinician knew the identity of the endangered party. For some, the dilemma arose solely in the context of partners who quite obviously had no reason to suspect that they had been placed at risk, the paradigmatic case being the female partner of a bisexual man. Other physicians extended their concern to those who might have reason to know but might nevertheless be ignorant of the risk to which they had been exposed, for example, the gay male partner in a long-standing, apparently monogamous relationship. The choices to be made would be all the more difficult given the extraordinary efforts that had been made to protect the confidentiality and rights of those infected with HIV. In fact, many early state statutes enacted to guard the privacy of HIV-related records precluded the exercise of professional judgment about whether confidentiality should ever be breached. This was the case in California, the home of the contemporary legal doctrine of the duty to warn or protect.

As legal scholars and ethicists confronted this issue, they often concluded that breaches of confidentiality could be justified. Writing in the *American Journal of Public Health,* Larry Gostin and William Curran concluded, "When there are strong clinical grounds for believing that a specific contact has not been informed who is in serious danger from exposure to HIV, the prudent course for the physician is to notify the contact of the positive serological status of the patient."[17] Grant Gillett made the strongest moral argument for breaking the prima facie duty to protect confidentiality in the case of an HIV-infected patient who refuses to modify his or her behavior or inform sexual partners:

> In asking that his affairs be concealed from others, a person is demanding *either* the right to preserve himself from the horrors that might befall him if the facts about his life were generally known *or* that his sensitivity as an individual be respected and protected. On either count it is inconsistent for him to claim some moral justification for that demand when it is made solely with the aim of allowing him to inflict comparable disregard or harm upon another.[18]

Margaret Somerville and her colleagues echoed this perspective when they stated, "The objective of medical confidentiality is perverted if it is used to facilitate the intentional transmission of disease."[19] The controversy continued, however, over the questions of whether such disclosures should be viewed as morally obligatory or discretionary; whether the morally obligatory should be made a legal duty; and whether, in warning contacts, the identity of the index patient should ever be revealed.[20]

Despite its opposition to the *Tarasoff* decision, the Board of Trustees of the American Psychiatric Association declared in 1987 that if a patient refused to change his or her behavior or to notify a party at risk known to the psychiatrist, it was "ethically *permissible* for the physician to notify [the persons] who the physician believes to be endangered"[21] [emphasis ours].

The American Academy of Family Physicians went further and declared in 1990 that if a physician failed to convince a patient to inform a partner at risk about his or her HIV infection, the imperative that these persons be informed "supersedes the patient's right to confidentiality."[22] Under such circumstances, the academy said, the physician is ethically obligated to warn partners at risk.

The Council on Ethical and Judicial Affairs of the American Medical Association (AMA) promulgated a more elaborate position, declaring that if a physician failed to get a patient to notify an endangered partner, efforts should be made to enlist the assistance of local public health departments to undertake the necessary warning. If such efforts were unsuccessful, then the physician should take whatever steps were necessary to inform the unsuspecting partner. This position was endorsed in mid-1988 by the AMA's House of Delegates. In commenting on the significance of this decision, the newly elected president of the AMA, James E. Davis, declared:

> This is a landmark in the history of medical ethics. We are saying for the first time that, because of the danger to the public health and the danger to unknowing partners who may be contaminated with this lethal disease, the physician may be required to violate patient confidentiality. . . . The physician has a responsibility to inform the spouse. This is more than an option. This is a professional responsibility.[23]

These moves by the medical establishment alarmed defenders of civil liberties and gay rights advocates. To those who had devoted themselves so assiduously to the effort to win the support of public health officials for iron-clad protections of confidentiality, and who had been so successful in achieving support for strict confidentiality enactments in many state legislatures (most notably in those states most affected by the AIDS epidemic), these professional assertions represented a dire turn of events.

As public health officials began to consider the issues posed by the warning of third parties who during the clinical work of physicians were discovered to be at risk, they sought to chart a response that was cognizant of both the centrality of confidentiality in the effort to control the spread of HIV infection and the importance of ensuring that known parties were informed of their possible exposure to HIV. In September 1988 mandatory notification was rejected in a report adopted by the Association of State and Territorial Health Officials, the National Association of County Health Officials, and the U.S. Conference of Local Health Officials.[24] Instead of mandatory notification, these public health officials argued for a "privilege to disclose," thus freeing physicians from liability for either breaching confidentiality or not warning those who were at risk. In so arguing, these officials were reasserting the principle that had guided public policy in the era before *Tarasoff* and that historically had guided physician behavior.

The doctrine of the privilege to disclose was a political compromise designed to meet the concerns of a number of constituencies, not all of whom shared assumptions about the appropriate role of physicians in protecting vulnerable third parties from HIV infection. For all clinicians, the doctrine offered the freedom to make complex ethical judgments without the imposition of state mandates. For clinicians committed to warning as many unsuspecting partners as possible, it offered the opportunity to act on their professional obligations without being burdened by the dictates of the state. For those who believed that breaches of confidentiality were acceptable only in the rarest of circumstances, the privilege to disclose permitted a principled recognition that disclosure could be justified without the dangers associated with an overbroad commitment to notification.

Between 1987 and 1989, twenty-one states adopted legislation explicitly confronting the issue of how and when physicians could warn unsuspecting partners. In all but two cases—North Dakota and South Carolina—mandatory notification was rejected. Five states explicitly prohibited the revelation of the identity of the infected party to the individual being notified.[25]

New York State's 1988 confidentiality law,[26] enacted after a complex process of political bargaining, carefully circumscribed the conditions under which notification might occur while prohibiting the revelation of the identity of the index case. Under the law, physicians may disclose the possibility of risk only when each of the following conditions has been satisfied: (1) the physician reasonably believes that notification is medically appropriate and that there is a significant risk of infection; (2) the patient has been counseled regarding the need to notify partners; (3) the physician has reason to believe that the patient will not notify partners; and (4) the patient has been informed of the physician's intent to notify partners and has been given the opportunity to express a preference as to whether the partners should be notified by the physician directly or by a public health officer. Although considerable latitude was thus provided for clinical judgment, the New York law clearly sought to avoid a situation of unbridled discretion, the kind of discretion that was of concern to Harold Edgar and Hazel Sandomire when they wrote, "What most surprises us is that so many legislatures are prepared to leave responsibility for the choice of whether contacts are made in the hands of physicians without . . . indicating the basis on which they are to make their choices."[27]

But the political compromise represented by the privilege to disclose was ultimately vulnerable to charges that in granting physicians broad discretion there was no way to ensure that individuals at risk would, in fact, be notified. Thus, Stephen Joseph, then commissioner of health in New York City, challenged the privilege-to-disclose doctrine that only a year earlier he had helped to fashion when he testified before the New York State legislature that the state's physicians were failing to make use of their privilege to warn. He urged a statutory revision, making the notification of endangered, unsuspecting third parties known to the physician a legal duty.[28]

Although federal health officials have clearly supported efforts on the part of the states to fashion policy in this realm, the PHS could most directly set policy for the clinical services provided by agencies such as the Indian Health Service, the National Institutes of Health, or the Health Resources and Services Administration. And here federal officials opted for required notification of known partners when treating physicians believed that their patients with newly detected HIV infection would not undertake the process themselves. At the same time, the PHS rejected the opinion of some officials as well as pressure from conservative political leaders to mandate the revelation of the identity of the index patient.[29]

The commitment to index-patient anonymity was further underscored by the response of James Mason, assistant secretary of health, to an American Bar Association (ABA) recommendation asserting that in some circumstances the effective warning of third parties under the privilege-to-disclose doctrine might require the revelation of the identity of the index patient. The ABA group had reasoned that there were circumstances in which a partner in an ongoing relationship would have no reason to suspect that a particular individual was the potential source of infection and that in these cases a failure to disclose such information would be tantamount to no warning at all.[30] In a letter to Walter H. Beckham, Jr., secretary of the ABA, on June 20, 1990, Mason responded by arguing that any support for a breach of confidentiality—even within the very limited clinical context dealt with by the ABA—might be construed by some as justifying such breaches in STD clinics where the contact-tracing tradition held sway. As a result, the willingness of individuals to participate in programs where cooperation was predicated on strict adherence to the principle of confidentiality could be affected.

CONCLUSIONS

Early identification of HIV infection in asymptomatic individuals will become increasingly beneficial in the changed clinical climate produced by the availability of antiviral therapy, prophylactic antimicrobials, and other therapeutic interventions. The case for partner notification becomes especially important as the incidence of HIV infection shifts from gay middle-class men to other populations, in which the level of awareness is lower and the capacity to act on whatever awareness exists may be limited. The needs of poor black and Hispanic women will bear special consideration.

As increasing numbers of individuals with HIV-related conditions come under the care of physicians in settings other than STD clinics, the question of the circumstances under which it is appropriate to breach confidentiality to warn unsuspecting partners will be faced repeatedly. Available evidence reveals that many persons who know themselves to be infected fail to inform their sexual partners of this fact.[31] Policymakers and clinicians will need to consider whether the process of notifying partners under such circumstances should be discretionary, as it now is under the doctrine of the privilege to disclose, or made mandatory. They will also have to consider whether identification of the index patient will be required if notification is to serve its protective function. Finally, they will have to determine whether clinicians themselves should undertake the process of notification when they know the identity of unsuspecting partners or whether that responsibility should be given to public health officials.

From the perspective of the ethics of the clinical relationship, those who may have been placed at risk unknowingly have a moral right to such information. They are entitled to such information so that they may take steps to protect themselves, so that they can seek HIV testing and clinical evaluation, so that they may commence treatment if necessary, and so that they may avoid the inadvertent transmission of HIV. The moral claim of those who have unknowingly been placed at risk entails the correlative moral duty of the clinician to ensure that the unsuspecting party is informed. Neither the principle of confidentiality nor the value attached to professional autonomy is an absolute.

Yet what seems so straightforward given the ethics of the clinical relationship is not so simple from the perspective of public health. As commentators have noted ever since the *Tarasoff* decision, it is possible that widespread awareness of the unconsented notification of third parties placed at risk (even when such notification is undertaken as a matter of professional obligation rather than legal duty) could discourage individuals from seeking care or from speaking candidly to their caregivers. Policymakers simply do not have sufficient data to resolve the question of whether unconsented disclosure would have this adverse impact. Thus, policy will have to be made in the face of uncertainty. It will therefore be crucial to undertake carefully designed investigations to study the impact of physician disclosures to third parties, so that public policy can be adjusted in the light of new evidence as it becomes available. Finally, since it is clear that private physicians are reluctant to undertake the process of notification—either because they believe it is beyond their professional responsibility and training or because the time involved is viewed as prohibitive—it will be necessary for public health departments to undertake the task of notification at the request of clinicians who know the identities of third parties who have been placed at risk. Despite its limitations, such an approach has the advantage of utilizing the skills of those who have been trained in partner notification and who are aware of how crucial confidentiality is to the process of informing contacts.

If the duty to warn poses difficult ethical questions, contact-tracing does not. Contact-tracing typically entails neither disclosure without the consent of the infected patient nor breaches of confidentiality. In fact, it can be argued that public health departments have a moral responsibility to undertake efforts modeled on the tradition of contact-tracing programs that can inform individuals at risk about matters crucial to their lives and to the lives of their sexual and needle-sharing partners without recourse to mandatory measures.

Such a moral injunction may create difficult choices for policymakers, who must try to balance these activities with other moral claims on limited resources. Whatever the strengths of contact-tracing, it is but one element in a much broader array of educational and programmatic efforts designed to limit the spread of HIV infection.[32] What proportions of the overall prevention efforts should be devoted to this labor-intensive and inevitably costly strategy? How are limited resources to be allocated among alternative strategies for achieving behavioral change? To these questions there can be no universal response, one that is applicable to all locales with their differing patterns of HIV infection. Targeted programmatic reviews based on local epidemiological conditions and resource availability will be required. But what an advance it will represent to face the question of partner notification without the misconceptions that bedeviled discussions during the first decade of the AIDS epidemic.

NOTES

1. Centers for Disease Control, "Recommendations for assisting in the prevention of perinatal transmission of human T-lymphotropic virus type III/lymphadenopathy-associated virus and acquired immunodeficiency syndrome," *MMWR* (1985), 34, pp. 721–726, 731–732.
2. *Surgeon General's Report on Acquired Immune Deficiency Syndrome* (Washington, D.C.: U.S. Public Health Service, October 1986), p. 33.
3. Institute of Medicine and National Academy of Sciences. *Confronting AIDS* (Washington, D.C.: National Academy Press, 1986).
4. *Report of the Presidential Commission on the Human Immunodeficiency Virus Epidemic* (Washington, D.C.: June 24, 1988).
5. "Rights v. duty: Colorado's effort to trace AIDS victims' contacts," *The Washington Post* (September 13, 1988).
6. J. Osborn, "AIDS, politics and science," *New England Journal of Medicine* (1988), 318, pp. 444–447.
7. Centers for Disease Control, unpublished document, April 30, 1987.
8. Ron Bayer, *Private Acts, Social Consequences: AIDS and the Politics of Public Health* (New Brunswick, N.J.: Rutgers University Press, 1990).
9. *Contact Tracing and Partner Notification* (Washington, D.C.: American Public Health Association, Special Initiative on AIDS, 1988), p. 5; J. K. Andrus, D. W.

Fleming, D. R. Harger, et al., "Partner notification: can it control syphilis?" *Annals of Internal Medicine* (1990), 112, pp. 539–543; A. Brandt. "Sexually transmitted diseases: shadow on the land, revisited," *Annals of Internal Medicine* (1990), 112, pp. 481–482.

10. N. Schram, "Partner notification can be useful tool against AIDS spread," *Los Angeles Times* (June 28, 1988).

11. States News Service (NEXUS database, December 14, 1989).

12. G. J. Annas, "When must the doctor warn others of the potential dangerousness of his patient's condition?" *Medicolegal News* (1975), 3(2), pp. 1–2.

13. 529 p2d553, 188 Cal Rptr 129 (Cal Sup Ct 1974).

14. V. Merton, "Confidentiality and the 'dangerous' patient: implications of *Tarasoff* for psychiatrists and lawyers," *Emory Law Journal* (1982), 31, pp. 263–343.

15. M. B. Lewis, "Duty to warn versus duty to maintain confidentiality: conflicting demands on mental health professionals," *Suffolk University Law Review* (1986), 20, pp. 579–615.

16. S. Landesman, "AIDS and the duty to protect," *Hastings Center Report* (1987), 17, pp. 22–23; J. S. Talbart, "The conflict between a doctor's duty to warn a patient's sexual partner that the patient has AIDS and a doctor's duty to maintain patient confidentiality," *Washington and Lee Law Review* (1988), 45, pp. 355–380; D. H. J. Hermann, "AIDS: malpractice and transmission liability," *University of Colorado Law Review* (1986)–1987), 58, pp. 63–107; R. L. North and K. H. Rothenberg, "The duty to warn 'dilemma': a framework for resolution," *AIDS Public Policy Journal* (1989), 4(3), pp. 133–141.

17. L. Gostin and W. Curran, "AIDS screening, confidentiality and the duty to warn," *American Journal of Public Health* (1987), 77, pp. 361–365.

18. G. Gillett, "AIDS and confidentiality," *Journal of Applied Philosophy* (1987), 4, p. 18.

19. H. P. Glenn, N. Gilmore, M. Somerville, and Y. M. Morisseppe, *HIV infection, AIDS and privacy* (Montreal, Quebec, Canada: McGill Centre for Medicine, Ethics and Law, 1990). Working paper.

20. B. M. Dickens, "Legal limits of AIDS confidentiality," *Journal of the American Medical Association* (1988), 259, pp. 3449–3451.

21. *Sexuality Today* (December 28, 1987–January 4, 1988), p. 1.

22. American Academy of Family Physicians, board meeting minutes, April 18–20, 1990.

23. *New York Times* (July 1, 1988), p. A1.

24. Association of State and Territorial Health Officials, National Association of County Health Officials, and U.S. Conference of Local Health Officials, *Guide to Public Health Practice: HIV Partner Notification Strategies* (Washington, D.C.: Public Health Foundation, 1988).

25. George Washington University, Intergovernmental Health Policy Project, unpublished files, 1987–1989.

26. New York State Public Health Law, Article 27-F, §2782, 2783, and 2785.

27. H. Edgar and H. Sandomire, "Medical privacy issues in the age of AIDS: legislative options," *American Journal of Law and Medicine* (1990), 16, pp. 155–221.

28. *New York Times* (December 14, 1989), p. B9.

29. R. Windom, assistant secretary for health, memorandum, August 16, 1988.

30. American Bar Association Report No. 124, resolution adopted by the House of Delegates (February 12–13, 1990).
31. G. Maks, J. L. Richardson, and N. Maldonado, "Self-disclosure of HIV infection to sexual partners," *American Journal of Public Health* (1991), 81, pp. 1321–1322.
32. G. Rutherford and J. M. Woo, "Contact tracing and the control of human immunodeficiency virus infection," *Journal of the American Medical Association* (1988), 260, p. 3275.

CHAPTER 7

Checkpoint at Inkster: Reasonable or Unreasonable?

ROGER CONNER

Drugs are a big business in the Detroit suburbs, as residents in Inkster, Michigan, can attest. This small, predominantly black city contained one of the busiest open-air drug markets in the Detroit metropolitan area. Wayne County Sheriff Robert A. Ficano chose to set up traffic checkpoints on the street most frequented by drug buyers. The checkpoints required every person driving down a public street to stop and show a uniformed police officer a valid driver's license, along with proof of insurance and registration. When Sheriff Ficano's critics accused him of grandstanding, he answered that they were insensitive to the needs of law-abiding residents.

Is this a case of citizens being asked to give up rights for the drug war, or a case of expanding the duties of citizens to free the community from drug dealing? Is it permissible for public officials to balance between the right of drivers to be free of suspicionless stops and the desire of residents to be free of drug-related crime, or is such a utilitarian analysis inappropriate when constitutional rights are implicated?

The facts of the case are not in dispute. The Demby Housing Project sprawls over Spruce and Hickory streets in Inkster. The drug dealers opened for business in the morning, and by midday twenty to twenty-five cars an hour were flowing through, according to a police survey; by nighttime it was busier yet. The residents of this publicly subsidized housing development are black. The customers are from more distant suburbs, and most of them are white.

Mable Foster, the manager of the development, explained how groups of young men would gather on the street, often with masks or bags over their heads, and dart out to greet cruising drivers for brief exchanges. With the growing drug market came vandalism, theft, and gunfire from fighting dealers. Some parents kept children inside during the day, even in summer, and others made youngsters sleep on the floor to avoid stray bullets. New organizations arose in local churches, including Mothers Against Sin and Shame (MASS), Mediators in Christ, and the Ministerial Alliance, which held all-night prayer vigils, called police with complaints, and held a parade with horns blaring and fingers pointed at alleged drug dealers.

The Wayne County sheriff is an elected official, and after Sheriff Robert Ficano was himself solicited by a drug dealer while driving down Spruce Street in a marked car, he decided to hold a press conference to announce that a traffic checkpoint would be established on Spruce, where each motorist who turned onto the street would be asked to produce the three documents lawfully required of each driver: a valid driver's license, registration, and proof of insurance.

Notwithstanding the publicity, over 100 cars turned onto Spruce between 1:00 and 4:00 P.M. on September 1989, only eight of which were registered to persons living in the neighborhood. All of the non-Inkster drivers were white, and forty-two citations for driving without valid licenses or registration were issued in this three-hour period. Although officers were instructed not to conduct any searches, one driver was arrested for having an unregistered pistol in plain view in his car.

The drug market was apparently disrupted as the drug dealers left, and after two hours nearby residents ventured out to offer verbal garlands to the officers. One senior citizen ventured onto her lawn to chat with a neighbor for the first time in two years, according to newspaper accounts. The organizer of Mediators in Christ, Juanita Cross, told a reporter, "The day after was just lovely. We walked outside and didn't see any pushers. The traffic was down. It was like . . . like peace, total peace."

Not everyone in Inkster agreed. On the following Monday, former Inkster Mayor Edward Bivens, Jr., filed a lawsuit asserting that the traffic check constituted an unreasonable search and seizure under the Michigan constitution. Bivens argued that the constitution does not permit police to stop a driver without a "showing of an individualized, articulate suspicion that the particular motorist was involved in some criminal activity." To him, it was redolent of Nazi Germany or pre-Gorbachev USSR that "the citizens of Michigan are being stopped and asked to, in effect, 'show me your papers' before exercising their right to drive down a certain street."

Courts have long held that for police to stop and question a motorist does constitute a "seizure" within the meaning of the constitutional ban on "unreasonable searches and seizure." The issue in the Inkster case is how to define "unreasonable." The plaintiff, Bivens, based his argument on two linked premises: the primacy of the individual right to privacy and the steepness of the slippery slope. "Every citizen is entitled to security of his person and property unless and until an adequate justification for disturbing that security is shown," he insisted. Stopping a driver "absent an individualized suspicion that some criminal wrongdoing had or was about to occur" is "simply repugnant to our system of government." Unless such a bright line is drawn, he contended, there will be no way to guard against the "petty tyranny of unregulated rummagers . . . executive officials who may act despotically and capriciously."

Citizens living in the nearby community countered that there is no absolute right to operate an automobile on the public highway, considering that drivers must pass tests, buy insurance, and submit to car inspections. And what about the right to live safely in one's own neighborhood? . . .

The sheriff conceded that constitutionally significant interests are at stake which require the policy to satisfy something more than a simple cost-benefit test. Drawing on U.S. Supreme Court cases involving border stops, he suggested that the stops can be approved if three criteria are met: The stops must be minimal in duration and extent, nondiscriminatory, and effectively serve a vital governmental need.

Plaintiffs countered that if the court would not accept the rule that stops without individualized suspicion are inherently unreasonable, it should at least add a fourth condition: "no less intrusive means are available." Their suggested alternatives for police were "confiscation of property, reverse undercover operations, observation booths on the street . . . video cameras for recording illegal activity, and writing down license plate numbers." As for local residents, the plaintiffs suggested "action such as getting out of [your] car and telling potential buyers in their cars 'you are not buying drugs here today,'" conducting "prayer meetings in the street," and trying to "run drug dealers off the corner when they try to come back." "When [citizens groups] are out there praying, the drug dealers are not present," notes the plaintiffs' trial brief.

The residents pointed out in reply that "this kind of activity has at least as much potential for abuse as checkpoints." The sheriff's response was caustic: "The [plaintiffs] would rather have Juanita Cross praying in the streets and single-handedly standing up to crowds of drug dealers, risking life and limb to demand her right to be free and safe in her own home and in her own neighborhood, than to have some innocent and some not-so-innocent drivers momentarily stopped and asked to show their license . . . in an area known to be an open-air drug market. Their position is either incredibly naive or deliberately ignorant of the gravity of the situation on Spruce and Hickory streets."

While the Inkster case was brought in state courts under the Michigan constitution, the issue is sure to surface elsewhere. Several cities, including Washington, D.C., are at some stage of planning or implementing similar devices. Your response?

CHAPTER 8

Free Speech, Equal Rights, and Water Buffaloes: University Regulation of Discriminatory Verbal Harassment

MARY ELLEN GALE

"Shut up, you black water buffaloes! . . . Go back to the zoo where you belong!"
—What an 18-year-old white male student yelled at black female students who held a midnight party below his dormitory window at the University of Pennsylvania, according to the five women, who eventually dropped a charge of racial harassment.

"Shut up, you water buffalo! . . . If you're looking for a party, there's a zoo a mile from here!"
—What the student said he yelled, characterizing it not as a racist comment but as a spontaneous translation from a mild insult in the language of his birthplace.

"Now is the time for healing."
—SHELDON HACKNEY, University of Pennsylvania president, conceding that the university's disciplinary system had failed to work to the benefit of the accusers, the accused, or the university.[1]

"[U]niversities are increasingly surreal."
—The male student's faculty adviser, prior to the dropping of the charge.[2]

"The heyday of campus speech codes is over."
—ROBERT M. O'NEIL, former president of the University of Wisconsin and founding director of the Thomas Jefferson Center for the Protection of Free Expression, when University of Wisconsin regents repealed a rule outlawing discriminatory harassment, including hate speech, after three turbulent years of dispute over the rule's language, its goals, its effectiveness, and its constitutionality.[3]

This could be a story about the sturdiness of the First Amendment at public universities like Wisconsin and the cultural values it invigorates at private universities like Pennsylvania that are not directly bound by First Amendment guarantees. It could be a story about the futility—even the danger—of trying to limit freedom of speech on the university campus, and a celebration of liberation from "enforced orthodoxy of thought and expression."[4] Some civil libertarians surely would think so. But is it?

Racism pervades American life and American speech. It colors our thoughts and haunts our dreams. It twists our perceptions and skews our politics. It framed our Constitution and constructed our laws. And now, more than a century after the first Reconstruction purported to erase it from the nation's legal ledger, racism still shapes our constitutional consciousness and deconstructs our recognition of individual responsibilities and rights. Even at universities and colleges where we may imagine ourselves safe from harm, free to inquire, and equal in our freedom, racism and similar prejudices seep in, poisoning the wells of knowledge.

The University of Pennsylvania story may seem too trivial, too ambiguous and fragmented. Why did the women students bring a charge of racial harassment? What harm did they suffer? They were, after all, making noise, disrupting sleep or study. The male student who yelled at them was born in Israel and speaks Hebrew. In the annoyance of the moment, he said, he translated a Hebrew epithet that has no racial overtones. But the women recollected that he spoke in the context of torrents of shouted abuse from others, "the 'N' word and sexually demeaning words, such as words used to describe our anatomy, and a word used to describe a female dog."[5] According to Elijah Anderson, a professor of sociology at the University of Pennsylvania, "The incident grows out of the unfinished business of the civil-rights movement and the incomplete inclusion of blacks into mainstream society."[6] And, he might have added, out of the incomplete acknowledgment of women, especially women of color, as the intellectual and moral equals of white men.

Other universities have their own stories of racial, religious, and sexual exclusion and harassment, many of them far more degrading than the "water buffalo" incident, some of them laced with overt bigotry or menace. The University of Wisconsin adopted its now-repealed rule against discriminatory verbal harassment after fraternities held a "Martin Luther Coon" party and a "slave auction" of pledges in blackface and Afro wigs, after some white students followed a black student down the hall, taunting him about quotas and saying, "We don't want your kind here," and after other white students hounded one black woman from a library study room with racial epithets and trailed another across campus shouting, "We've never tried a nigger."[7] At other universities, there were other incidents: someone carved "KKK" on a dormitory room door and scrawled an anonymous note to the two black residents, "African monkeys, why don't you go back to the jungle?" A fraternity elected a "Jewish American princess" to mock and degrade. Jewish students have been confronted with swastikas. Gay students have been denounced as "faggots" and told they don't belong at the university.[8]

Across the nation, hundreds of similar incidents have demonstrated the resurgence of racism, sexism, homophobia, and religious prejudice. Dozens of colleges and universities have responded with rules against discriminatory harassment and intimidation that reach beyond actions to words alone.[9] But even as the antidiscrimination regulations were being drafted, civil libertarians attacked them as "speech codes" that, at public schools, directly and seriously violate the First Amendment rights of even bigoted students to free speech. Libertarians defended verbal racism as democratic discourse, the constitutionally valued expression of political dissent and personal autonomy. Quoting Supreme Court Justices Oliver Wendell Holmes, Jr., and Hugo L. Black, libertarians demanded "freedom for the thought that we hate" to ensure protection of "the ideas we cherish."[10] And when the rules were sifted through the constitutional screens of the judiciary, they failed to make the grade. Federal trial courts struck them down.[11]

Perhaps most damaging to the constitutional credibility of campus antiharassment rules was the Supreme Court's 1992 decision in *R.A.V. v. City of St. Paul*,[12] invalidating a city ordinance that resembled many university regulations. St. Paul outlawed the use of burning crosses, Nazi swastikas, or any other symbol (presumably including words, at least if tangibly represented) "which one knows or has reasonable grounds to know arouses anger, alarm or resentment in others on the basis of race, color, creed, religion or gender."[13] The city sought to bring the ordinance within the long-acknowledged (though long-disputed) First Amendment exception for the category of "fighting words"—assaultive speech that inflicts injury or incites a violent response during a direct personal confrontation.[14] But the Supreme Court would have none of it. A five-justice majority reiterated the Court's traditional hostility to speech regulations based on political subject matter or viewpoint. The majority rejected the St. Paul ordinance as censorship of racist expression, an unconstitutional blunder raising "the specter that the Government may effectively drive certain ideas or viewpoints from the marketplace."[15] Concurring separately, the remaining four justices agreed to discard the law as "fatally overbroad" because it condemned not only fighting words but also expressive activity that merely "causes hurt feelings, offense, or resentment."[16]

It was left to three justices in a third, overlapping opinion to point out the obvious: despite absolutist rhetoric, First Amendment law permits regulation based on the content of some messages that our society finds sufficiently harmful. Even though words alone may accomplish the deed, the First Amendment "does not protect the right to 'fix prices, breach contracts, make false warranties, place bets with bookies, threaten, [or] extort.' "[17] Or, the justices might have added, to deny education or employment on the basis of race or sex. Although St. Paul's ordinance was too sweeping, the three justices suggested that a narrower ban on discriminatory threats or harassment might survive constitutional scrutiny—precisely because such expressive acts cause especially severe harm to individuals, to the stigmatized groups, and to society.[18]

In a separate opinion, Justice John Paul Stevens challenged the Supreme Court's First Amendment jurisprudence. He argued that although a categorical approach may "create safe harbors" for free expression, life and language are "more complex and subtle," requiring attention to the social context. Instead of trying to divide speech into protected categories (like political debate) and unprotected ones (like fighting words or obscenity), Justice Stevens suggested, the Court should look more closely at the particulars of each case: the purpose of the regulation challenged, the content of the speech it regulated, and the nature and intensity of the harm inflicted in the circumstances. Applying his approach to the facts of *R.A.V.*, Justice Stevens characterized the particular cross-burning—aimed at "a single African-American family trapped in their home"—as direct intimidation that the First Amendment need not protect.[19] Justice Harry A. Blackmun voiced the suspicion that the Court majority had "manipulated doctrine to strike down an ordinance whose premise it opposed, namely, that racial threats and verbal assaults are of greater harm than other fighting words." The Court, he suggested, had succumbed to "the temptation to decide the issue over 'politically correct speech' and cultural diversity.' "[20]

Did the Supreme Court, in effect, decide that universities may no longer pursue racial and sexual justice and equality through regulations of harassing speech? The Court majority rejected regulations defined by the content of *any* speech, even if earlier decisions placed that category of speech beyond First Amendment protection. But the majority also provided exceptions to its new rule—if the reason for singling out particular subjects for special regulation is the same reason the entire category (like fighting words) is unprotected, if regulation serves some government purpose unrelated to stifling free expression (like a ban on loudspeakers in residential neighborhoods), or if no realistic possibility exists that the regulation will suppress ideas at all.

University regulation of discriminatory verbal harassment appears to fit all three exceptions. But, puzzlingly enough, so does the type of ordinance involved in the *R.A.V.* case itself—even if the broadly phrased St. Paul version went too far in potentially eliminating particular words or symbols from public discourse (and thus unconstitutionally constricting our expressive vocabulary).[21] Fighting words were originally excepted from First Amendment protection because they inflict instant injury or incite immediate violence and are of "slight social value as a step to truth."[22] Prejudiced harassment—on or off the campus—seems analogous: it causes similar harms, and seems equally irrelevant to social enlightenment. After the *R.A.V.* decision, either we must constitutionally differentiate university regulations of discriminatory verbal harassment from general laws against it—or we must seek a new understanding of the First Amendment.

Or perhaps we can do both. In the discussion that follows, I argue on the basis of two intertwined but competing intuitions: that traditional conceptions of the First Amendment can accommodate a deeper, clearer, and more egalitarian vision of the meaning of free expression, and that if they cannot, we need to reconstruct the First Amendment to provide a sounder basis for community and individual justice, equality, and freedom.

Consider first an idealized version of the St. Paul ordinance, narrowed to avoid outlawing expression that merely annoys or offends others and redrafted to focus on harassment and intimidation rather than on the use of particular words or other symbols. Discriminatory fighting words intensify the harm of speech intended to evoke violence or cause direct personal injury. They can inflict damage that goes beyond "hurt feelings" to invade fundamental interests, such as equal housing rights or personal peace and security in one's home.[23] They unravel both the equal protection of the laws promised by the Fourteenth Amendment and the social fabric of mutual respect that binds the nation together. Combatting the effects of racial prejudice is an especially important government purpose—in legal jargon, a "compelling interest"—unrelated to suppressing ideas. For example, we demand compliance with federal laws against employment discrimination without requiring employers or workers to refrain from criticizing or challenging them. And no one who reads a newspaper or sees a television news program can be unaware that racist and sexist opinions still flourish in the United States. Banning intimidation of specific individuals on the basis of racial or similar prejudices, though scarcely designed to encourage bigotry as an idea, runs no serious risk of suppressing it.

The analysis of most university antiharassment regulations can proceed along similar lines. Discriminatory verbal assaults directed at particular individuals or groups and based on their race, sex, sexual orientation, or religion can have devastating consequences, both for the victims and for our constitutional ideals. At least since the Reconstruction Amendments, with their promises of an end to racial subordination and of a new national commitment to equality and freedom, our fundamental law has envisioned a diverse society that transcends prejudice and guarantees fair access for all citizens to such basic social goods as a public university education. As Michael Walzer has observed, "The primary good that we distribute to one another is membership in some human community."[24] What makes racist and similarly biased verbal assaults so harmful is that they subordinate the needs and dreams of some Americans, effectively excluding them from the community of true citizens. Both the cross-burning in the R.A.V. case—directed at one of the few African-American families living in a particular neighborhood—and most of the incidents described at the beginning of this essay send the message of exclusion in unmistakable terms. The often covert, sometimes overt, text is this: you don't belong here. You belong somewhere else, in the ghetto, the kitchen, the bedroom, or the zoo—not in the library, not in the classroom, not at the party, not in the university, not in the neighborhood. Not in our educational or political community. Not in our shared vision of citizenship, entitlement, freedom, or equality.

Moreover, those who speak the words very often have the power to make them true—even just by saying them. Conventional First Amendment doctrine attempts to draw a sharp line between protected speech, including nonverbal acts that are wholly or primarily expressive, and unprotected conduct, including some communicative acts that do independent harm (such as political assassination). But that doctrine too often gives little credence to the familiar philosopher's insight that some speech in context is intrinsically performative rather than communicative or expressive.[25] Words can do something as well as say something. Just as an oral or written contract can bind parties and change their legal relationship—for instance, by marrying them to each other[26]—words of exclusion and subordination can exclude and subordinate.

And they have done so. Cross-burnings like the one that occurred in *R.A.V.* and similar incidents of harassment and intimidation have contributed to residential segregation throughout the country, driving members of minority groups back to ethnic enclaves that often have disproportionately little political power within states, cities, or school systems. Residential segregation is a leading cause of segregation in public elementary and secondary schools, segregation that violates the moral spirit—though not, in modern jurisprudence, the law—of *Brown v. Board of Education,*[27] the Supreme Court decision that abolished official American apartheid but, sadly, left ostensibly private structures of discrimination and prejudice intact. The racial segregation of public schools has contributed not only to their decline but also to "savage inequalities" in public education.[28] Those inequalities limit or destroy the chances of many racial minority children to escape their assigned role as perennial outsiders in American life. For those who survive inferior education to attend a predominantly white college or university, in the hope that higher education will free them at last, the searing experience of racial exclusion, subordination, and intimidation can lead not just to disappointment but to despair—and to the permanent loss of educational opportunities. Even for those whose outsider status stems from other histories—women, lesbians and gays, religious minorities, persons with AIDS or other disabilities—the harm can cut much deeper than mere offense or even resentment. To characterize the misery inflicted, the lifetime losses that may be suffered, as mere "hurt feelings" is to embrace the cruel morality of the playground[29] and give it undeserved constitutional recognition.

Some of the worst incidents at universities have terrorized students into psychological collapse. Some victims leave school altogether, forfeiting their educational rights, while others flee to the comparative safety of home ground—schools where their own race, sex, or religion predominates. Some students remain on campus but adjust their own conduct to minimize the threat of repeated verbal aggression, dissembling their views, displacing their racial, cultural, or sexual identity, and denying—perhaps even to themselves—their own pain and withdrawal. When the victims of hate speech relinquish the opportunity they once sought to confront new ideas and to share their own ideas with people of different backgrounds and viewpoints, democratic discourse is diminished—not expanded. An interpretation of the First Amendment that celebrates this result as a victory for political dissent and individual autonomy is worth little respect. In the name of promoting liberty from government constraint, it uses the power of government to perpetuate unjust inequalities through concessions to private prejudices. It sacrifices the liberty and silences the voices of genuine dissenters and outsiders—those to whom our constitutional system too often has promised much and delivered much less.

If not mesmerized by the critics of "political correctness," who seek tolerance for bigotry and shelter for discrimination by invoking traditional liberal conceptions of free speech, we might reject the Supreme Court's First Amendment analysis in *R.A.V.* as fundamentally incorrect. Either the Supreme Court has misinterpreted the First Amendment—that is, it already means something different from what the Court supposes—or the time has come to reimagine the First Amendment, to recapture lost meanings, or to inscribe new ones that better serve our constitutional democracy.

We can reimagine the constitutional guarantee of free expression by considering the values that have been attributed to it. Free speech has been justified as crucial to democracy because it encourages political debate and dissent, moral inquiry, and participation in self-government; limits and diffuses government power, and exposes government oppression and abuse of power; promotes tolerance, diversity, self-doubt, and self-restraint; provides information, advances knowledge, nourishes artistic experimentation, stimulates intellectual exploration, and discovers truth; and respects individual autonomy and self-fulfillment—the development of our identities, talents, and goals, and of our power to determine our own destinies. Beneath all these purposes lie two central tenets of liberal constitutionalism: an abiding distrust of government[30] and, especially, distrust of the passions of temporary legislative majorities, and a commitment to representative democracy as an openended quest, pluralistic, various, and forever incomplete, providing no fixed or final answers to our moral and political questions.

The commitment to democracy as process rather than to particular political results and the distrust of government combine to produce a conception of the First Amendment that emphasizes negative liberty—the freedom from government restraints—and deemphasizes positive liberty—the freedom to choose how we construct our lives—except insofar as negative liberty enhances positive liberty.[31] Government's only legitimate role, then, is to facilitate public discourse, to provide "the framework for all possible forms of politics"[32] in a broad sense—the interplay of asserted ideas, facts, feelings, and opinions. In this conception, the First Amendment functions primarily to forbid government interference with individual communicative choices and to ensure government neutrality when regulation that may be necessary to serve some other, compelling government interest limits freedom of expression. The libertarian First Amendment prevents the government from favoring or disfavoring any particular contribution to public discourse on the basis of its content or its viewpoint, and leaves us all free to speak, to listen, and to judge for ourselves. Thus, the Constitution, in its majestic impartiality, prevents public universities from regulating discriminatory verbal harassment—just as it prevented them from censoring students who protested against the war in Southeast Asia or on behalf of civil rights twenty-five years ago.

But this conception of the First Amendment seems inadequate in at least three respects. It abstracts the guarantee of free expression from the values it purports to serve. It ignores the social reality that private concentrations of power and privilege indirectly supported by the government can subordinate the needs and interests of the less powerful and unprivileged as surely as direct government regulation can suppress political dissent. And it separates the First Amendment from the Constitution of which it is an organic part, distancing it from the Thirteenth and Fourteenth amendments' explicit guarantees of equal justice and equal liberty.

If we consider the social context, as Justice Stevens admonished, university regulations of discriminatory verbal harassment may seem better designed to serve First Amendment values than the speech they discourage—speech that contributes only marginally, if at all, to political, moral, or cultural debate and does nothing to further political participation, expose government abuse, advance knowledge, discover truth, or promote tolerance of divergent views. Although even insults may be culturally innovative (like "water buffalo") or may contribute to the speaker's self-expression and self-discovery, they may also undermine the dignity and freedom of the victim. In the absence of harassment and discrimination, First Amendment distrust of government regulation may prevail. But speech that inflicts the special harms of prejudice tells another story, of unjustified dominance and exclusion that itself detracts from First Amendment values. The libertarian First Amendment reenacts the existing distributive injustice by expanding the speech of those who already command substantial expressive resources and by exacting the price from those who already suffer disproportionate disadvantages. Equal freedom of expression is not furthered by muffling the voices of outsiders or discrediting them in advance as members of despised and disadvantaged groups whose words and ideas, interests and rights, do not matter because they do not belong in our university or in our society.

The libertarian argument for government neutrality appeals to the civil rights and antiwar protests of the 1960s, and to more recent Supreme Court decisions that protected political dissidents who burned the American flag.[33] Libertarians warn that the same logic that would protect the victims of discrimination from assaultive speech would allow political majorities to legislate against insistent and compelling critics of the government. But the cases are not truly similar. Discriminatory harassment is directed at particular persons—often, at particularly powerless individuals or groups—because of their innate identity. It is not directed at government officials acting in their official roles, at government policies, or at government symbols like the national flag. Its victims are often what the Supreme Court has described as a "captive audience"— people who either cannot avoid the expressive acts that harm them or who, like a family at home, employees in a work place, or students seeking a college education, must remain in that setting to obtain a particular social benefit, one to which they may well have a statutory or constitutional right. Its perpetrators are not political debaters seeking to assert ideas, to attract adherents, or to anger their opponents. Instead, they are intentional harassers seeking to hoard social benefits for themselves and to deny them to others—not on the basis of need or merit but in furtherance of arbitrary prejudice and willful exclusion. The harm inflicted is not mere offense or annoyance but loss or diminution of important opportunities and rights—to a peaceful place to live, to an interesting job that pays a decent wage, to an education that enriches individual skills and choices for a lifetime. More speech—the usual remedy prescribed by the First Amendment—cannot restore the damage done to self-respect, identity, and equal citizenship.

Of course, we can hypothesize circumstances that make it difficult to draw the line between spirited argument and targeted harassment. Political debate is often polarized and personal, and may include attacks on opponents who hold no government power. As the different versions of the "water buffalo" incident illustrate, some remarks will fall close to the line. Changing a word or two may change our analysis. But hard cases do not exempt us from moral responsibility. Discriminatory verbal assaults seldom simulate two-way discussion. If they do, or if the harm inflicted seems minimal, we can adopt a skeptical stance that requires clear evidence of intentional threats or harassment based on central personal characteristics or choices like race, sex, or religion, which have been used by dominant individuals or social groups—as well as by governments—to inflict unjustified harms.

The libertarian appeal to First Amendment history seems misplaced or romanticized. Many civil rights activists and war protesters lost their claims or won protection only after years of litigation. Only five of the nine Supreme Court justices in 1989 and 1990 ruled that flag-burning is protected political expression, and three of the votes came from liberal justices who have since left the Court. The First Amendment has often functioned, both in its application and in its exceptions, to serve the interests of wealth, power, and popular prejudice rather than to open public discourse to dissident voices.[34] The complex realities of racism, sexism, and similar prejudices—the deep structures of belief and opinion inscribed by our culture—influence our choices and responses at an unconscious as well as a conscious level.[35] Even without direct government authorization, prejudiced acts by persons and groups throughout society, sanctioned by a laissez-faire interpretation of the First Amendment, can effectively serve as an informal system of censorship. They skew or destroy the supposed free marketplace of ideas by legitimating a rule of nonrecognition—that the feelings, perceptions, and expressions of disadvantaged individuals and groups may be routinely discounted by those who wield determinative market power.

The university, whether private or public, has a special duty to ensure that the liberty of some students is not furthered at the expense of the equality and liberty of others. The university is dedicated not only to universal freedom but also to universal education—to equal opportunities and equal rights of participation and self-realization for students of all races, religions, and economic classes, both sexes, and any sexual orientation. The ideal university would welcome everyone seeking knowledge and the wisdom to use it, without regard to characteristics like race or sex that may deeply affect identity and experience but are nonetheless essentially irrelevant to the desire and capacity to learn. The ideal university would educate its students for a wide variety of jobs and lives, based on their diverse talents, needs, and choices. It would guide intellectual exploration, stimulate artistic expression, instill political awareness and moral complexity, and channel, protect, and encourage the risk-taking and experimentation through which we discover and create ourselves. It would ask and expect its students to talk to each other across the boundaries of race, sex, class, and religion, to hear and to value dissonant voices. It would teach them to participate vigorously, effectively, and civilly in their shared community, while preparing them to thrive in the world outside and to restructure that world together as democratic citizens. Even the real university, which must cope with the stubborn distractions of everyday life, may aspire to these ideals.

The Fourteenth Amendment, no less a part of the Constitution than the First, helps to define and enforce the right to an equal education. With the Thirteenth Amendment, it directly disestablishes a regime of racial hierarchy and exclusion. At public universities, the Constitution requires those who share the university's benefits not to deny them to others. Even private colleges and universities are subject to the cultural ideals of the Constitution, if not to its direct constraints.

The First Amendment, like the Fourteenth, protects equality as well as liberty. Free speech is guaranteed not just to one speaker or to one class of speakers but by simple inference to all speakers. In refusing deference to the most obvious choice for hierarchical control—the democratically elected government—the First Amendment implicitly rejects all other hierarchies as well, especially those built on prejudices that encode social narratives of dominance and subordination. Free speech and equal opportunity, as constitutional values, can be interpreted as promises of more than procedural justice. They resonate beyond mere negative liberty or freedom from government controls. They aspire to just outcomes, to substantiate a vision of positive liberty that enables democratic participation and enhances moral autonomy, individual dignity, and personal choice.

Although most proponents of university regulation have appealed to the First Amendment exception for fighting words, this analysis suggests that discriminatory harassment may be more accurately described as itself a violation of constitutional rights. By silencing and stigmatizing outsiders and imposing the constraints of racism, sexism, and similar prejudice on its victims, it transgresses both the First and the Fourteenth amendments. The social and individual interests in deterring prejudice and ensuring that college students have a true and equal opportunity to learn are at least as important as the interests in preventing criminal behavior, physical violence, or employment discrimination that we have long believed can justify limited regulation of free expression.

Perhaps, after *R.A.V.* and the judicial rejection of antiharassment regulations at Wisconsin, Michigan, and other universities, "the heyday of campus speech codes" really is over. The abandonment of restrictions that sweep casual remarks and classroom discussions within their prohibitions may even be a true victory for the First Amendment. But modest regulations that forbid targeted harassment of particular individuals or groups on the basis of racism, sexism, and similar prejudices can help to counteract centuries of injustice, to discourage cruelty and exclusion, and to ensure equal liberty and equal education for all students.

Distrusting government is not a virtue for all seasons; it does not always enhance freedom and democracy. As women and minorities have learned in the long struggle for political and civil rights, government power sometimes offers us the only resources to dismantle private structures of dominance and discrimination that deny us equal membership in our human community. Only through civil rights laws enacted at last by reluctant majorities did we finally gain some measure of freedom.[36] The First Amendment, reimagined as a guarantee of both equality and liberty of expression, enjoins us to generate new political, legal, and moral strategies that will empower all our voices.

NOTES

1. The first three quotations appear in Michael deCourcy Hinds, "Five Blacks at Penn Drop Charge in a Racial Incident," *The New York Times* (May 25, 1993), p. A6.
2. David G. Savage, "Penn Board Refuses to Dismiss Harassment Claim," *Los Angeles Times* (May 15, 1993), p. A2.
3. Barry Siegel, "Fighting Words," *Los Angeles Times Magazine* (March 28, 1993), pp. 14, 46–48.
4. Ibid., p. 44.
5. Hinds, "Five Blacks at Penn."
6. Elijah Anderson, "Can We All Get Along? Not Yet," *Los Angeles Times* (May 26, 1993), p. B7. In another incident at Penn, often discussed in tandem with the "water buffalo" remark, the university declined to pursue disciplinary action against a group of black students who destroyed 14,000 copies of the student

newspaper to protest a conservative columnist's views. See Hinds, "Five Blacks at Penn"; Richard Bernstein, "Play Penn," *The New Republic* (August 2, 1993), pp. 16, 17. Some libertarians have characterized this as a "double standard" applied to favor minorities and diminish free speech (Bernstein, "Play Penn," p. 17). Despite the appeal of this analysis (it's hard to defend book-burning in any guise), it's worth noting that the black students apparently believed they had no other recourse after the columnist and the university rejected their request for a meeting to discuss the exacerbation of racial tensions on campus. See Bernstein. First Amendment absolutism sometimes conceals an elitist form of egalitarianism, which assumes a symmetry of resources and opportunities that our collective history and individual experience of racial prejudice contradict.

7. Thomas C. Grey, "Civil Rights vs. Civil Liberties: The Case of Discriminatory Verbal Harassment," *Social Philosophy & Policy* (Spring 1991) 8(2), pp. 81, 84 (also discussing incidents at Stanford University); Siegel, "Fighting Words," p. 16.
8. See generally Anti-Defamation League of B'nai B'rith, ADL Conference on Campus Prejudice (1990); Mari Matsuda, "Public Response to Racist Speech: Considering the Victim's Story," *Michigan Law Review* (1989), 87, p. 2320; Darryl Brown, Note, "Racism and Race Relations in the University," *Virginia Law Review* (1990) 76, pp. 295, 315–316; "Lessons from Bigotry 101," *Newsweek* (September 25, 1989), p. 48. In a recent survey of 550 college newspaper editors, 64 percent of those at schools with more than 10,000 students and 49 percent overall reported that race relations on campus were "fair" or "poor." "Race on Campus," *U.S. News & World Report* (April 19, 1993), pp. 52, 53 (also listing incidents).
9. Siegel, "Fighting Words," p. 16 (estimating that 200 universities adopted "hate-speech" codes in the late 1980s and early 1990s).
10. *Communist Party v. Subversive Activities Control Bd.*, 367 U.S. 1, 137 (1961) (Black, J., dissenting); *United States v. Schwimmer*, 279 U.S. 644, 655 (1929) (Holmes, J., dissenting).
11. For example, *UWM Post, Inc. v. Board of Regents of the Univ. of Wisconsin Sys.*, 774 F.Supp. 1163 (E.D. Wis. 1991); *Doe v. University of Michigan*, 721 F.Supp. 852 (E.D. Mich. 1989).
12. 112 S.Ct. 2538 (1992). After this chapter was written, the Supreme Court upheld the constitutionality of a seemingly similar "hate crime" statute that increased penalties for criminals who select their victims on the basis of race or other protected characteristics, including religion, disability, and sexual orientation (but not gender). *Wisconsin v. Mitchell*, 113 S.Ct. 2194 (1993). The Court distinguished *R.A.V.*, reasoning that the St. Paul ordinance "was explicitly directed at expression," whereas the Wisconsin statute "aimed at [otherwise criminal] conduct unprotected by the First Amendment." 113 S.Ct. 2194, p. 2201. The Court reasoned that the state could properly inflict more severe punishments on the ground that bias-motivated crimes cause "greater individual and societal harm" by inciting community anger or retaliation and inflicting distinctive emotional harms on victims. Ibid., p. 2201. Such statutes may also be distinguishable because they focus on a criminal's biased choice of victim rather than on statements, thoughts, or opinions that explain the choice. See Daniel A. Farber, "Foreword: Hate Speech After *R.A.V.*," *William Mitchell Law Review* (1992), 18, pp. 889, 896–897. Another possibility, of course, is that *R.A.V.* and *Mitchell* exemplify judicial inconstancy in

analyzing the interplay of antidiscrimination laws and principles of free expression, and testify (though not eloquently) to the need for a searching reexamination of the First Amendment's guarantee of free speech.

13. 112. S.Ct., p. 2541.
14. Both the arguments and the decision ignored the possible distinction between spoken words and tangible symbols—for the good reason that there is no meaningful difference between them for purposes of First Amendment analysis.
15. 112 S.Ct., p. 2545.
16. Ibid., pp. 2550, 2559–2560 (White, Blackmun, O'Connor, and Stevens, JJ., concurring in the judgment).
17. Ibid., p. 2563, quoting Frederick Schauer, "Categories and the First Amendment: A Play in Three Acts," *Vanderbilt Law Review* (1981), 34, pp. 265, 270.
18. See 112 S.Ct., p. 2565.
19. Ibid., pp. 2566–2570 (Stevens, J., concurring in the judgment).
20. Ibid., pp. 2560–2561 (Blackmun, J., concurring in the judgment).
21. See *Cohen v. California*, 403 U.S. 15 (1971) (First Amendment protects the use of profane, sexually explicit words to express political dissent).
22. *Chaplinsky v. New Hampshire*, 315 U.S. 568, 572 (1942).
23. See Charles H. Jones, "Proscribing Hate: Distinctions Between Criminal Harm and Protected Expression," *William Mitchell Law Review* (1992), 18, pp. 935, 950–958.
24. Michael Walzer, *Spheres of Justice: A Defense of Pluralism and Equality* (New York: Basic Books, 1983), p. 31.
25. See J. L. Austin, *How to Do Things with Words: The William James Lectures Delivered at Harvard University in 1955* (Cambridge, Mass.: Harvard University Press, paperback 2nd ed. 1975); J. L. Austin, "Performative Utterances," in *Philosophical Papers* (Oxford: Clarendon Press, paperback 3rd ed. 1979), pp. 233, 235; Cynthia Brodsky Lacour, "Doing Things with Words: 'Racism' as Speech Act and the Undoing of Justice," in Toni Morrison, ed., *Race-ing Justice, En-gendering Power: Essays on Anita Hill, Clarence Thomas, and the Construction of Social Reality* (New York: Pantheon Books, 1992), pp. 127, 134–142.
26. Austin, "Performative Utterances," pp. 235–238.
27. 347 U.S. 483 (1954).
28. See generally Jonathan Kozol, *Savage Inequalities: Children in America's Schools* (New York: Crown Publishers, 1991).
29. See Derrick Bell, "A Kindergarten Cliquebuster," *The New York Times* (September 6, 1992), Section 7 (Book Review), p. 6, reviewing Vivian Gussin Paley, *You Can't Say You Can't Play* (Cambridge, Mass.: Harvard University Press, 1992).
30. See generally Frederick Schauer, *Free Speech: A Philosophical Inquiry* (Cambridge: Cambridge University Press, 1982), pp. 157–158.
31. See generally Isaiah Berlin, "Two Concepts of Liberty," in *Four Essays on Liberty* (London: Oxford University Press, paperback ed. 1969), p. 118.
32. Robert C. Post, "Racist Speech, Democracy, and the First Amendment," *William & Mary Law Review* (1991), 32, pp. 267, 314.
33. See *United States v. Eichman*, 110 S.Ct. 2404 (1990); *Texas v. Johnson*, 109 S.Ct. 2533 (1989).
34. Richard Delgado and Jean Stefancic, "Images of the Outsider in American Law and

Culture: Can Free Expression Remedy Systemic Social Ills?" *Cornell Law Review* (1992), 77, pp. 1258, 1285–1288; Charles R. Lawrence III, "If He Hollers, Let Him Go: Regulating Racist Speech on Campus," *Duke Law Journal* (1990), pp. 431, 466–467.

35. Mary Ellen Gale, "Reimagining the First Amendment: Racist Speech and Equal Liberty," *St. John's Law Review* (1991), 65, pp. 119, 119–121; Charles R. Lawrence III, "The Id, the Ego, and Equal Protection: Reckoning with Unconscious Racism," *Stanford Law Review* (1987), 39, pp. 317, 321–323, 329–331.

36. See Willie Abrams, "Racial Equality over Hate Speech," *William Mitchell Law Review* (1992), 18, pp. 979, 980; Walzer, *Spheres of Justice*, pp. 15–16.

CHAPTER 9

Pornography: Free Speech versus Civil Rights?

SHARON J. PRESSNER

Is pornography a form of sexual discrimination that violates the civil rights of women, or is it free speech protected by the First Amendment? For those who believe pornography constitutes sexual discrimination, the central issue is whether pornography encourages violence toward women. They point to studies—such as those by Daniel Linz and N. M. Malamuth—that suggest that pornographic images often provoke rape, domestic violence, and sexual harassment. Civil libertarians argue that the pivotal issue is preserving the right to free speech, and they cry out against the potential for government control of expression. For both sides, the problem is the same: How can we both prevent violence against women and yet ensure that our First Amendment rights are not jeopardized?

Defining pornography as a civil rights issue would allow victims of sex crimes who can prove a link between the crime and pornography to sue the producers and distributors of the material for damages. Legislation based on this approach includes the Pornography Victims Compensation Act, promoted by Republican Senator Mitch McConnell of Kentucky, which was introduced in 1991 but never reached the Senate floor for a vote. This bill would have allowed victims of sexual violence who could trace the crime to child pornography or obscenity the possibility of suing the producers and distributors of the material.

Along the same lines, the Civil-Rights Antipornography Ordinance, which covers all forms of pornography, is the work of feminist activists Catharine MacKinnon and Andrea Dworkin. Versions of this ordinance were adopted in Minneapolis in 1983 and in Indianapolis in 1984, and then later repealed. The former was vetoed, and the latter was found to be unconstitutional. Another version is currently under consideration in Massachusetts. MacKinnon enjoyed a recent success in Canada where, with her legal assistance, the Supreme Court expanded its obscenity code to include material "that would apparently fail the community standards test not because it offends against morals, but because it is perceived by public opinion to be harmful to society, particularly to women." The efforts of the antipornography feminists are being supported by conservatives who aim to ban pornography—such as Phyllis Schlafly and members of the religious right—a rather unlikely coalition.

PORNOGRAPHY AS A FORM OF EXPRESSION

Pornography, free-speech feminists and civil libertarians insist, should be protected just like any other form of expression, "no matter how objectionable or offensive it may be to some or even most of us," as the ACLU says. In response to the bill pending in the Senate, the ACLU states, "Under the First Amendment, expression cannot be punished or suppressed unless it is intended to and will incite imminent harm." The civil rights approach, the ACLU concludes, "might seem attractive but, like all other anti-pornography measures, it could easily backfire by empowering the state to control speech, and to use its power to limit more than just the speech we abhor." Some raise the additional question of how such an ordinance would treat violent pornographic images that, arguably, have social value. For example, the movie *The Accused* uses explicit rape scenes to convey an anti-rape message. Others fear this legislation would allow lawmakers to censor any explicit material they consider offensive, perhaps even including textbooks used to teach sex education.

In addition, law professors Nan Hunter and Sylvia Law submitted a brief objecting to the Indianapolis ordinance on grounds that such legislation does a disservice to men by underestimating their self-control: "Men are not attack dogs, but morally responsible human beings. The ordinance reinforces a destructive sexist stereotype of men as irresponsible beasts, with 'natural physiological responses' which can be triggered by sexually explicit images of women, and for which the men cannot be held responsible." According to Hunter and Law, the end result of such legislation is to absolve men from responsibility for their actions and displace the blame for sexual violence onto the producers of pornography.

Joining the ACLU in its opposition to such ordinances is the group Feminists for Free Expression, which includes Betty Friedan, Susan Jacoby, and Nora Ephron. They contend that women, varied in their tastes and in their definitions of sexism, do not require "protection from explicit sexual materials." In fact, granting women special protections implies that women are not able to protect themselves. Others in this alliance against antiporn legislation are publishing organizations such as the American Booksellers Association and the Association for American Publishers; gay and lesbian groups, whose erotica would probably be first on the list to be restricted; and proponents of sex education, whose campaigns against AIDS and teen pregnancy often use explicit images and materials.

PORNOGRAPHY AS SEX DISCRIMINATION

The antiporn ordinances attempt to deflect the issue of free speech by defining pornography in nonspeech terms, as "the graphic sexually explicit subordination of women, whether in pictures or in words," depicting women enjoying "pain or humiliation." However, to invalidate the Indianapolis ordinance, the U.S. Court of Appeals relied on the categorization of pornography as a form of expression. Judge Frank Easterbrook apparently recognized the negative effects of pornography on women but ruled that the law was an unconstitutional violation of the guarantee of free speech: "The state may not ordain preferred viewpoints in this way. The Constitution forbids the state to declare one perspective right and silence opponents."[1] What is of central concern here, say those who would make pornography a civil rights issue, is the harmful consequences of pornography to women; pornography, therefore, is an issue of discrimination, not a First Amendment issue. MacKinnon, testifying before Attorney General Edwin Meese's Commission on Pornography in 1985, stated:

> These abuses include coercion into performing pornography, the pervasive forcing of pornography on individuals, the assaults it directly causes, and the targeting for rape, battery, sexual harassment, sexual abuse as children, forced prostitution and the inferiority that is endemic to this traffic in female sexual slavery. . . . Because these injuries are disproportionately inflicted on women, but also on everyone whom it victimizes, on the basis of their sex . . . we have proposed a new approach: That pornography be civilly actionable as sex discrimination and recognized as a violation of human rights. Civil-rights legislation does not threaten the freedom of speech through censorship or a morals squad, they maintain. It allows women to act in response to proof that they have been harmed.

IS THERE A LINK BETWEEN
SEXUAL VIOLENCE AND PORNOGRAPHY?

Proponents of civil rights legislation seek to demonstrate the correlation between pornography and violence. In one experiment conducted by Daniel Linz and colleagues, groups of college-age males were shown five extremely violent R-rated commercial films and were told to rate aspects of the film and their own mood. This study showed that the men soon became desensitized to the violence against women; they rated the fifth film as less offensive and degrading, and even found some of the material humorous and enjoyable.[2]

N. M. Malamuth and colleagues conducted studies showing that exposure to pornography depicting violent rapes reduces men's aversion to rape. They presented an audiotape, using a male voice, of different stories, including one of consensual sex and a fantasy in which a woman appears to enjoy being raped. About 40 percent of the subjects found the rape fantasy to be very arousing.[3] A similar study found that 30 percent of their subjects were very aroused by both the male fantasy rape and by another story in which a man assaults a woman.[4]

In addition to the social science experiments, those who advocate making pornography a civil rights issue point to links between violent porn and sex crimes in some select incidents. In 1988 police found in the possession of a man accused of raping, molesting, or robbing four women, nude photographs of other women, along with the equipment he had used to take pictures of some of his own victims; he had asked at least one to "smile pretty." A 1989 serial murder suspect in Delaware had a collection of sadistic pornography that portrayed abuses similar to the ones he inflicted on his victims. Infamous serial killer Ted Bundy blamed pornography for his violent behavior. Furthermore, antiporn advocates point out that police say many similar incidents of crime influenced by pornography go unreported.

Civil libertarians, including the ACLU, are skeptical of such evidence. Researchers in other countries, such as Britain and Denmark, have found no clear connection between pornographic images and violence. Rather than encouraging rape, pornography "is an aphrodisiac, that is, food for the sexual fantasy of persons," writes Berl Kutchinsky, professor of the Institution of Criminal Science at the University of Copenhagen.[5] Pointing to the experiences of other countries, Harvard law professor Alan Dershowitz wrote: "Many countries that have stringent laws against pornography—such as the Soviet Union, Saudi Arabia and China—have high levels of rape and poor records on feminism. Other countries more tolerant of pornography—such as the Scandinavian and Western European countries—have lower levels of violence against women and more respect for equality and feminism."[6]

Opponents of pornography also argue that degrading images encourage men to view women as objects and institutionalize men's supremacy over women. The judge who overturned the Indianapolis ordinance conceded that "depictions of subordination tend to perpetuate subordination. The subordinate status of women, in turn, leads to affront and lower pay at work, insult and injury at home, battery and rape on the streets."

All said and done, the antipornography draft legislation leaves many questions unanswered. Will it reduce the mistreatment of women? Will subjecting producers and distributors to lawsuits diminish sexual abuse or at least curb the pornography market—or will the black market continue to supply the goods in demand? How would such legislation distinguish between various types of pornography—that with social value, or hard- versus soft-core pornography? But before we dismiss this legislative approach outright, can we continue to tolerate brutal images that may contribute to incidents of sexual violence against women?

NOTES

1. *Hudnut v. American Booksellers Association, Inc.*, 1986.
2. Linz, David, "The Effects of Multiple Exposures to Filmed Violence Against Women," *Journal of Communication*, no. 34, 1984, pp. 130–147.
3. Malamuth, N. M. and J. V. P. Check, "First Penile Tumescence and Perceptual Responses to Rape as a Function of Victim's Perceived Reactions," *Journal of Applied Social Psychology*, 10(6), pp. 528–547.
4. Malamuth, N. M., J. V. P. Check, and J. Briere, "Sexual Arousal in Response to Aggression: Ideologies and Aggressive and Sexual Correlates," *Journal of Personality and Social Psychology*, 50(2), pp. 330–340.
5. "Can Pornography Lead to Violence?" *Washington Post*, July 21, 1992.
6. Dershowitz, Alan, "Feminist Fig Leaves," *This World*, July 8, 1984.

CHAPTER 10

The Misunderstandings of the "Property Rights" Movement

DONOVAN D. RYPKEMA

By almost any definition, community implies the existence of a place—a physical place made up of land, buildings, and public spaces. In most American communities, the vast majority of the place is in the ownership of individuals—private property.

Since virtually the beginnings of the rights of private ownership of land, there has been some restriction on the use of that property. Historically, restrictions have been enacted in order to protect the interests of the community from the adverse potential impacts a private property might generate. Today a fundamental challenge to the concept of public restrictions on private land is emerging.

The burgeoning private property rights movement is making a three-pronged attack on land-use regulation throughout the United States. The first assault comes from lawyers and developers, who contend that the regulation of private property has become a "taking" entitling the owner to "just compensation" for loss of property value. This prong of the attack is wending its way through the court system—both state and federal—and no doubt will continue to do so for years to come.

The second wave of the attack is on the political front. If the first part of the argument could be rephrased as, "The government does not have the right to pass such regulations," the second rephrasing might be, "Even if the government has the authority to enact such regulations, it should not exercise that right." This political question will ultimately be decided in state legislatures and by city councils.

The third tier of the property rights advocates' attack is the economic argument. In simplified terms, the argument is as follows: "This land-use regulation diminishes the economic value of my asset. I am entitled to use [develop] my asset to its 'highest and best use.' It is wrong for the government to deprive me of that opportunity."

The legal prong of the property rights argument will be decided (and then probably redecided) in the court room. The political prong will be decided at the ballot box.

But it is the economic prong that the property rights proponents are using and abusing with increasing frequency. And it is this prong of attack that, to date, has received inadequate response from the advocates of land-use regulations.

It is stating the obvious to say that land-use regulations apply to land. But an acknowledgment of that reality is critical to an understanding of the source, justification, and economic impact of these regulations. Land is an asset like no other. (The terms *land, real estate,* and *property* will be used interchangeably throughout this essay.) Among the singular attributes of real estate are:

Every parcel is unique.

It is fixed in place.

It is finite in quantity.

It will last longer than any of its possessors.

It is necessary for virtually every human activity.

Contrast those traits with any other investment vehicle—stocks, bonds, gold, insurance policies, commodities futures, oil, fine art, treasury bills, certificates of deposit. None of them possesses all of real estate's attributes; most possess none at all.

In part because of its peculiar attributes, real estate has always been treated differently than any other asset in law, taxation, lending, political perspective, and philosophy. But real estate has been treated differently for two fundamental economic reasons as well:

the impact of land use on surrounding property values; and

the primary source of value of real estate being largely external to the property boundaries.

Imagine two next-door neighbors, each owning a series of assets. One owns IBM stock, government bonds, gold coins, and antique watches; the other owns GM stock, corporate bonds, gold ingots, and baseball cards. The investment decisions of one have absolutely no measurable effect on the value of the assets of the other. One neighbor probably neither knows nor cares about the investment portfolio of the other. There is no need for one neighbor to urge the enactment of public restrictions on the use to which gold ingots can be placed since the neighbor's decisions will not affect his or her own asset value.

Now suppose that in addition to the assets above each neighbor owns a parcel of real estate abutting the parcel of the other. Every decision one owner makes has an immediate impact on the economic value of the asset of the other. To the extent possible, one owner will try to limit the potential adverse effect that the neighbor's land-use decisions might have on his or her own property value.

Historically, the initial purpose of land-use regulation was public health and safety. Although it is conveniently forgotten by the proponents of the economic prong of the private property rights argument, the mitigation of adverse economic impacts caused by proximate land use is also at the core of land-use limitations.

There is an old principle of private rights that says, "My right to swing my fist ends where your nose begins." Certainly, the same principle applies to the regulation of land use.

The sheer complexity of trying to establish individual agreements with every property owner whose decisions might affect the value of one's real estate asset quickly reaches the point of mathematical absurdity. Therefore, the common-sense approach for real estate investment protection has been land-use regulations instituted by the public to protect the composite economic value of private land and to mitigate the risk of substantial value decline caused by actions on nearby properties.

Those who loudly proclaim, "It's my land and you can't tell me what to do with it," are quick to appear before the City Council when a homeless shelter is moving in next door or a hazardous waste disposal site is proposed next to their summer cottage. And their argument won't be, "I'm against the homeless," or "Hazardous waste shouldn't be disposed of," but rather, "That action will have an adverse effect on my property value, and you, City Council members, need to prevent that."

Land-use regulations protect property values. But where does real estate value originate? Some landowners would have you believe that the value of their asset somehow emerges from within the boundaries of their site and, because that value was created within their lot lines, they are entitled to the highest returns available. Nothing, in fact, could be further from the truth. Consider two five-acre parcels of desert land, one in the middle of the Sahara and the other in the middle of Las Vegas. Within the lot lines, both have the same physical characteristics: flat, dry, and, in their natural state, incapable of supporting human habitation. Do they have the same economic value? Obviously not. But the differences between the two lie entirely outside the boundaries of the property. Everyone has heard the old adage that "the three most important characteristics of real estate are location, location, location." The reality of that maxim is well illustrated by the two desert parcels.

It is not the land but the activity around the land that gives considerable value to one parcel and next to none to the other. In other words, the millions of dollars the Las Vegas site is worth stems not from the investment of the deed holder of the site but almost entirely from the investment of others—the city of Las Vegas, employers, owners of other properties, residents of Las Vegas. The creation of value in real estate is to a large extent *external* to the property itself.

The scenario can be changed somewhat by adding a 40-story hotel to the site. Surely in Las Vegas the property is now worth millions more than the bare land prior to the building being erected. But what is the value of the land and hotel in the middle of the Sahara? Next to nothing—regardless of the cost of construction. The economic value of the property was created not from within the property lines but from without.

Restrictions on the use of land represent an appropriate dividend on the investment others have made which has generated the economic value of an individual parcel.

Students of real estate economics have identified the "forces of value" that push the economic value of a single parcel up or down. These forces are social, economic, physical, and political. Land-use regulations reflect the political and, to a lesser extent, the social forces of value. Does the enactment of a land-use regulation affect value? Absolutely—in both directions! The rezoning of a parcel of land from General Agricultural to Light Industrial will change the economic value of the property; in all likelihood, the value will increase. That land-use decision increased the value of the site. Note that the land itself did not change. The permitted use changed, and, therefore, the economic value of the property changed. When was the last time you heard a property owner say, "Because of rezoning, my land went from being worth $10,000 to being worth $100,000. But because it was the action of the Planning Commission and not some investment I made that increased the value, I'm writing a check to the city for $90,000." No landowner has ever said that, nor should he or she have said it. The political force of value is one of the risks inherent in the ownership of real estate, and it has upside opportunity as well as downside potential.

To suggest that a decline in value resulting from the enactment of a public land-use limitation entitles a property owner to "just compensation" is to ask for a floor under the risk of real estate ownership. Where then is the offsetting ceiling limiting the enhanced value generated from the same source? No property rights pamphlet has advocated that equitable exchange.

Does the enactment of a historic preservation statute, a wetlands protection law, or a downzoning ordinance ever reduce the value of an individual parcel of real estate? Certainly. But every day hundreds of governmental decisions affect individual investments of all kinds, and often adversely. What happens to the value of Lockheed Corporation bonds when McDonnell Douglas is chosen instead to build a new bomber? It goes down! What happens to the value of the local Ford dealer's franchise when the city decides to buy Chevrolets? It goes down! What happens to the value of the utility company stock when the state utilities commission refuses to grant a rate increase? It goes down! In every instance, a political decision by a public body acting in what it deemed "the public interest" had an effect on somebody's assets. Real estate owners have no inherent right not to be adversely affected by political decisions.

To return to the forces of value, it is the social, political, and economic context within which a property exists that gives it value. Of the four forces, only the physical is primarily contained within the property lines. To claim that the adverse impact of public decisions (the political force of value) is somehow unwarranted, unfair, or undemocratic is to fail to understand (by accident or by design) the fundamental nature of real estate economics. The potential adverse impact of political decisions is simply one of the risks inherent in the ownership of real estate.

This does not mean that it is not possible to have a land-use decision that is fundamentally unfair. Of course, that can happen, and when it does it is incumbent on the property owner to demonstrate to the decision-making body that what he or she loses as a result of those restrictions is much greater than what the public (for whom the public body is acting) has to gain. No one should dispute an individual landowner's right to testify against his or her property's being subject to a particular land-use constraint. But to object solely because of a claim of potential loss of value demonstrates a basic misunderstanding of the nature of real estate.

Often at land-use hearings those seeking to rezone their property (or oppose historic districting, environmental restrictions, etc.) proclaim some divine right to use their property to its "highest and best use." Based on their orations, one could quickly reach the conclusion that "highest and best use" means the greatest return imaginable. That simply is not so. "Highest and best use" is a real estate appraisal term that has a very specific definition: It is the use that, at the time of the appraisal is the most profitable *likely* use to which the property may be placed. The word *likely* is a key one. The first constraint on "likelihood" is what is legally permitted, that is, what is allowed under land-use limitations. It would be a fundamental violation of appraisal practice to estimate the value of the property, assuming a use not currently permitted, unless it were probable that the land-use restriction would be changed. Just the possibility of current regulation being changed is not sufficient; the appraiser would have to demonstrate the probability of change. In other words, for the owner of an undeveloped 40 acres currently zoned General Agriculture to argue that the "highest and best use" of his or her property is as a suburban office park when that use is not permitted by current restrictions, nor is it probable that those restrictions will be changed, is simply misusing and misrepresenting the vocabulary of real estate. "Highest and best use" is not the maximum value imaginable; it is the most profitable use for which there is market demand and legal authority. If the "maximum imaginable value" were the standard, we would have adult bookstores, hazardous waste disposal sites, steel mills, and sewage disposal plants in every residential neighborhood in America. . . .

But the concept of highest and best use is but one of the principles of

value misrepresented by the property rights advocates. There doesn't seem to
have been much attempt to understand either the theory or the practice of
real estate valuation. For example, two principles of real estate appraisal are
particularly germane to this discussion: the principle of balance and the principle of conformity. The principle of balance establishes that land value is created and maintained when there is an appropriate balance among types and
uses of land in the affected area. Comprehensive plans and zoning laws are an
important element in sustaining that balance.

The principle of conformity affirms that areawide values are greatest when
there is a reasonable degree of land-use compatibility and architectural homogeneity. Conformity in use establishes and sustains the composite value of the
neighborhood and the individual affected parcels within.

Usually, in the heat of land-use arguments, the property rights advocates
frame the debate in terms of "property owners versus the 'government.'"
Defining the dispute in that context conjures up visions of faceless bureaucrats
in Washington dictating how far a garage has to be set back from Elm Street
and deciding what color one's house can be painted. An 80-year-old home-
owner can be forgiven for having that misunderstanding when that's what he
or she has been told. But the leaders of the property rights movement know
full well that is a bogus argument. Virtually all land-use controls are enacted
and implemented at the local level. It is not Washington bureaucrats but
citizens from the town or the county who pass zoning laws, subdivision ordinances, and historic district provisions.

Even the National Register of Historic Places, one of the few pieces of
federal legislation affecting properties at all, places no restriction whatsoever
on what a property owner may do with his or her property. The owner, in fact,
is even completely free to demolish historic structures.

This "property owners versus the government" argument is a blatant mis-
representation of the issue in another sense. It is not for the sake of the local
government that land-use restrictions are put into place but rather to protect
the value of the investment of one property owner from the adverse economic
impact of the actions of another. Well-drawn land-use controls may very well
reduce the maximum potential value of a single parcel, but the composite value
of the sum of the affected properties will be enhanced. Property rights advocates often call land-use restrictions a "fairness" issue. In that they are certainly
right. But it is not the "fairness" of the local government potentially reducing
the uppermost value of a single parcel; it is the fairness of allowing a single property owner to receive a windfall at the expense of his or her neighbors. The local
government is unaffected by how far I swing my fist; but my neighbor is not.

In virtually every objective evaluation of the economic impact of land-use
controls—and particularly of historic districts—the composite value of the
affected properties was protected at worst and significantly enhanced at best.
It is the difference between individual value maximization for a few property
owners and value optimization for all of the owners.

But even if land use were viewed as the rights of the "public" versus the rights of the private property owner, that public is entitled to a return on the value that public expenditures largely created. It is the streets, sewers, water lines, sidewalks, curbs, streetlights, and parking lots, which were, in the main, paid for with tax dollars, that have created much of the value of any given property. The contribution of public expenditures to the value of private property was well recognized by the father of laissez-faire economics, Adam Smith, who wrote in *The Wealth of Nations:* "Good roads, canals, and navigable rivers, by diminishing the expense of carriage, put the remote parts of the country more nearly upon a level with those in the neighborhood of the town. They are upon that account the greatest of all improvements."

Yet today "roads, canals" and their contemporary infrastructure counterparts remain "the greatest of all improvements" for which the regulation of land use is an appropriate recompense.

There is another fact of economic life where the interests of the individual and the interests of the public at large coincide. In economics it is the differentiated product that commands a monetary premium. Any good advertising agency, manufacturer, retailer, or service vendor will tell you the economic value of its product is enhanced by identifying and capitalizing on the differences between its product and that of the competitors. Much land-use legislation, particularly historic preservation districts, has at its heart the identification and maintenance of the differences between that community and any other. It is that product differentiation that has created an economic premium—from which both the public and private sector benefit—from Charleston, South Carolina, to Guthrie, Oklahoma, from Seattle, Washington, to Fredericksburg, Virginia.

It is easy rhetoric to proclaim, "This country was built on the unencumbered rights of private landowners. It is un-American to limit what I can or cannot do with the land I own. We need to return to the frontier days of the homesteaders who developed their land without the interference of 'big brother' in their decisions."

In fact, certainly the most severe and limiting land-use restrictions ever enacted by the federal government were those placed on the homesteaders of the western frontier. To be able to lay claim to their 160 acres, the men and women of the western expansion had to clear, cultivate, and live on their land for five years. Almost no current land-use control is that demanding. It wasn't for money that the Homestead Act placed those restrictions. The federal government paid less than 3 cents an acre for each of those 160-acre parcels— an amount most homesteaders could have afforded to pay. A homesteader was not allowed the option of paying $4.50 instead of abiding by the land-use controls. The actions were required because of the recognition of the interrelationship of properties and the desire to meet the social, political, and economic needs of the sum of the landowners (and the nation as a whole), even if it meant restricting the "freedom" of the individual landholder.

The property rights debate is about fairness, about equity. Specifically, it is about the fairness of allowing a single property owner to affect adversely the values of a multitude of owners. It is about the fairness of the public getting a return on its investment which created much of the individual value to begin with. It is about the fairness of one owner's windfall against a group of owners' maintenance of value. It is about the fairness of a single individual destroying the "product differentiation" of a community, built up over generations, in order to create a carbon copy locally of somewhere else. It is about the fairness of the owner of real estate demanding compensation if his or her asset declines in value because of a public policy decision when the holders of the Lockheed bond, the Ford dealer, and the owner of utility company stock have no such protection.

In fact, land-use controls are a capitalist plot to optimize the property values of the majority of real estate owners, not a communist conspiracy to deprive individuals of some imaginary "property rights."

Adam Smith perceptively observed that "As soon as the land of any country has all become private property, the landlords, like all other men, love to reap where they never sowed." That doesn't mean we are depriving them of rights when we tell them no.

PART III

Moral Infrastructure

Seeking and maintaining the balance between individual rights and social responsibilities is a mainstay of communitarian thinking and policies. Shoring up the practices and institutions that sustain a civil society is equally important. At the root of the communitarian position on these issues is the keen observation that values do not fly on their own wings; rather, they must be continuously reinforced in our daily lives.

Robert Goodin's argument provides a response to those who argue that the society (or state) should not interfere when individuals express their preferences, whether it is to smoke, ride motorcycles without helmets, or drink to oblivion. Of course, the impact of actions on others must be taken into account, but Goodin goes a step further. He argues that when there is clear evidence that one of us is seeking to overcome an addiction or any other debilitating habit, the community is entitled to intervene in order to assist the individual.

If people have grown dependent on welfare, Isabel Sawhill asks, how far may we go to wean them off it? Some argue that we should not impose our middle-class values on those with a different background and that the behaviors involved (from drug use to welfare dependency) are difficult to modify. Others contend that if we allow people on welfare to remain dependent, we are hobbling their future and loading them with unfair burdens. Society seems to be moving irrevocably toward imposing greater social demands on its welfare clients. But where do we draw the line? Should we, for instance, cut mothers with children off welfare if they cannot find work after a grace period (or training period) of two years or so? Should they be offered community jobs if no private-sector work is available, even if these jobs add to the costs of the welfare program?

William Galston opens a discussion of the vital building blocks of a civil society, arguing that nuclear families are essential. True, some single parents do a better job of bringing up their children than the "old-fashioned" family of two parents. Statistically, however, a two-parent home is more effective at child-rearing. (Here we are referring not to the traditional family but to one in which both fathers and mothers have equal rights and duties: both dedicated to their children.)

121

The second societal building block is the school, where the character education begun at home is continued—or initiated, when a family has failed to provide any. William Damon raises many of the same questions brought up by critics of moral education in public schools (in which about 88 percent of the young study). He points out, however, that moral education in schools is inevitable. We may not be aware of the signals the school is sending but without doubt schools are engaged in value education. All schools provide some sort of moral education, whether it is deficient and misguided or nurturing and ennobling. The public debate over moral education is nowhere stormier than on the touchy issue of the parents' role in the education of their children, the subject of a report by John Leo.

Does a return to community imply a return to the "good old days"? John Gardner suggests that much of our past has been authoritarian and oppressive, whereas a true community is democratic and open to all. He spells out the key elements that make a community responsive to its members. The list could be augmented, but few would alter the basic concepts.

To speak of community is to evoke the fear not only of traditionalism but also of exclusion. This is not merely a matter of "allowing" members of minorities to buy properties freely and move into white neighborhoods. It is a deeper question of whose values will prevail in the community at large, the American society. Until recent years, one answer has been that of a melting pot in which all differences are dissolved into one big white blend. This approach seems unnecessarily homogenizing. At the same time, the contrary notion of unbounded diversity with tribes of distinct racial and ethnic backgrounds, each merely celebrating its own tradition, seems to be dangerously divisive. Diane Ravitch provides a communitarian model that enables each group to maintain its subculture with pride, while not breaking the bonds that tie us together. Dennis Farney provides a vivid illustration of how difficult, complex, and enriching a heterogeneous community really is.

If we view our nation as a community of communities rather than as a large group of individuals, communitarians must concern themselves with what will maintain national bonds. Shared core values are crucial, but these need to be embodied in practices and institutions. Social bonds are also needed. National service is a social instrument that might serve to bring people of divergent backgrounds to know one another as people and to serve shared national goals. Benjamin Barber examines national service not as a tool for doing good for others, but as an essential element of one's civic growth. Suzanne Goldsmith's case provides an illuminating view of what service is actually like, at least in the case she studied and experienced. Communitarianism also recognizes nongovernmental methods for achieving community ideals. Robert Wuthnow takes service to the nation a step further by stressing the importance of voluntarism. In his view, this fundamental feature of American life, commonly treated with cynicism by critics, fulfills a vital role by reinforcing basic human values that are beyond the reach of political and economic institutions.

CHAPTER 11

In Defense of the Nanny State

ROBERT E. GOODIN

Paternalism is desperately out of fashion. Nowadays notions of "children's rights" severely limit even what parents may do to their own offspring, in their children's interests but against their will. What public officials may properly do to adult citizens, in their interests but against their will, is presumably even more tightly circumscribed. So the project I have set for myself—carving out a substantial sphere of morally permissible paternalism—might simply seem preposterous in present political and philosophical circumstances.

Here I shall say no more about the paternalism of parents toward their own children. My focus will instead be on ways in which certain public policies designed to promote people's interests might be morally justifiable even if those people were themselves opposed to such policies. Neither will I say much more about notions of rights. But in focusing on people's interests rather than on their rights, I shall arguably be sticking closely to the sorts of concerns that motivate rights theorists. Of course, what it is to have a right is itself philosophically disputed, and on at least one account (the so-called interest theory) to have a right is nothing more than to have a legally protected interest. But on the rival account (the so-called choice theory) the whole point of rights is to have a legally protected choice. There, the point of having a right is that your choice in the matter will be respected, even if that choice actually runs contrary to your own best interests. It is that understanding of rights which leads us to suppose that paternalism and rights are necessarily at odds, and there are strict limits on the extent to which we might reconcile the two positions. Still, there is substantial scope for compromise between them.

Those theorists who see rights as protecting people's choices rather than promoting their interests would be most at odds with paternalists who were proposing to impose on people what is judged to be objectively good for them. That is to say, they would be most at odds if paternalists were proposing to impose on people outcomes that are judged to be good for those people, whether or not there were any grounds for that conclusion in those people's own subjective judgments of their own good.

Rights theorists and paternalists would still be at odds, but less so, if paternalists refrained from talking about interests in so starkly objective a way. Then, just as rights command respect for people's choices, so too would paternalists be insisting that we respect choices that people themselves have or would have made. The two are not quite the same, to be sure, but they are much more nearly the same than the ordinary contrast between paternalists and rights theorists would seem to suggest.

That is precisely the sort of conciliatory gesture that I will be proposing here. In paternalistically justifying some course of action on the grounds that it is in someone's interests, I shall always be searching for some warrant in that person's own value judgments for saying that it is in that person's interests. "Some warrant" is a loose constraint, to be sure. Occasionally, we will find genuine cases of what philosophers call "weakness of will": people being possessed of a powerful, conscious present desire to do something that they nonetheless just cannot bring themselves to do. Then public policy forcing them to realize their own desire, though arguably paternalistic, is transparently justifiable even in terms of people's own subjective values. More often, however, the subjective value to which we are appealing is one that is present only in an inchoate form, or will only arise later, or can be appreciated only in retrospect.

Paternalism is clearly paternalistic in imposing those more weakly held subjective values on people in preference to their more strongly held ones. But, equally clearly, it is less offensively paternalism thanks to this crucial fact: at least it deals strictly in terms of values that are or will be subjectively present, at some point or another and to some extent or another, in the person concerned.

THE SCOPE OF PATERNALISM

When we are talking about public policies (and maybe even when we are talking about private, familial relations), paternalism surely can be justified only for the "big decisions" in people's lives. No one, except possibly parents and perhaps not even they, would propose to stop you from buying candy bars on a whim, under the influence of seductive advertising and at some marginal cost to your dental health.

As far as public policy is concerned, certainly, to be a fitting subject for public paternalism, a decision must first of all involve high stakes. Life-and-death issues most conspicuously qualify. But so do issues that substantially shape your subsequent life prospects. Deciding to drop out of school or to begin taking drugs involves high stakes of roughly that sort. If the decision is also substantially irreversible—returning to school is unlikely, the drug is addictive—then that further bolsters the case for paternalistic intervention.

The point in both cases is that people would not have a chance to benefit by learning from their mistakes. If the stakes are so high that losing the gamble once will kill you, then there is no opportunity for subsequent learning. Similarly, if the decision is irreversible, you might know better next time but be unable to benefit from your new wisdom.

EVALUATING PREFERENCES

The case for paternalism, as I have cast it, is that public officials might better respect your own preferences than you would have done through your own actions. That is to say, public officials are engaged in evaluating your surface preferences, judging them according to some standard of your own deeper preferences.

Public officials should refrain from paternalistic interference and allow you to act without state interference, only if they are convinced that you are acting on

> relevant preferences;
>
> settled preferences;
>
> preferred preferences; and, perhaps,
>
> your own preferences.

In what follows, I shall consider each of those requirements in turn. My running example will be the problem of smoking and policies to control it. Nothing turns on the peculiarities of that example, however. There are many others like it in relevant respects.

It often helps, in arguments like this, to apply generalities to particular cases. So in what follows I shall further focus in on the case of one particular smoker, Rose Cipollone. Her situation is in no way unique—in all the respects that matter here, she might be considered the prototypical smoker. All that makes her case special is that she, or, more precisely, her heir, was the first to win a court case against the tobacco companies whose products killed her. In summarizing the evidence presented at that trial, the judge described the facts of the case as follows:

> Rose . . . Cipollone . . . began to smoke at age 16, . . . while she was still in high school. She testified that she began to smoke because she saw people smoking in the movies, in advertisements, and looked upon it as something "cool, glamorous and grown-up" to do. She began smoking Chesterfields . . . primarily because of advertising of "pretty girls and movie stars," and because Chesterfields were described . . . as "mild." . . . Mrs. Cipollone attempted

to quit smoking while pregnant with her first child . . . , but even then she would sneak cigarettes. While she was in labor she smoked an entire pack of cigarettes, provided to her at her request by her doctor, and after the birth . . . she resumed smoking. She smoked a minimum of a pack a day and as much as two packs a day.

In 1955, she switched . . . to L&M cigarettes . . . because . . . she believed that the filter would trap whatever was "bad" for her in cigarette smoking. She relied upon advertisements which supported that contention. She . . . switched to Virginia Slims . . . because the cigarettes were glamorous and long, and were associated with beautiful women—and the liberated woman. . . .

Because she developed a smoker's cough and heard reports that smoking caused cancer, she tried to cut down her smoking. These attempts were unsuccessful. . . .

Mrs. Cipollone switched to lower tar and nicotine cigarettes based upon advertising from which she concluded that those cigarettes were safe or safer . . . [and] upon the recommendation of her family physician. In 1981 her cancer was diagnosed, and even though her doctors advised her to stop she was unable to do so. She even told her doctors and her husband that she had quit when she had not, and she continued to smoke until June of 1982 when her lung was removed. Even thereafter she smoked occasionally—in hiding. She stopped smoking in 1983 when her cancer had metastasized and she was diagnosed as fatally ill.[1]

This sad history contains many of the features that I shall be arguing makes paternalism most permissible.

RELEVANT PREFERENCES

The case against paternalism consists in the simple proposition that, morally, we ought to respect people's own choices in matters that affect themselves and by and large only themselves. But there are many questions we first might legitimately ask about those preferences, without in any way questioning this fundamental principle of respecting people's autonomy.

One is simply whether the preferences in play are genuinely relevant to the decision at hand. Often they are not. Laypeople often make purely factual mistakes in their means–ends reasoning. They think—or, indeed, as in the case of Rose Cipollone, are led by false advertising to suppose—that an activity is safe when it is not. They think that an activity like smoking is glamorous, when the true fact of the matter is that smoking may well cause circulatory problems requiring the distinctly unglamorous amputation of an arm or leg.

When people make purely factual mistakes like that, we might legitimately override their surface preferences—the preference to smoke—in the name of their own deeper preferences—to stay alive and intact. Public policies designed to prevent youngsters from taking up smoking when they want to, or to make it more expensive or inconvenient for existing smokers to continue smoking when they want to, may be paternalistic in the sense of running contrary to their own manifest choices in the matter. But this overriding of their choices is grounded in terms of their own deeper preferences, so such paternalism would be minimally offensive from a moral point of view.

SETTLED PREFERENCES

We might also ask whether the preferences being manifested are "settled" preferences or whether they are merely transitory phases people are going through. It may be morally permissible to let people commit euthanasia voluntarily, if we are sure they really want to die. But if we think that they might subsequently have changed their minds, then we have good grounds for supposing that we should stop them.

The same may well be true with smoking policy. Although Rose Cipollone thought smoking was both glamorous and safe, youngsters beginning to smoke today typically know better. Many of them still say that they would prefer a shorter but more glamorous life and that they are therefore more than happy to accept the risks that smoking entails. Say what they may at age 16, however, we cannot help supposing that they will think differently when the pigeons eventually come home to roost. The risk-courting preferences of youth are a characteristic product of a peculiarly daredevil phase that virtually all of them will, like their predecessors, almost certainly outgrow.

Insofar as people's preferences are not settled—insofar as they choose one option now, yet at some later time wish that they had chosen another—we have another ground for permissible paternalism. Policymakers dedicated to respecting people's own choices have, in effect, two of the person's own choices to choose between. How such conflicts should be settled is hard to say. We might weigh the strength or duration of the preferences, how well they fit with the person's other preferences, and so on. Whatever else we do, however, we clearly ought not privilege one preference over another just because it got there first. Morally, it is permissible for policymakers to ignore one of a person's present preferences (to smoke, for example) in deference to another that is virtually certain to emerge later (as was Rose Cipollone's wish to live, once she had cancer).

PREFERRED PREFERENCES

A third case for permissible paternalism turns on the observation that people not only have multiple and conflicting preferences but also preferences for preferences. Rose Cipollone wanted to smoke, but judging from her frequent (albeit failed) attempts to quit, she also wanted not to want to smoke. In this respect, it might be said, Rose Cipollone's history is representative of smokers more generally. The U.S. surgeon general reports that some 90 percent of regular smokers have tried and failed to quit. That recidivism rate has led the World Health Organization to rank nicotine as an addictive substance on a par with heroin itself.

That classification is richly confirmed by the stories that smokers themselves tell about their failed attempts to quit. Rose Cipollone tried to quit while pregnant, only to end up smoking an entire pack in the delivery room. She tried to quit once her cancer was diagnosed and once again after her lung was taken out, even then only to end up sneaking an occasional smoke.

In cases like this—in which people want to stop some activity, try to stop it, but find that they cannot stop—public policy that helps people implement their own preferred preference can hardly be said to be paternalistic in any morally offensive respect. It overrides people's preferences, to be sure. But the preferences that it overrides are ones that people themselves wish they did not have.

The preferences that it respects—the preference to stop smoking, like preferences of reformed alcoholics to stay off drink or of the obese to lose weight—are, in contrast, preferences that the people concerned themselves prefer. They would themselves rank those preferences above their own occasional inclinations to backslide. In helping them to implement their own preferred preferences, we are only respecting people's own priorities.

YOUR OWN PREFERENCES

Finally, before automatically respecting people's choices, we ought to make sure that they are really their own choices. We respect people's choices because in that way we manifest respect for them as persons. But if the choices in question were literally someone else's—the results of a posthypnotic suggestion, for example—then clearly there that logic would provide no reason for our respecting those preferences.

Some people say that the effects of advertising are rather like that. No doubt there is a certain informational content to advertising. But that is not all there is in it. When Rose Cipollone read the tar and nicotine content in advertisements, what she was getting was information. What she was getting when looking at the accompanying pictures of movie stars and glamorous, liberated women was something else altogether.

Using the power of subliminal suggestion, advertising implants preferences in people in a way that largely or wholly bypasses their judgment. Insofar as it does so, the resulting preferences are not authentically that person's own. In consequence, those implanted preferences are not entitled to the respect that is rightly reserved for a person's authentic preferences. Such thoughts might lead some to say that we should therefore altogether ignore advertising-induced preferences in framing our public policy. I demur. There is just too much force in the rejoinder that "wherever those preferences came from in the first instance, they are mine now." If we want our policies to respect people by, among other things, respecting their preferences, then we will have to respect all of those preferences with which people now associate themselves.

Even admitting the force of that rejoinder, however, there is much that might still be done to curb the preference-shaping activities of, for example, the tobacco industry. Even those who say, "They're my preferences now" would presumably have preferred, ahead of time, to make up their own minds in the matter. So there we have a case, couched in terms of people's own (past) preferences, for severely restricting the advertising and promotion of products—especially those that people will later regret having grown to like but that they will later be unable to resist.

CONCLUSIONS

What, in practical policy terms, follows from all this? Well, in the case of smoking which has served as my running example, we might ban the sale of tobacco altogether or turn it into a drug available only by prescription to registered users. Or, less dramatically, we might make cigarettes difficult and expensive to obtain, especially for youngsters whose purchases are particularly price-sensitive. We might ban all promotional advertising of tobacco products, designed as it is to attract new users. We might prohibit smoking in all offices, restaurants, and other public places, thus making it harder for smokers to find a place to partake and providing a further inducement for them to quit.

All of those policies would be good for smokers themselves. They would enjoy a longer life expectancy and a higher quality of life if they stopped smoking. But that is to talk the language of interests rather than of rights and choices. In those latter terms, all those policies clearly go against smokers' manifest preferences, in one sense or another. Smokers want to keep smoking. They do not want to pay more or drive further to get their cigarettes. They want to be able to take comfort in advertisements constantly telling them how glamorous their smoking is.

In other more important senses, however, such policies can be justified even in terms of the preferences of smokers themselves. They do not want to die, as a quarter of them eventually will (and ten to fifteen years before their time), of smoking-related diseases; it is only false beliefs or wishful thinking that make smokers think that continued smoking is consistent with the desire not to avoid a premature death. At the moment, they may think that the benefits of smoking outweigh the costs, but they will almost certainly revise that view once those costs are eventually sheeted home. The vast majority of smokers would like to stop smoking but, being addicted, find it very hard now to do so.

Like Rose Cipollone, certainly in her dying days and intermittently even from her early adulthood, most smokers themselves would say that they would have been better off never starting. Many even agree that they would welcome anything (like a work place ban on smoking) that might now make them stop. Given the internally conflicting preferences here in play, smokers also harbor at one and the same time preferences pointing in the opposite direction; that is what might make helping them to stop seem unacceptably paternalistic. But in terms of other of their preferences—and ones that deserve clear precedence, at that—doing so is perfectly well warranted.

Smoking is unusual, perhaps, in presenting a case for permissible paternalism on all four of the fronts canvassed here. Most activities might qualify under only one or two of the headings. However, that may well be enough. My point here is not that paternalism is always permissible but merely that it may always be.

In the discourse of liberal democracies, the charge of paternalism is typically taken to be a knock-down objection to any policy. If I am right, that knee-jerk response is wrong. When confronted with the charge of paternalism, it should always be open to us to say, "Sure, this proposal is paternalistic—but is the paternalism in view permissible or impermissible, good or bad?" Thinking along the lines sketched here, I think we will find that paternalism proves perfectly defensible much more often than not.

NOTE

1. *Cipollone v. Liggett Group,* Civil Action No. 83-2864, 683 F. Supp. 1487; 1988 U.S. Dist.

CHAPTER 12

The New Paternalism: Earned Welfare

ISABEL V. SAWHILL

In the early 1990s, a new debate has broken out about what welfare recipients should and should not be expected to do. In part, it is prompted by a fiscal crunch at the state level that has given new impetus to a whole new set of proposals to link welfare benefits to "good" behavior—the so-called new paternalism. In Wisconsin and Ohio, for example, welfare benefits may be withheld if recipients or their children fail to attend school on a regular basis. The Republican governor of Wisconsin has proposed both to cap benefits after the first child and to provide a marriage bonus. In California, another Republican governor, Pete Wilson, has announced a ballot initiative that would not only cut welfare benefits by up to 25 percent but would also, among other things, deny extra benefits to those who have additional children while on welfare and require teenagers on welfare to live with a parent or guardian. New Jersey recently passed a statute, endorsed by both Democrats and Republicans, that disallows extra benefits for mothers who have children while on welfare but couples this with job training and more generous benefits for those who marry or go to work. And the Democratic governor of Maryland has joined the movement by proposing a cut in welfare benefits for those who fail to get preventive health care, pay their rent regularly, or keep their children in school.

The reaction to these proposals is at least as interesting as the measures themselves. Critics, including many experts, have noted the sometimes punitive nature of these "reforms," have worried about their possibly racist overtones, and have scoffed at the social engineering involved. Defenders, including most ordinary middle-class citizens, see such proposals as eminently fair and as a constructive response to the self-destructive behaviors that give rise to much poverty and welfare dependency in the first place. Who is right, and how should we evaluate these proposals?

SOME HISTORY

The debate is not a new one. When the architects of the social security system in the 1930s decided that most of its benefits would be based on a history of individual work-related contributions, they made an exception for payments to widows and their children. What began as a small program of aid to dependent children—one that was supposed to fade away when their widowed mothers again became some breadwinners' dependents—mushroomed into a major part of the social safety net as divorce and out-of-wedlock childbearing swelled the ranks of eligible single parents. Although few questioned the appropriateness of such assistance during the 1960s and 1970s, by the 1980s these changes in family composition, and a concomitant increase in the welfare rolls, had etched themselves on the national consciousness, setting the stage for a conservative backlash. And a backlash there was. The Reagan administration, with the help of its conservative allies in the intellectual community, began to articulate a new view of the welfare system, arguing that it was the cause of poverty and not the solution. Mainstream scholars countered that there was little or no empirical evidence to support this charge.

By the end of the decade, the debate seemed to have reached a new equilibrium with the passage of the Family Support Act of 1988. This legislation emphasized the responsibility of fathers to pay child support and of mothers to participate in education and training that would move them toward self-sufficiency. At the same time, the government committed itself to funding the training and other services that would make self-sufficiency possible. Welfare in return for work, or the willingness to prepare for work, was the new rule. With so many middle-class mothers in the workforce, taxpayers were less willing to pay low-income mothers to stay home with their children. A welfare system out of step with middle-class norms and behaviors could not survive. The new paternalism of the 1990s is also an attempt to bridge this gap.

MOST BEHAVIOR IS DIFFICULT TO MODIFY

One reason why supporters of the Family Support Act prevailed was because there was evidence that training programs for welfare mothers worked. This is much less clear in the case of the new proposals. Several studies suggest that decisions to marry and to have children are, at best, only modestly affected by the kinds of incentives one can build into the welfare system. Decisions to work or to stay in school may be somewhat more open to such influence. The effects on behavior also depend on the magnitude of the incentive provided and the way in which it is delivered. A big enough incentive delivered in a user-friendly and supportive fashion can have an impact. There are numerous examples of programs that have changed people's lives, among them the "I

Have a Dream" program that promised college tuition to those who finished high school, the workfare experiments of the early 1980s, and even (some claim) a Planned Parenthood program in Colorado that paid teenagers not to become pregnant. Each of these programs uses carrots rather than sticks and combines rewards with heavy doses of counseling and other services.

On the other hand, a legislatively mandated evaluation of the Wisconsin Learnfare program, designed to improve the school attendance of family members on AFDC (Aid to Families with Dependent Children) "did not find improvements in attendance" in high school or middle school students studied. In a congressional hearing presided over by Senator Daniel Patrick Moynihan (D-N.Y.), a diverse panel of welfare experts all agreed that government attempts to change personal behavior, such as childbearing or marriage, with a system of rewards and punishments probably would not do much. As one panelist argued, "[T]he most likely effect is no effect at all. We have every reason to believe that recipients will resist changes in their personal behavior." All said and done, although we don't know everything we should about the potential of these and other interventions to move people toward self-sufficiency, it is clear that many of the simpleminded economic incentives that the public believes will change people's behavior may not.

PUBLIC ATTITUDES MATTER

If the public were convinced of this, how much difference would it make? Would more exposure to information about the relationship between welfare benefits and marriage cause the citizens of California to reject their governor's ballot initiative? I doubt it: "Effectiveness" is not the only issue here. Morality, or conformity with social norms, also matters. The public wants to distinguish between the deserving and the undeserving poor and to set conditions on the use of its "hard-earned" money. (Paul Taylor of the *Washington Post* reports that when President Bush condemned welfare dependency in his 1992 State of the Union address, he received his second highest marks of the evening from a focus group armed with devices that provide instant feedback.) Whether one likes it or not, this is a fact of political life. Community expectations and values are registered through the political process and cannot be ignored. Advocates for the poor have long had to live with the reality that single mothers are considered more deserving than equally poor men and that assistance for the elderly poor is more popular than that for their younger counterparts.

Such distinctions apply not just to who deserves assistance but also to the form in which such assistance is provided. The public is willing to provide noncash benefits to the poor, such as food stamps, even though there is no evidence that such earmarked benefits increase spending on food. Indeed, providing cash instead of food stamps would be administratively cheaper, provide more freedom of choice, and be less demeaning to the poor. But liberals have long since learned that to cash out the food stamp program would almost certainly diminish the total amount of assistance available. In the same way, they may come to accept the idea that conditioning assistance on behavior may be the political price they have to pay for continued support of the welfare system, even when they disagree with the moral premises of the policy itself.

What I am asserting here is the community's right (subject to constitutional limitations) to express its values through the political system. If its sentiments and beliefs are wrongheaded, then it is up to those who disagree to change rather than to override public opinion. In recent decades, those liberals who have aggressively asserted individual rights over community concerns have ended up alienating much of the public. In his book, *Liberal Purposes*,[1] William Galston has articulated the problem well:

> In the past generation . . . important forces within both American academia and public life have embraced understandings of liberalism perceived, with some justification, as hostile to traditional moral understandings. The result has been a disaster for progressive politics. If self-styled liberals cannot accommodate, and recognize their dependence on, the moral restraints espoused by ordinary citizens, liberalism cannot regain in practice the general acceptance needed to guide public life in a constitutional democracy.

Liberals are aware of the erosion of public support for progressive policies, but their most common reaction has been an attempt to rebuild support by emphasizing more universal policies rather than by accommodating the moral sensibilities of the middle class. Social security is the historical paradigm of a universal program that has done more to help the poor than all of the means-tested programs put together, but that has bedrock public support because of its inclusiveness. Proposals for universally subsidized day-care, national health insurance, and tax credits for families with children are the modern analogues. The problem is that such programs are enormously expensive. Moreover, the popularity of social security may have as much to do with its contributory character as with its broad coverage. Even if we could afford a guaranteed income for every American along the lines proposed by George McGovern, it would almost certainly not pass muster. Public support cannot be bought by delivering assistance to everyone. It can be bought by making such assistance conditional on work or other widely approved behaviors.

Political support for the new paternalism is not the only issue. There can be such a thing as too much government by public opinion. The popular will should be filtered through the legislative process. The fact that Governor Wilson's proposals are being put on the ballot rather than debated in the legislature is significant because it eliminates the kind of considered judgments and education of the citizenry by its elected representatives that we should expect in a democracy. The voters are currently not as well informed as the people they elect. For example, the possibility that the public expects far more behavioral change from the new paternalism than it can possibly deliver has already been noted. Moreover, the tensions between individual rights and community concerns are real and cannot be resolved except by considering each case on its merits and evolving reasonable compromises.

INDIVIDUAL LIBERTIES MUST BE PROTECTED

Another reaction from rights-oriented liberals has been to conjure up worst-case scenarios and anecdotes as arguments against the new paternalism. It is not hard to paint a portrait of America circa 1994 that would give George Orwell a run for his money: welfare mothers being forced to have abortions or sterilizations because otherwise they would be denied extra money for additional children; parents being blackmailed by their potentially truant children into appropriately submissive behavior ("I will buy you a gun if you go to school tomorrow"); teenage mothers being forced to live with abusive parents as a condition of receiving assistance; and so forth.

In the end, we must decide which is the greater threat to democracy and the individual freedoms that democracy promises: occasional specific abuses of the coercive power of the state by those who support reasonable versions of the new paternalism or a broader backlash against the entire system fomented by the David Dukes of the world and fueled by resentment of the life-styles of the poor. Specific abuses can be curtailed by administrative safeguards (such as exceptions, in cases of conflict or abuse, to the rule that teen mothers must live with a parent). But the only defense against a populist backlash is to align policy with mainstream values.

PATERNALISM SHOULD BE EVENHANDED

One issue is fairness. If paternalism is good for the poor, it should be good for the rich and the middle class as well. Indeed, if it is not applied in an even-handed way, then charges of racism, classism, and sexism carry more weight. If tax policies are moving in the direction of making allowances for family size among the working poor and the middle class, as they seem to be these days, then denying the welfare population equal treatment seems unfair. Or, to take another example, imagine denying college aid from public sources to middle-class kids who cut their classes or medicare to elderly citizens who don't get annual checkups. The precise analogies to the new paternalism may seem a bit farfetched, but the general point is not. Proposals to tie public health insurance to personal life-style (e.g., smoking) or college loans from public sources to academic performance in high school have as much merit as the new paternalism for welfare recipients. Imposing similar conditions only on the poor smacks of just the kind of tyranny of the majority that a rights-based liberalism correctly warns us against.

INCENTIVES NEED TO BE ACCOMPANIED
BY SPECIFIC FORMS OF HELP

One way to guard against discriminatory policies is to apply the Rawlsian test—that is, to imagine oneself on welfare and to ask what conditions one would consider fair. As far as it goes, this is a reasonable criterion. The problem I see is that most of us who have achieved a middle-class life-style or better have a tendency to imagine that all our normal cognitive and psychological resources would be preserved intact if we were poor and that all we would lack would be money. But poverty often is corrosive, not only because of material deprivation, but more important, because it affects a person's self-image and sense of control. Policies should not assume a capacity to adapt immediately to middle-class norms on the basis of purely economic incentives. People need to be helped to take control of their lives, and not simply rewarded for doing so. If work is the goal, then training and assistance with finding a job may be the means to make this possible. If reducing teenage childbearing, and the welfare dependency that so often follows, is the goal, then making family-planning services more accessible, and poor women's life prospects more promising, may be essential.

Moreover, people should be given opportunities to prove their competence in small increments that, because they are rewarded, are systematically reinforced. As Douglas Besharov of the American Enterprise Institute has emphasized, the behavior that we are trying to achieve needs to be within realistic reach of the recipient, and the incentives that are offered should encourage new modes of behavior that can be internalized in the long run. He also notes the importance of being able to track the behavior in question. If truancy, for example, can't be accurately monitored by school authorities and reported to welfare offices, then bonuses for school attendance cannot be effectively administered.

INNOCENT VICTIMS NEED TO BE PROTECTED

The current welfare system is not neutral; it rewards childbearing. We would not give a welfare family a bigger grant if they went out and bought a car, but we do when they decide to have a baby.

Cars and babies, it will be argued, are different. To begin with, babies are not always planned. However, this is true of much impulsive consumption as well. Beyond this, children are the innocent victims of any curtailment of welfare benefits for larger families. In theory, one can argue that the costs imposed on children penalized under such a regime may be more than compensated for by the reduction in the number of children growing up in poor families. After all, we endanger the lives of hostages in order to deter further hostage taking. But if smaller welfare benefits for larger families do little to deter additional childbearing, this argument carries little weight. The costs imposed on children seem too high a price to pay for encouraging more responsible fertility decisions among their parents. We are left, then, with a dilemma. We do not want to reward childbearing among those unable to support their children, but we must reward it in order to protect their offspring. One way out of this dilemma is to link welfare benefits not to the number of children born but to a willingness to use effective family planning.

Seen in this context, the proposal of a Kansas legislator to give extra money to welfare mothers who agree to use Norplant is more reasonable than it might seem at first blush. (Norplant is a new long-term, virtually fail-safe, contraceptive implant that is as safe as the Pill and completely reversible.) Opponents of the plan argue that poor women would need the money so badly that they would, in effect, be coerced into forfeiting their right to have children. But where is the right established to have children at someone else's expense? Many middle- and working-class families are financially constrained from having additional children, and their paychecks are not adjusted upwards should an unexpected baby arrive on the scene. Should John Doe be expected to pay for a welfare mother to have two children when, partly because of the taxes he pays, he can only afford one?

If we are serious about protecting innocent victims, we should reward contraception, not penalize children; at a minimum, people should have the means to effectively and safely plan their families.

PATERNALISM SHOULD BE USED SPARINGLY

Finally, we would be wise to use behavioral incentives sparingly. The criteria for their use have been thoughtfully laid out by Robert Goodin in Chapter 11 of this book. Paternalistic policies are justified, he argues, in cases in which the stakes are high and individual preferences are unstable or inconsistent. Take once more the case of early childbearing. The stakes are certainly high both for society and for individual mothers and their children. The public costs of supporting a family begun by a teenager (in present value terms) averaged $17,000 in 1989. Moreover, the life prospects of both the mother and her children are likely to be constrained. As a result, many women later regret having a baby as a teenager and find it inconsistent with their desire to obtain an education, hold a job, or marry someone other than the child's father.

Similarly, surveys show that most welfare recipients want to work and that most drug addicts want to kick their habits. People's behaviors and their deep-seated preferences are not always consistent. Policies that accord with the latter are only paternalistic in the best sense of the word (assuming that people's deep-seated preferences can be reliably known). We understand this in dealing with our own children, especially adolescents, who are the group most at risk of prematurely damaging their lives. Public policies should be based on similar principles. Using the welfare system to get people to pay their rent on time, however, does not seem to meet either the "high stakes" or the "deep-seated preferences" criterion.

IN CONCLUSION

In the end, my view is that the new paternalism must be seriously considered because welfare programs that are not consistent with mainstream values will never be politically viable and will certainly not be adequately funded. At the same time, such approaches are justified only under certain conditions. Most important, there must be some evidence that the policies will actually work to change behavior or that there is a willingness to combine them with services, counseling, or other measures that can help welfare recipients achieve the goals of the program. Otherwise, they are nothing more than a way of pandering to public opinion. In addition, paternalistic policies are likely to be more acceptable and be more appropriate when:

1. They are introduced as a means to reward rather than punish and are not used as a means to balance budgets on the backs of the poor.
2. They are applied in an evenhanded way that does not discriminate against the poor.
3. They are designed in ways that do not produce an infringement of individual liberties or create a new set of innocent victims.
4. The stakes are high.

In the past, many experts and advocates, because they have largely ignored community values, have failed to develop welfare policies that are effective, respectful of individual rights, and acceptable to the public at large. This is no mean task. But if we fail now, a new paternalism that does not work, or is patently unfair, is not only what we will get but also what we will deserve.

NOTE

1. Galston, William. *Liberal Purposes: Goods, Virtues, and Diversity in the Liberal State*, New York: Cambridge University Press: 1991.

CHAPTER 13

A Liberal-Democratic Case for the Two-Parent Family

WILLIAM A. GALSTON

WHY LIBERAL DEMOCRACIES NEED STRONG FAMILIES

I am here chiefly concerned with a traditional issue: the role of the family as a moral unit that transmits (or fails to transmit) the beliefs and dispositions needed to support oneself and to contribute, however modestly, to the community. This moral concern is linked to a broader political thesis. A healthy liberal democracy, I suggest, is more than an artful arrangement of institutional devices. It requires, as well, the right kinds of citizens, possessing the virtues appropriate to a liberal democratic community. A growing body of empirical evidence developed over the past generation supports the proposition that the stable, intact family makes an irreplaceable contribution to the creation of such citizens, and thus to the promotion of both individual and social well-being. For that reason, among others, the community as a whole has a legitimate interest in promoting the formation and sustaining the stability of such families.

As in many other spheres of American life over the past generation, family relations have witnessed a tremendous expansion of individual rights and liberties. In the process, some long-festering problems have been addressed. But these gains have not come without costs, many of which have been borne by America's children. It is time, I suggest, to put the family at the center of our thinking about social policy, and children at the center of our thinking about the family. As we do so, we discover a discourse of responsibilities that supplements and, in some measure, supplants the language of individual rights.

So understood, responsibility is a two-way street. The liberal democratic community has a wide range of responsibilities to families: not to tax away the money they need to raise children; to ensure that full-time work provides a nonpoverty family income; to decrease as far as possible the current tension between family and work; to increase supportive services available to families experiencing severe stress; and to nurture rather than undermine the network of intermediary associations ("civil society") within which families function best.

I have discussed the policy implications of these community responsibilities elsewhere (see "Putting Children First," published by the Progressive Policy Institute, September 1990, and co-authored with Elaine Ciulla Kamarck). My focus here is on the responsibilities of parents to their children and to the community, among which are: to make every effort to stay married; to acknowledge or establish paternity; to contribute adequately to their children's financial support; to refrain from activities such as substance abuse that harm their children; and to involve themselves in their children's education and socialization.

To say that the community ought to take a legitimate interest in parental discharge of these responsibilities is to leave open the possibility that this interest may assume the form of law. In the first issue of *The Responsive Community*,[1] James Childress distinguishes between policies that "express" community and those that "impose" community. There can be little doubt that, whenever a meaningful choice exists, it is preferable to create moral incentives for socially desirable behavior rather than to employ directly coercive measures. But in family policy as elsewhere, this choice is not always available. The law—the moral voice of the state—must sometimes command as well as cajole. The hope is that over time, this legal demonstration of community commitment will evoke a higher level of normative internalization and voluntary compliance.

At some point, legal demands may jeopardize a liberal democracy's dedication to a wide sphere of individual freedom. What begins as the expression of legitimate community interest can become inappropriate and counterproductive meddling. State action must therefore be justified in light of widely shared public purposes, and the line separating such public purposes from personal moral preferences must be vigilantly safeguarded.

THE DECLINE OF THE AMERICAN FAMILY

In 1990, the *Washington Post* published the results of a nationwide inquiry into the public mood. The title: "Introspective Electorate Views Future Darkly." The thesis: The public believes America is in the grip of "moral decay." The public's prime explanation of moral decay: "the breakdown of the family." These worries are hardly the product of an overheated public imagination. Last year, more than one-quarter of all infants were born out of wedlock. For black infants, that figure exceeded 60 percent. Divorce trends paint an equally alarming picture. From 1940 to 1960, the U.S. annual divorce rate was essentially stable.

From 1960 to 1985, by contrast, it skyrocketed by 250 percent. In 1960, the United States had 35 divorced persons per 1,000 married persons. By 1985, that figure had nearly quadrupled, to 130. So when we talk about the "breakdown of the family" and its consequences for children, family breakup is just as significant as the failure of families to form in the first place.

To be sure, similar trends may be observed in virtually every advanced industrialized country except Japan. But it has proceeded farther in the United States. Even today, French and (West) German divorce rates are actually lower than were U.S. rates in 1960, and Swedish rates, popularly believed to be stratospheric, are, in fact, less than one-half those of the United States. As Constance Sorrentino of the Bureau of Labor Statistics summarizes the situation, "Based on recent divorce rates, the chances of a first American marriage ending in divorce are today about one in two; the corresponding ratio in Europe is about one in three to one in four."

We have known for some time about the economic consequences of family breakdown. As David Ellwood of Harvard University observes, "The vast majority of children who are raised entirely in a two-parent home will never be poor during childhood. By contrast, the vast majority of children who spend time in a single-parent home will experience poverty." In 1984, the rate of poverty before government transfer payments in single-parent families was about 50 percent, whereas the comparable figure for two-parent families was 15 percent.

A closer look at the statistics only intensifies the difference. Eighty percent of children growing up in two-parent families experienced no poverty whatever during the first ten years of their lives, whereas only 27 percent of the children in single-parent households were so fortunate. Conversely, only 2 percent of children in two-parent households experienced persistent poverty (seven years or more), whereas a full 22 percent of children in single-parent households literally grew up poor. It is no exaggeration to say that the best antipoverty program for children is a stable, intact family. Conversely, family disintegration is a major reason why, after a decade-long economic expansion, the poverty rate is nearly twice as high among children as it is among elderly Americans.

If the economic effects of family breakdown are clear, the noneconomic effects are just now coming into focus. Although scholars over the past generation have disagreed over the consequences of divorce, work done during the 1980s on balance reinforced the view that children of broken families live under major noneconomic disadvantages. Writing recently in the *American Enterprise*, Karl Zinsmeister summarizes this emerging consensus: "There is a mountain of scientific evidence showing that when families disintegrate, children often end up with intellectual, physical, and emotional scars that persist for life. . . . We talk about the drug crisis, the education crisis, and the problems of teen pregnancy and juvenile crime. But all these ills trace back predominantly to one source: broken families."[2]

In 1981, John Guidubaldi, then president of the National Association of School Psychologists, picked a team of 144 psychologists in thirty-eight states, who gathered long-term data on 700 children, half from intact families and the other half from children of divorce. Preliminary results published in 1986 showed that the effects of divorce on children persisted over time and that the psychological consequences were significant even after correcting for income differences. The results also indicated that during grade-school years, boys were significantly less able than were girls to cope with divorce, in large measure because divorce almost always means disrupted relations with the father rather than with the mother. Boys need on-the-scene fathers and are highly vulnerable in their absence.

The problems engendered by divorce extend well beyond vanishing role-models. Children need authoritative rules and stable schedules, which harried single parents often have a hard time supplying. As Guidubaldi puts it, "One of the things we found is that children who had regular bedtimes, less TV, hobbies and after-school activities—children who are in households that are orderly and predictable—do better than children who [did] not. I don't think we can escape the conclusion that children need structure and oftentimes the divorce household is a chaotic scene." The results of the Guidubaldi study have been confirmed and deepened by Judith Wallerstein's ten-year study of sixty middle-class divorced families. Among her key findings published in *Second Chances: Men, Women, and Children a Decade After Divorce*[3]

> Divorce is a wrenching experience for many adults and almost all children. It is almost always more devastating for children than for their parents . . .

> The effects of divorce are often long-lasting. Children are especially affected because divorce occurs during their formative years. What they see and experience becomes a part of their inner world, their view of themselves, and their view of society . . .

> [A]lmost half the children entered adulthood as worried, underachieving, self-deprecating, and sometimes angry young men and women . . .

> Although boys had a harder time than girls, suffering a wider range of difficulties in school achievements, peer relationships, and the handling of aggression, this disparity in overall adjustment eventually dissipated . . .

> Adolescence is a period of grave risk for children in divorced families; those who entered adolescence in the immediate wake of their parents' divorces had a particularly hard time. The young people told us time and time again how much they needed a family structure, how much they wanted to be protected, and how much they yearned for clear guidelines for moral behavior . . .

Given the profound psychological effects of divorce, it is hardly surprising that recent studies confirm what many teachers and administrators have suspected for some time: the disintegrating American family is at the root of the

United States' declining educational achievement. There is nothing new about this proposition. Ever since James Coleman and his coauthors published their seminal study nearly a quarter century ago, research has consistently indicated the importance of family background for student achievement. An overwhelming body of data suggests that the "hidden curriculum of the home," which consists largely in the development of language skills, is directly related to children's later success in school. Untangling just what it is about family structure that makes for high or low educational achievement is a difficult task. Family economic status is clearly important; children from poor families consistently do less well than do children from nonpoor families. Still, income is not the whole story. After controlling for income, significant differences in achievement remain between children from single-parent families and those from intact families—especially for boys.

To summarize: Evidence indicates that from the standpoint of the psychological development and educational achievement of children as well as their economic well-being, the intact two-parent family is generally preferable to the available alternatives. It follows that a prime purpose of sound family policy is to strengthen such families by promoting their formation, assisting their efforts to cope with economic and social stress, and retarding their breakdown whenever possible. This "prime" purpose is not the only purpose: Family policy must also seek to ameliorate the consequences of family breakdown for children while recognizing that some negative effects cannot be undone.

To avoid misunderstanding, I want to make it clear that a general preference for the intact two-parent family does not mean that this is the best option in every case. That proposition would be absurd. Nor does it mean that all single-parent families are somehow "dysfunctional"; that proposition would be not only false, but also insulting to the millions of single parents who are struggling successfully against the odds to provide good homes for their children. The point is that at the level of statistical aggregates and society-wide phenomena, significant differences do emerge, differences that can and should shape our understanding of social policy.

Nor, finally, should the endorsement of the two-parent family be mistaken for nostalgia for the single-breadwinner, "traditional" family of the 1950s. Setting aside all other variables, it cannot be doubted that much of the surge of women into the workforce in the past three decades has come in response to economic stress. As inflation-adjusted hourly wages have fallen in response to international competition and stagnant productivity, only increased female labor force participation has enabled families to maintain their purchasing power. For better or worse, the new reality for most American families is that two earners are now needed to maintain even a modestly middle-class way of life—and that many of their marginal economic gains are being eroded by work-related expenses. As Barbara Whitehead has documented in *Family Affairs,* the economic benefits are counterbalanced by a sense of increasing stress brought about by decreased time available for family life. The point of a policy that takes its bearings from the two-parent family is not to turn the clock back, but rather to enable such families to deal more effectively with the economic and social challenges of the 1990s.

Having entered these disclaimers, I want to stress that my approach is frankly normative. The focus is on what must be a key objective of our society: raising children who are prepared intellectually, physically, morally, and emotionally to take their place as law-abiding and independent members of their community, able to sustain themselves and their families and to perform their duties as citizens. Available evidence supports the conclusion that, on balance, the intact two-parent family is best suited to this task. We must then resist the easy relativism of the proposition that different family structures represent nothing more than "alternative life-styles"—a belief that undermined the Carter administration's efforts to develop a coherent family policy and that continues to cloud the debate even today.

In taking this position, I associate myself not just with scholarly evidence, but also with the moral sentiments of most Americans. Over the past few years, Barbara Whitehead has conducted one-on-one and focus-group discussions with a cross-section of middle-class parents. Her overall finding: "Our national debate on the family is being conducted in two separate languages. The first is official language, spoken by experts and opinion leaders in politics, the media and academia. The second is family language, spoken by ordinary middle class families." "Official" language speaks mainly of economics and public policy; "family" language focuses on culture and values. Official language is self-consciously relativistic; family language is unabashedly judgmental:

> In the official debate, . . . the remembered past is almost always considered a suspect, even unhealthy, guide for the present or the future. . . . these memories harken back to what the official language is pleased to term the "mythical" or "nostalgic" family of the past sentimental fiction that blinds us to the real challenges of modern life. But the mothers and fathers I met do not hesitate to look back at their own childhoods. And in a majority of cases, they report that, compared to today, families then were stronger, children better off, and neighborhood and community life far more supportive of family well-being. In the official language, the family isn't getting weaker, it's just "changing." Most parents I met believe otherwise.

The reasons for this belief are not hard to identify. Most Americans are neither moral fanatics nor moral experimentalists. They are tolerant of individual and group differences, and they don't want to impose their views on others. But they do have moral views, strongly held and deeply rooted in the nation's cultural heritage. And they regard many family changes of the past generation as violations of these convictions.

With regard to the family, these views go roughly like this: A primary purpose of the family is to raise children, and for this purpose families with stable married parents are best. Sharply rising rates of divorce, unwed mothers, and runaway fathers represent abuses of individual freedom, for they are patterns of adult behavior with profoundly negative effects on children. The character of the family, these Americans believe, is the key to raising children successfully. Families have primary responsibility for instilling such traits as discipline, ambition, willingness to abide by the law, and respect for others—a responsibility that cannot be discharged as effectively by auxiliary social institutions such as public schools. This responsibility entails a sphere of legitimate parental authority that should be bolstered—not undermined—by society. It requires personal sacrifice and delay of material and emotional gratification on the part of parents. But this responsibility can be fulfilled, even in the face of daunting odds. Generations of Americans have shown that economic and social hardships are compatible with strong families raising competent children—and that such families are the key to overcoming these hardships.

This, then, is the core of average Americans' moral understanding of the family. But these same Americans do not, for the most part, see contemporary society as supportive of this understanding. On the contrary, they see their efforts to transmit moral values to their children counteracted by many of our society's most powerful forces. They are experiencing what might be termed a "cultural squeeze."

As Barbara Whitehead's work has shown, two principal objects of parental concern are rampant materialism and the dominance of the media. As these parents express it, reports Whitehead: "They are losing the struggle to pass on their family values to their children—losing it to an aggressive and insidious consumer culture. In their eyes, their children are no longer acquiring an identity at home as much as they are attempting to buy one in the marketplace."

Other evidence suggests an even broader indictment: of a society that seems unable to control drugs, that cannot even guarantee their children's physical security in school and on the way to it, that fails to reinforce discipline and high standards, that emphasizes instant gratification over working for the future, that flaunts transitory sexuality at the expense of lasting commitment.

One consequence of this cultural squeeze was graphically illustrated in a recent Rand Corporation study. Contrary to conventional wisdom, it turns out that during the late 1980s more than two-thirds of the young adults charged with drug dealing in the District of Columbia actually held legitimate, full-time jobs with hourly compensation averaging $7—twice the prevailing minimum wage. Rather than being a response to desperation born of employment and economic deprivation, drug dealing was a "lucrative underground form of moonlighting" designed to support expensive patterns of consumption. For example, the typical drug dealer reported spending more money on clothes than on housing or food—on average, $275 per month, or $3,300 a year!

The authors of the report draw the obvious conclusion: In these circumstances, even the creation of jobs paying three times the minimum wage would hardly dent the problem. In the short term, stricter sanctions and swifter, surer punishment for dealers and users may help. But in the long run, there is simply no substitute for moral education that effectively conveys values such as delay of gratification and respect for law to the next generation of children.

For all these reasons, I suggest, we must reject the moral relativism characterizing much "official" discussion of the family. We should reject, as well, the thesis that questions of family structure are private individual matters not appropriate for public discussion and response. After all, the consequences of family failure affect society at large. We all pay for systems of welfare, mental and physical disability, criminal justice, and incarceration; we are all made poorer by the inability or unwillingness of young people to become contributing members of society; we all suffer if our society is unsafe and divided. There is a fundamental distinction between social institutions and practices that affect only the consenting parties to them and those that affect everyone else. Whenever institutions and practices have such pervasive consequences, society has the right to scrutinize them and, where possible, to reshape them in light of its collective goals.

This suggests that from a moral viewpoint, there is a deep difference between families with children and those without them. Families without children may be regarded as consensual arrangements that touch the vital interests of their immediate members only, and principles of individual freedom and choice may be most appropriate. By contrast, families with children are engaged in activities with vast social consequences. Moral categories such as duty, continuing responsibility, and basic interests come into play in addition to, and as restraints on, freedom of choice. Society may then be justified in treating these two types of families quite differently in the structure of law and policy.

THE RETURN TO RESPONSIBILITY: DIVORCE LAW REFORM

One prime candidate for this strategy of differentiation is the law of divorce. To begin with, because of the shattering effects of divorce on children, it would be reasonable to introduce "braking" mechanisms that require parents contemplating divorce to pause for reflection. There is a transatlantic precedent for such procedures. A report from Britain's Law Commission has recommended that such couples

> Notify the courts of their intention, then spend at least nine months resolving crucial details of the divorce. Their first obligation would be to decide the future of their children before settling questions of property and mainte-

nance. Only then could couples return to court for a divorce. As a recent account notes, "By encouraging parents to look at the consequences of a family breakup rather than at the alleged cause or excuse for it, the commission hopes couples will improve their prospects of saving the marriage.[4]

Of course, such pause for reflection will not always—perhaps not usually— succeed in warding off divorce. It is then necessary to turn to phase two—the reform of procedures affecting the economics of divorce for families with children. For these families, the divorce revolution of the past generation has been a disaster. As Lenore Weitzman has shown in *The Divorce Revolution: The Unexpected Social and Economic Consequences for Women and Children in America* "Divorce has radically different economic consequences for men and women. . . . divorced men experience an average 42 percent rise in their standard of living in the first year after the divorce, while divorced women (and their children) experience a 73 percent decline."[5]

Moreover, this large disparity between men and women post-divorce was calculated under the assumption that the noncustodial father actually fulfilled his mandatory financial responsibilities, which is far from universally true. The real gap is almost certainly larger.

Even after the limited federal and state reforms of the 1980s, the child support system is a mess. More than one-third of all absent fathers simply ignore their legal obligation to support their children, and many others pay only a fraction of what they owe. The average annual contribution of those who do pay is only $2,300, and many use delays or arbitrary reduction in support payments to achieve other bargaining objectives vis-à-vis the custodial parent. If a reasonable level of collections and payments were achieved, absent fathers would contribute at least $25 billion more each year than they do today. And if the system were made less discretionary and more uniform, a major source of uncertainty, conflict, and distress for custodial parents would be removed. The fundamental norm that should guide our efforts is this: The responsibility of biological parents for their children does not cease simply because of divorce, separation, or out-of-wedlock birth. As David Ellwood argues,[6] to give voice to—and to enforce—this basic moral proposition, our society should create a far more uniform and straightforward method of child support. Among the major steps toward reform:

Society would commit itself to identifying every child's father and mother. In the future, the social security numbers of both parents would appear on each child's birth certificate.

All absent parents would be expected to contribute a portion of their income, which would vary with the number of children they fathered (or bore).

Payments would be collected by employers, just like social security taxes, and remitted to the federal government, which would then send the money directly to custodial parents. All absent or noncustodial parents would be included, not just delinquents. Failure to pay would be an offense comparable to tax evasion.

These and other reforms will require fundamental changes, not just in what we legislate, but in how we think as well. As Mary Ann Glendon, a leading American student of the law of divorce, has observed in *Abortion and Divorce in Western Law*,[7] "When almost three-fifths of all divorces in the United States involve couples with minor children, it is astonishing that our spousal support law and marital property law treat that situation as an exception to the general rule." She goes on to recommend a set of guidelines for divorces with children:

> A "children first" principle should govern all such divorces. . . . the judges' main task would be to piece together, from property and income and in-kind personal care, the best possible package to meet the needs of the children and their physical custodian. Until the welfare of the children had been adequately secured in this way, there would be no question or debate about "marital property." All property, no matter when or how acquired, would be subject to the duty to provide for the children.

COERCION AND THE MORAL VOICE OF THE LAW

I offer divorce law reform as an illustrative example of what a turn toward a responsibility-based family policy would mean. By becoming parents, individuals assume certain responsibilities, among which Glendon's "duty to provide for the children" bulks large. And because the failure to fulfill this duty entails such negative consequences for children and for the community, society has a right—indeed, a responsibility—to take an active interest in its fulfillment.

It would be wonderful if a simple hortatory expression of that interest—society's collective moral voice—were sufficient to achieve general compliance. But our experience gives us little warrant for believing this to be the case. Indeed, mandatory declarations—laws with teeth—are typically needed to convince citizens that the community is serious about its professed standards of responsibility. From drunk driving to racial discrimination, vigorous enforcement backed by sanctions has proved essential in changing behavior.

To say that social responsibility must sometimes begin with a measure of public coercion is not to say that it must always remain there. The post–*Brown* history of U.S. race relations offers some grounds for hoping that, over time, changed behavior can lead to changed belief—that is, to a genuine internalization of previously external norms. Laws such as the Civil Rights and Voting Rights acts have turned out to be schools for a new and widely shared understanding of a more equal citizenship for all.

But, to repeat, the force of these laws rested on more than the moral norms they articulated. Without the demonstration of deep seriousness in the form of the coercive power of the state, few if any changes in public attitudes would have occurred.

Thus, to return to the matter at hand, I do not doubt that the coercive features of the family proposals I have advanced will arouse deep misgivings in many quarters. Forcing individuals to discharge their responsibilities is not a prospect that anyone can regard with equanimity, let alone satisfaction. But the alternative seems to be a society in which one group of citizens can inflict grave damage on a second group and then force a third group to bear the collective costs. The long-term prospects of a community unwilling to act forcefully against such abuses cannot be regarded as bright.

NOTES

1. *The Responsive Community*, vol. 1, issue 1, Winter 1990/1991.
2. Zinsmeister, Karl. "Raising Hiroko: The Child Centered Culture of Japan," *The American Enterprise*, vol. 1, March/April 1990.
3. Wallerstein, Judith. *Second Chances: Men, Women, and Children a Decade After Divorce*, New York: Ticknor and Fields, 1989.
4. Gardner, Marilyn. "Putting Children First: The New English Precedent," *Christian Science Monitor*, March 30, 1990.
5. Weitzman, Lenore. *The Divorce Resolution: The Unexpected Social and Economic Consequences for Women and Children in America*, New York: Free Press, 1989.
6. Ellwood, David. *Poor Support: Poverty in the American Family*, New York: Basic Books, 1988.
7. Glendon, Mary Ann. *Abortion and Divorce in Western Law*, Cambridge, MA: Harvard University Press, 1987.

CHAPTER 14

Moral Guidance for Today's Youth, In School and Out

WILLIAM DAMON

In our public concern over the moral state of our younger generation, we have politicized the age-old endeavor of moral education in a most divisive way. Our divided response, rather than helping to correct the decline that we see in young people's behavior, further feeds it. The most valuable legacy that a community of elders can give a younger generation is a steady consensus of shared values that the young can look to with certainty for guidance. In our present societal climate, we instead are offering them angry squabbles about values and mixed messages rife with discord and confusion.

To ensure the moral futures of our young, we need to build what one social scientist has called a "youth charter." In a study of over 300 American cities and towns, Frances Ianni found that an unwritten community consensus, or "charter," is a far stronger predictor of wholesome youth behavior than are such heralded factors as affluence, ethnicity, geography, or family social status.[1] This will come as no surprise to anyone who appreciates the many sources of lasting influence on children's social development during their formative years.[2] Young people receive messages about what is right and what is wrong from *all* the people in their lives. It is important that the multiple messages work in synchrony to guide a child coherently and in a beneficial direction.

In the abstract, the notion of projecting a consensus of values to guide the young may seem unrealistic at best and totalitarian at worst. How could such a fractious society as ours achieve consensus about anything value-laden? Whose rights of dissent might be trampled on in the process? But I do not refer to a consensus on every subtlety or nuance of human choice about which people may legitimately disagree. I refer, rather, to a consensus about those basic precepts of right and wrong that virtually all responsible members of civilized society want their children to abide by. These include qualities such as a commitment to truthfulness; a respect for authority; a concern for others; a sense of fairness; and a dedication to common decency. The fact is that we already have a societal consensus about such matters, but we have failed to join hands in communicating it strongly and effectively to our young. On such matters, there is no reason for adults to withhold guidance from the young and every reason vigorously to assert it. For this is where our gravest danger lies today: in the core matters of civility and decency that determine the quality of any society and that are increasingly in short supply in contemporary social life.

A fifty-year comparison reported in the spring of 1993 by the *Congressional Quarterly Researcher* tells the story in stark simplicity.[3] In 1940 public school teachers named gum chewing, littering, breaking in line, violating dress codes, talking too loudly, and running in the halls as their students' major behavioral shortcomings. By 1990 the list of student conduct disorders had become considerably more weighty. Teachers at the beginning of the 1990s worried about suicide, assault, robbery, rape, premature pregnancy, alcoholism, and drug abuse. Now, in the mid-1990s, the downward trend is quickening further and shows no sign of abating.

If we were to take a walking tour around a typical American school, city or suburban, in this final decade of the twentieth century, we would not use up much shoe leather before encountering one or more of the following incidents: A counselor is calling a student's home about some apparently excused absences, only to find that the parent's letters have been forged. A young boy is in the principal's office for threatening his teacher with a knife. Three students are separated from their class after hurling racial epithets at a fourth. A girl is complaining that her locker has been broken into and all her belongings stolen. A small group of boys are huddling in a corner, shielding an exchange of money for drug packets. In the playground, two girls grab a third and punch her in the stomach for flirting with the wrong boy. Throughout the corridors and classrooms, there is a palpable spirit of apathy, disorderliness, and disrespect.

Is there a responsible citizen in our society who would not find any of this appalling? There can be no controversy in educating youth away from such behaviors and toward more virtuous ones. Precisely this is the first and foremost charge for moral education in our schools. I believe that it is an incontestable one.

Now it is true that this is not the stuff of the juicy ideological debates on moral education that has made for all the good news stories over the past decade. Politicians looking for cultural "wedge" issues would rather air their views on condom distribution, abortion, school prayer, cultural diversity, and the other polarizing disputes that are tearing our social fabric apart. In this case as in others, politics and education do not mix.

Schools have a societal mandate to create orderly environments where children can learn. To create an orderly environment for youth in today's societal climate is no easy task, but schools have many means of doing so. In the course of the school day, many natural opportunities arise for discussing and enacting core values such as truthfulness, respect for authority, concern for others, fairness, and academic ethics. Teachers can communicate a world of moral meaning in their manner, in the quality of their relationships with students, and in their interpretations of the curricula. The hot mix of cultural, religious, and sexual controversies that have so obsessed the media may be left to the institutions where they properly belong—to our families, our churches, and to our many valuable community associations for youth. If our schools simply did well what they are supposed to do on their own territory, all of our young people would have at least one place in their lives where they would experience at first hand the core values of decency. And it is through such first-hand experiences that a child's character begins to be shaped.

A child's character development cannot end with the child's school experience, of course, nor, even, with the child's family experience. There is an Old World folk saying that claims, "It takes a whole village to raise a child." In fact, the acid test of whether there is a community at all is the extent to which moral guidance for the young is shared among all who come in contact with the young. . . .

Unfortunately, moral guidance for the young has become too scarce a commodity in contemporary culture. This is shameful and unnecessary, for the principles underlying beneficial moral guidance are neither complex nor elusive. Moreover, they remain essentially the same in all the settings where children come into contact with the world of adults.

SOME SOUND PRINCIPLES FOR OFFERING
MORAL GUIDANCE TO THE YOUNG

Moral education builds on the child's formidable natural capacities for moral awareness. In *The Moral Child*, I made the case that children start life predisposed to respond toward others in a moral fashion.[4] They are born with the capacity for empathy and sympathy; they quickly develop moral emotions such as shame, guilt, and outrage; and they acquire strong positive feelings about authority and fairness by the time they have entered preschool. As James Q. Wilson elegantly demonstrates in a more expansive argument than I have made, the "moral sense" is fundamental to the human species.[5]

Accordingly, moral guidance does not start from ground zero. We have much to work with in the constitution of every child. The constitutional forces are important, although they are certainly not sufficient for full moral development. In order for children to reach their best potential as responsible citizens of society, they need proper adult guidance throughout their entire childhood and adolescence.

Moral guidance must begin by building bridges to the child's native proclivities; and it must first of all develop in the child a firm respect for authority. My own phrase for the sort of bridge-building that recognizes the child's own moral strengths and draws them into an adult's framework of guidance is *respectful engagement.*

The elements of respectful engagement are:

1. The creation of a dialogue in which the adult and the child share a common interest.
2. The structuring of that dialogue in ways that introduce the adult's intellectual or moral agenda to the child.
3. The encouragement of the child's active participation in the dialogue, including the child's free expression of beliefs (however wrong these beliefs may seem).
4. The clear expression, in ways that the child can comprehend, of the adult's own perspective.

All four conditions are necessary for effective moral education.

Respectful engagement establishes a climate of tolerance for divergent opinions. But tolerance in instructional dialogues need not imply, as some have wrongly deduced, that teachers and other adults should practice values neutrality while discussing ethical conflicts with the young. In fact, displays of values neutrality from teachers and other adults have an opposite effect to that intended. By failing to confront children with real values, genuinely held, such displays engender in children an attitude of passive indifference—and even cynicism—toward the enterprise of moral choice. Why should a child bother working through a moral problem, or risk taking a stand, when the child's supposed moral mentor refrains from publicly doing so?

To have a lasting effect, moral educators must confront children with basic values that are clearly stated and sincerely held. The principle of respectful engagement assumes that a primary goal of moral instruction must be to foster in children the deep understanding of everyday moral issues. The child must learn to find the moral issue in an ambiguous situation, to apply basic moral values to unfamiliar problems, and to create moral solutions when there is no one around to give direction. The only way to master these key challenges is to develop an ability to interpret, understand, and manage moral problems.

Among moral educators, one contentious debate over the past decade has been between those who would emphasize training children to have good habits versus those who would emphasize helping children to develop the capacity for moral reasoning and reflection.[6] Predictably, the debate has been roughly along conservative/liberal lines. I can understand the opposition, for it is true that habit and reflection are two distinct psychological systems, with distinct developmental roots.[7] Acquiring the capacity for one does not ensure the capacity for the other. Yet I would find it catastrophic if we were forced to choose between the two.

Naturally, we want young people to act right habitually, as a matter of course. I agree that the moral life is built primarily on good habits. We want young people to resist immoral behavior in the same automatic way that most people refrain, without hesitation, from robbing a helpless beggar for easy gain. But reflection, when grounded in good values, supports rather than deflects the habitual moral response. Moreover, it can prevent that periodic human tendency to blindly stumble into horrendous moral mistakes. When habit and reflection marry, sustained moral commitment becomes possible.[8] It is this commitment, and no less, that we must work for in ourselves and in our young.

THE SPECIAL CASE OF SCHOOLS AND TEACHERS

Skepticism about our schools is so rife these days that many have given up entirely on the possibility of schools' promoting moral growth. But there is nothing unrealistic about the idea that schools can teach children good values. Nor should this idea seem controversial to us. By their very existence, schools present students with important values such as respect for others, honesty, responsibility, and orderliness. Beyond these implicit standards, schools also introduce children to many of the values necessary for constructive participation in a democratic society—values such as equal rights, freedom of speech, and respect for legitimate authority. By also teaching children the social and historical context of such values, schools prepare young people for full citizenship.

Many wonder whether it is appropriate for public schools to take positions on human values. "Whose values?" is the question most often raised. Shouldn't a public school teacher be "values neutral"? In fact, many school districts throughout the land have adopted moral education approaches that advocate values neutrality for teachers. ("Values clarification" is the best known of such approaches.) The results have not been good. Children have not come away with improved understanding, firmer beliefs, or better conduct. Rather, they have become confused and cynical about the school's message (or lack thereof).

Values neutrality is unnecessary and misguided because there is widespread consensus among civilized people everywhere about the importance of core values such as truthfulness, respect, kindness, and responsibility. In a democratic society such as ours, there also is a widespread endorsement of democratic values such as liberty, equality, and justice. When schools focus their efforts on teaching these central values, there is little cause for disagreement or concern. On the other hand, it is important to keep in mind that public schools have no business proselytizing about controversial matters of religious or political ideology. Nor need they do so in order to teach children the key values they need for conducting their affairs decently and civilly.

Some wonder, nevertheless, whether there is any point to the exercise. How much can schools really accomplish in the face of all the other influences on a child's moral capacities? As noted above, children are born with native dispositions toward empathy, shame, outrage, and other moral emotions. On top of these natural inclinations, children's religious, family, peer, and community engagements powerfully shape the child's morality. Can schools add anything useful to this mix?

The answer is decidedly yes. There is much that children need to learn about the task of applying natural feelings to complex social problems. A young child might respond with concern to another person in distress without knowing how to help effectively. Schools can teach children skills for translating moral feelings into effective action. They can also teach children how to recognize a moral problem beyond the immediate circle of the child's own friends and family. If children know nothing about conditions in remote parts of the world, they can hardly be expected to empathize with people living there. In school, children acquire knowledge about the world at large.

The curriculum itself may also be used to communicate values.[9] Each discipline has moral and ethical issues embedded within it. Literature is full of interpersonal problems that may be examined in terms of the core human values that they express. History can be viewed in light of how people struggle for rights and determine the responsibilities of citizenship. Science raises moral issues such as truthfulness and ethical ones such as the future of biomedical technology. A good teacher will be quick to draw students' attention to such issues when they arise naturally in readings or classroom discussion. Such discussions of values need neither dominate the curriculum nor detract from its integrity. Rather, they can enhance the curriculum by revealing another key dimension in the subject matter's significance for human affairs.

Although it is by now commonly accepted that teaching has a moral dimension, there is still a curious ambivalence in the profession concerning a teacher's proper stance on moral issues. I have seen this ambivalence most clearly in moral education seminars that I have taught for student teachers. I often begin such seminars by asking whether it is appropriate for teachers to bring their values into the classroom at all. When phrased in this general manner, the question provokes a wide range of opinion and disagreement. It is normal for student teachers to express great reservations about any assertion of moral or personal values in the classroom. This is commonly considered unprofessional and unfair to pupils who would not share the teacher's values.

But when the seminar moves on to consider the general goals of teaching, it quickly becomes clear that there is widespread support for the universal assertion of at least two values. In every discussion of teaching goals that I have had with teachers or student teachers, I have found strong consensus that teaching should foster, if nothing else, tolerance and critical thinking. Within our educational culture, these two goals are so widely accepted, and so little questioned, that I often have trouble getting teachers to see that they are values at all. It always astonishes me that many teachers, for example, see a commitment to absolute tolerance in the classroom as perfectly consistent with the belief that teachers should not allow their values to affect their classroom judgments and behavior. Similarly, teachers often show a tendency to place the goal of critical thinking in a kind of natural "metacategory" outside the realm of values, as if there were no rational choice to be made in the matter. Because critical thinking is seen as an objective procedure for subjecting choices to the tests of reason and truth, it is not usually seen as itself being subject to evaluation.

The anecdote that I tell my seminars on this point is an incident that I witnessed at a conference in Toronto, Canada, about ten years ago. It is one of those rare stories that is more timely now than when it first occurred. The occasion was a presentation by a researcher from the Ontario Institute for Studies in Education (OISE) about new methods for fostering critical thinking in adolescents. Her ideas seemed noncontroversial enough to me, but they were met with indignation and even some outrage from a pair of local school board members. Didn't these new techniques, they asked, inculcate what at the time was called "divergent thinking?" And didn't Canada, that loose affiliation of diverse cultures, need to encourage more *con*vergent thinking in its young people? Who was this researcher to interject her own antinationalistic values into curriculum materials designed for public schooling?

No doubt many of the non-Canadians in the audience were oblivious to the shifting fault lines that even then were threatening to tear that sprawling nation apart. But even many of the Canadians there that day also dismissed this objection as nationalistic hyperanxiety. I suspect that, if the same incident were to take place at the present time, many more might be persuaded. My point here, however, is not to argue for or against these particular nationalistic concerns. Rather, my point is that even the most assumed virtues can come under attack in contexts where the virtues do not function in ways that are perceived to be adaptive (and therefore valued). Who is to say that nationalism should not be an educational priority in a certain time and place? And who is to say that critical thinking may not undermine nationalistic sentiment?

All educational choices—from direct moral instruction to curricular priorities—reflect values; and no matter how unassailable such values may appear at a particular time and place, they may well be questioned at a different time and place. This can be a jarring experience when a person has assumed that certain choices are beyond question. The first challenge of teaching is acquiring a coherent framework of values for making educational choices. Like any members of society, teachers do not (and need not) construct their frameworks independently: there is a solid legacy of values available to them from their communities. Still, in the daily press of schooling, there is always a wide latitude of personal interpretation and choice. In the final section of this essay, I suggest three principles for guiding these interpretations.

THREE PRINCIPLES FOR MORAL GUIDANCE IN TEACHING

All instruction flows from relationships. In turn, all relationships have distinguishable features that give them their moral quality. By its very nature, the teacher–student relationship has certain features that affect its moral quality. Most importantly, in any teacher–student relation, the teacher maintains a position of authority over the student, regardless of how nondirective or egalitarian the teacher tries to be. The moral nature of the teacher–student relationship derives from the legitimacy of the teacher's authority and the manner in which it is wielded.

Legitimate authority in the teacher situation has three benchmarks: *fairness, specificity,* and *truthfulness.* Let us examine each of these three in the context of teaching.

Fairness is a moral imperative of all relationships. In a teaching situation, it usually arises in issues of evenhandedness while dealing with different students and in concerns of judiciousness while doling out rewards or punishments. A common example is a teacher's response to uncompleted homework. There are many reasons why a teacher may be more patient with some students than with others, ranging from the teacher's history with particular students to the forcefulness of a student's excuses. Some of these reasons may be good ones and even necessary. But students are highly sensitive to such variations in response, and unless they perceive the variations as benignly motivated and justly administered, the teacher places her moral authority at risk.

Specificity is one of the benchmarks determining the legitimacy of authority in asymmetrical relationships. It means that an authority's directives to those under its command must be restricted to specific areas in which the holder of authority has a legitimate claim to leadership. A legitimate claim can derive from a number of socially recognized attributes, such as competence, experience, and status. All such claims hold only for properly designated spheres of authority. They do not constitute a license for the unconstrained exercise of power. Authority figures must not overstep the boundaries of their specific area of command. It is fine for a teacher to tell a student what classroom to be in on Tuesday morning but not what church to be in on Sunday morning or whom to vote for in the next election.

Like fairness, the third benchmark—*truthfulness*—is also a general moral criterion of human relationships. Yet truthfulness raises a particular set of problems in instructional relations. These problems revolve around the most difficult and important moral challenge that teachers face: pursuing moral ends with moral means. Teachers, and other adults as well, often shade the truth when talking to children, out of the common conviction that the whole truth can lead young minds astray. No matter how well-intentioned, this is a mistaken and dangerous conviction. It inevitably imparts a harmful moral message and can jeopardize the students' trust in their teachers.

Truth shading can take many forms in the classroom. A science teacher working with a health curriculum may exaggerate the risks of unsafe behavior (smoking, drinking, eating high-fat foods) for the benign purpose of getting the warning across in a dramatic way. A history teacher may skip over facts that could cast revered figures in the wrong light. The acute sensitivity of many groups in a pluralistic society creates constant pressure on social studies teachers to tread lightly, if at all, on possibly derogatory facts about historical figures that the groups hold up as heroes.

My purpose here is not just to inveigh against the common but morally questionable practice of "shading the truth." More to the point, I wish to focus on the special instructional risks that doing so can create. The teacher–student relationship is based on trust. In this regard, it is like any other relationship. But since the purpose of the teacher–student relationship is to communicate knowledge, it is essential to the viability of the relationship that the accuracy of the knowledge be trusted. This trust can easily be undermined by an awareness that the teacher is more committed to a certain message—however noble—than to the truth.

Beyond the risks to instructional credibility, truth shading undermines a large part of the moral significance inherent in the teacher–student relationship. In many ways, the developmental effects of relationships on individuals derive directly from the interactional qualities of the relationship. The medium of exchange, in a sense, is the moral message. This is what Piaget meant when he wrote that relationships characterized by constraint can only engender unilateral respect, moral realism, and a host of other "heteronomous" leanings; whereas relationships characterized by cooperation lead directly to mutual respect and an autonomous moral orientation.[10] The forms of interaction within the relationship themselves have a moral meaning and *in the course of development become internalized by the relationship's participants.*

The greatest educational pitfall of a dishonest communication is that it will embody, and therefore transmit, a value of untruthfulness. This is a powerful form of moral education in the wrong direction. The demoralizing legacy of a dishonest communication far outweighs any verbal exhortation toward honesty that a teacher could convey. Yet, in my observations, it is the single most common miseducative experience that students encounter during their education and the single most difficult misstep for teachers to avoid in their practice. It is common and it is difficult to avoid for the same reason: In human affairs, there are always compelling reasons why certain momentous ends seem to justify any means.

In human relationships generally, absolute consistency between means and ends may not always be within reach. Certainly there are times, for example, when deceit has served an essential moral purpose, as when a lie saves a refugee from the hands of an evil dictator.[11] But here I wish to point to the *particular* moral risks of dishonesty between teacher and student, risks that derive from the purpose and nature of the instructional enterprise. The purpose of the enterprise, most educators agree, is to foster the student's intellectual and moral development; and the nature of the enterprise, as I have noted, is a communicational relationship in which the teacher takes on an authoritative role. Dishonest communications weaken and corrupt every aspect of the enterprise because they impart a message that truth is not valued; they create a miseducative encounter between teacher and student; and they undermine the teacher's legitimate authority in the classroom. It is difficult for me to imagine any shading or distortion of the truth that could be justified in an instructional relation where the teacher has assumed responsibility for the student's development. The means and ends of instruction are so intertwined that their congruence is essential—for effective teaching as much as for the usual moral considerations.

Of all the complex issues that arise in classrooms, ethical problems are the ones that teachers often say they are least prepared to deal with. Yet such problems offer unparalleled openings into students' values. The rule of thumb is similar to that concerning the teacher's general manner when engaging with students: teachers do best by modeling the values that they are trying to impart. As long as they respond to classroom problems with principles of fairness, respect, and honesty, they may feel confident that their responses are serving the purpose of moral guidance.

The enterprise of teaching children values in schools is more often than not an indirect one. Where core values are concerned, teachers communicate more by their manners than through explicit messages. A habit of being scrupulously honest with one's students is far more powerful for teaching the value of truthfulness than a thousand lectures on the subject. Students are acutely aware of times when teachers are shading the truth, when they are favoring some students over others, and when they are turning a cold shoulder on students in need. Students are equally aware of their teachers' efforts to be honest, fair, and caring. Such efforts are the school's surest and most lasting means of communicating good values to children.

No matter how well they function, schools can be only a limited part of the solution to today's youth crisis. The problem is too large for any one institution alone; and, in any case, many central areas of moral guidance are better left to a young person's family, friends, and spiritual leaders. *All* the institutions that come in contact with young people must play a constructive role in their moral growth. Schools cannot shoulder the entire responsibility themselves. We should neither expect this of them nor blame them for every ill consequence that follows from our inaction.

But neither can schools shirk the responsibility that legitimately falls on their turf. Until and unless schools dedicate themselves to creating within their own walls a climate of positive moral guidance for their students, it will be difficult, if not impossible, to stop the downward drift.

NOTES

1. F. Ianni, *The Structure of Experience* (New York: Free Press, 1989).
2. See William Damon, *Social and Personality Development* (New York: W. W. Norton, 1993).
3. Cited in *Forbes* magazine, 24 May 1993, and in the *Wall Street Journal* the previous month.
4. William Damon, *The Moral Child* (New York: Free Press, 1988).
5. James Q. Wilson, *The Moral Sense* (New York: Free Press, 1993).
6. E. Turiel, M. Killen, and P. Davidson. "Morality: Its Structure, Function, and Vagaries," in J. Kagan and S. Lamb, eds., *The Emergence of Morality in Young Children* (Chicago: University of Chicago Press, 1987).
7. Damon, *Social and Personality Development.*
8. See Ann Colby and William Damon, *Some Do Care: Contemporary Lives of Moral Commitment* (New York: The Free Press, 1992).
9. For a useful early statement of this idea, see William J. Bennett, "The Teacher, the Curriculum, and Values Education," *New Directions for Higher Education* (1980), 8, pp. 27–34.
10. Jean Piaget, *The Moral Judgment of the Child* (New York: Free Press, 1932/1965).
11. S. Oliner and P. Oliner, *The Altruistic Personality* (New York: Free Press, 1988).

CHAPTER 15

Schools to Parents: Keep Out

JOHN LEO

In his new book, *Free Speech for Me—But Not for Thee*,[1] Nat Hentoff tells the story of a Pennsylvania high school pressuring two fundamentalist students to read *Working*, a Studs Terkel book containing a chapter on prostitutes and a good deal of blasphemous language. Backed by their parents, the teenagers asked in conscience to opt out from reading it. The school, vengeful to the end, wanted to withhold the students' diplomas and settled for failing them in the course. Along the way, the school board said haughtily that "with all deference due the parents, their sensibilities are not the full measure of what is proper education."

That's a rather conventional attitude among educational bureaucrats: We are the professionals; parents are the nettlesome amateurs to be mollified or brushed aside. These days the attitude is on vivid display in the debate about condoms and AIDS-prevention programs, with schools and health officials cutting many corners to get the programs they want.

A friend reports that his 11-year-old daughter came home from school one day and announced that she put a condom on a banana in her fifth-grade class. My friend was not consulted or even told that the preteens were learning how to protect a roomful of tropical fruit from venereal disease. These things have a way of happening without parental input, possibly because the sensibilities of parents, poor yahoos that they are, aren't as good as the sensibilities of enlightened bureaucrats in instructing the young about sex. Besides, you can get a lot more done if parents don't know what's going on. At least my friend had the advantage of dealing with a private school he could yank his daughter out of. At public schools, the stakes are higher. When you send a child to a state school, do you yield all authority over the child's sexual education?

Sexual rights. In New York City, some parents noticed their children coming home from school with a pamphlet outlining a sexual "bill of rights" for teenagers, including "I have the right to decide whether to have sex and who to have it with." Parents were surprised to learn that all children had the inalienable right to sleep around, and wondered who, exactly, had bestowed it. As it turned out, the new "rights" sprang full-grown from the head of someone at the City Department of Health. The pamphlets were printed with federal money and made their way into the schools.

The list includes "the right to ask for help if I need it." This sounds harmless on the face of it, but it has the effect of inviting a student–school alliance on sex, with parents cut out of the loop. A critic of these alleged new rights, Irene Impellizzeri, vice president of the city's Board of Education, translated it as "I can go behind my parents' back." She argued that ethnic groups get ahead in American society by not allowing schools and other institutions to get between child and parent: "Any school policy that shields children from their parents' traditional values and authority—any practice of addressing children over the heads of their parents—tends to hinder the progress of the group and to 'emancipate' more and more of its children into the underclass."

Washington, D.C., has just acted firmly to emancipate students from parental objections to condom distribution. Dr. Mohammad Akhter, the city's public health commissioner, overrode the arrangement allowing parents to get their children exempted from the condom program in District schools. The superintendent of schools said parents could opt out of the condom program by writing him a letter. But Akhter ordered school nurses to disregard any such notes. The head of the District's Congress of Parents and Teachers complained, in effect, that parents with moral or religious objections had been mugged. Columnist William Raspberry argued that Akhter's "doctor-knows-best arrogance" in brushing parents aside will have the effect of weakening the authority of mothers in the eyes of children.

Many school systems are notably honest and open with parents about sex programs. The city of Baltimore, for example, has that reputation. Partly as a result of working closely with parents, it has avoided the uproar over contraceptives that has hit New York, Los Angeles, and Boston. But other school systems like to hide from parents the exact details of what their children are being taught and offered.

Impellizzeri says she found out about New York's teen "bill of rights" only because a teacher slipped it to her privately, asking her not to tell where she got it. She says graphic material on how to perform anal sex is showing up, unapproved, inside city schools. Under various other programs around the country, children can be taught the use of "dental dams" for oral sex or referred for counseling to a gay activist without parents knowing.

David Blankenhorn, president of the Institute for American Values, thinks parents are quite intentionally kept in the dark. Educational bureaucrats, he says, "accept the proposition that parents are kind of backward, repressed, held back by religion, and have to be handled." Look for more stealth programs in schools.

NOTE

1. Hentoff, Nat. *Free Speech for Me—But Not for Thee: How the American Left and Right Relentlessly Censor Each Other* New York: HarperCollins, 1992.

CHAPTER 16

Building a Responsive Community

JOHN GARDNER

THE TRADITIONAL COMMUNITY

Setting about the contemporary task of building community, one discovers at once that the old, beloved traditional model will not serve our present purposes well. Nostalgia for "the good old days" will not help us through the turbulent times ahead.

The traditional community was homogeneous. Today most of us live with heterogeneity, and it will inevitably affect the design of our communities. Some of the homogeneity of traditional communities was based on exclusionary practices we cannot accept today.

The traditional community experienced relatively little change from one year to the next. The vital contemporary community will not only survive change but, when necessary, seek it.

The traditional community commonly demanded a high degree of conformity. Because of the nature of our world, the best of our contemporary communities today are pluralistic and adaptive, fostering individual freedom and responsibility within a framework of group obligation.

The traditional community was often unwelcoming to strangers, and all too ready to reduce its communication with the external world. Hard realities require that present-day communities be in continuous and effective touch with the outside world, and our values require that they be inclusive.

The traditional community could boast generations of history and continuity. Only a few communities today can hope to enjoy any such heritage. The rest, if they are vital, continuously rebuild their shared culture and consciously foster the norms and values that will ensure their continued integrity.

In short, much as we may value the memory of the traditional community, we shall find ourselves building anew, seeking to reincarnate some of the cherished values in forms appropriate to contemporary social organization. The traditional community, whatever its shortcomings, did create, through the family, through the extended family, and through all the interlocking networks of community life a structure of social interdependency in which individuals gave and received support—all giving, all receiving. With that no longer available, we must seek to reconstruct comparable structures of dependable interdependency wherever we can—in the work place, the church, the school, the youth-serving organizations, and so on.

THE INGREDIENTS OF COMMUNITY

I have spoken of the building and rebuilding community, but so far haven't said what we might expect as a result of our rebuilding. Let me be specific. I think of community as a set of attributes that may appear in diverse settings—a school, a congregation, a town, a suburb, a work place, a neighborhood. I'm going to list ten attributes of a community that would be viable in the contemporary world. There is no value neutrality in my description of the ingredients, but I believe the values explicit in these pages are widely shared. My interest is not to depict Utopia. My interest is to get us away from vague generalizations about "community" and to identify some ingredients we can work on constructively.

One of my purposes is to provide a list of characteristics against which observers can measure any setting in which they find themselves. Many readers, as they review the list, will be asking themselves what steps might be taken in their own setting. So at the same time that I describe the ingredients, I shall be suggesting—under the heading Steps Toward Solutions—some of the ways in which those ingredients might be made to emerge—methods of building community. I do so with some hesitation because my thoughts at this writing are preliminary and incomplete. Yet they may lead to more developed ideas as the subject is pursued further.

Some methods buy community at too high a price, and I shall not advocate them. It is always possible, for example, to build community by creating (or exaggerating) an outside threat. Many cults force new members to divest themselves of old ties and to cast off old identities. Many totalitarian societies create community by cutting off other options for their members.

1. Wholeness Incorporating Diversity

We live in a world of multiple, interacting systems. On the international scene, nations function interdependently or collide. In the city, government officials, business, labor, ethnic groups, and community organizations find—or fail to find—ways of living together. Russia seeks a way of dealing with the Ukraine, Canada a way of dealing with Quebec. Los Angeles copes with its multiple cultures. One encounters religious congregations that are split along class, racial, or doctrinal lines.

In our system, "the common good" is first of all preservation of a system in which all kinds of people can—within the law—pursue their various visions of the common good *and* at the same time accomplish the kinds of mutual accommodation that make a social system livable and workable. The play of conflicting interests in a framework of shared purposes is the drama of a free society. It is a robust exercise and a noisy one, not for the fainthearted or the tidy-minded. Diversity is not simply "good" in that it implies breadth of tolerance and sympathy. A community of diverse elements has greater capacity to adapt and renew itself in a swiftly changing world.

But to speak of community implies *some* degree of wholeness. What we seek, at every level, is pluralism that achieves some kind of coherence, *wholeness incorporating diversity*. I do not think it is venturing beyond the truth to say that wholeness incorporating diversity is the transcendent goal of our time, the task for our generation—close to home and worldwide.

"Wholeness" does not characterize our cities today. They are seriously fragmented. They are torn by everything from momentary political battles to deep and complex ethnic rifts. Separate worlds live side by side but fail to communicate or understand one another. The list of substantive issues facing the city are not the city's main problem. Its main problem is that it can't pull itself together to act on any of the issues. It cannot think as a community or act as a community.

As we look at the world's grimmest trouble spots, wholeness incorporating diversity seems a hopeless quest. But there are a good many cities and even nations where markedly heterogeneous populations live and work together quite peaceably.

Steps Toward Solutions

To prevent the wholeness from smothering diversity, there must be a philosophy of pluralism, an open climate for dissent, and an opportunity for subcommunities to retain their identity and share in the setting of larger group goals.

To prevent the diversity from destroying the wholeness, there must be institutional arrangements for diminishing polarization, for teaching diverse groups to know one another, for coalition-building, dispute resolution, negotiation and mediation. Of course the existence of a healthy community is in itself an instrument of conflict resolution.

A clear part of the problem, particularly in our cities, is the fragmentation of leadership. Most leaders are one-segment leaders, fattening themselves on the loyalty of their own little segment and exhibiting little regard for the city as a whole. Indeed, sometimes they thrive on divisiveness. But in any city there are leaders capable of a broader perspective, capable of joining with leaders of other segments (in and out of government) to define and solve the larger problems of the community. Such networks of responsibility can serve as a kind of constituency for the whole.

In our pluralistic system, each group is given the right to pursue its purposes within the law. Each group may demand recognition, may push for its rights, may engage in the healthy conflict implicit in pluralism—but then, in a healthy community each group will reach back to the whole community of which it is a segment and ask, "How can we help? How can we sing our part in the chorus?"

The nonprofit or voluntary sector can be a significant ally in accomplishing wholeness that incorporates diversity. It is a natural arena for diversity, but it is also capable of the "knitting together" that brings us back to some semblance of wholeness.

2. A Reasonable Base of Shared Values

To require that a community agree on everything would be unrealistic and would violate our concern for diversity. But it has to agree on something. *There has to be some core of shared values. Of all the ingredients of community this is possibly the most important.* The values may be reflected in written laws and rules, in a shared framework of meaning, in unwritten customs, in a shared vision of what constitutes the common good and the future.

To say that the community is characterized by those shared ideas and attributes puts the matter too passively. It will be more truly a community if members see it as an active defender of the shared ground. There should be a sense of social purpose. In our own society, we expect that the community will not only respect but actively pursue such ideals as justice, equality, freedom, the dignity of the individual, the release of human talent and energy, and so on. Thus, programs in education, civil rights, and the like build community. Rampant crime, fraud, and corruption tear it down.

The community teaches. If it is healthy it will impart a coherent value system. If it is chaotic or degenerate, lessons will be taught anyway—but not lessons that heal and strengthen. We treasure images of value education in which an older mentor quietly instructs a child in the rules of behavior, but that is a small part of a larger and more turbulent scene. The child absorbs values, good and bad, on the playground, through the media, on the street— everywhere. It is the community and culture that hold the individual in a framework of values.

None of this should be taken to mean that healthy communities should suppress internal criticism or deny their flaws or agree on everything. Irving Janis has shown how easily shared beliefs can become shared delusions.

Steps Toward Solutions

If the community is very lucky—and few will be in the years ahead—its shared values will be embedded in tradition and history and memory. But most future communities will have to build and continuously repair the framework of shared values. Their norms will have to be explicitly taught. Values that are never expressed are apt to be taken for granted and not adequately conveyed to young people and newcomers. Individuals have a role in the continuous rebuilding of the value framework, and the best thing that they can do is not to preach values but to exemplify them. Teach the truth by living it. All of us celebrate our values in our behavior. It is the universal ministry. The way we act and conduct our lives is saying something to others—perhaps something reprehensible, perhaps something encouraging.

Today we live with many faiths, so we must foster a framework of shared secular values—liberty, justice, and so on—while leaving people free to honor diverse deeper faiths that undergird those values.

3. Caring, Trust, and Teamwork

In some of the primitive tribes studied by anthropologists, the group was almost wholly self-sufficient. The community was responsible for all of the functions essential to human life: the provision of food and shelter, the resolving of internal conflicts, common defense in a hostile environment (human and other), the passing on of survival skills as well as provision of a context of meaning, allegiance, identity, and emotional fulfillment.

Today the community has been stripped of many of these functions by federal and state government, by distant suppliers, by media external to the community, and so on. It is all the more important then that we give attention to the functions that remain. Prominent among those remaining functions is providing the climate of caring, trust, and teamwork that ensures the accomplishment of group purpose.

The members of a good community deal with one another humanely, respect individual differences, and value the integrity of each person. A good community fosters an atmosphere of cooperation and connectedness. There is recognition and thanks for hard work, and the members are aware that they need one another. There is a sense of belonging and identity, a spirit of mutual responsibility. There is the altruism that is so consistently urged by major world religions. There is trust and tolerance and loyalty. Everyone is included. There is room for mavericks, nonconformists, and dissenters; there are no outcasts. Obviously, this describes an ideal community, perhaps beyond our reach. The best communities we know have a long way to go.

But even the approximation of such an environment is powerfully rewarding to individuals and can counteract the tendency of members to drift away that afflicts most American communities today.

Research shows that much of the basis for positive and generous adult relationships can be traced back to a warm and nurturing environment in childhood. But there are measures that can be taken at the adult level.

Steps Toward Solutions

In seeking the goal of caring, trust, and teamwork, the first necessary step is to give all subgroups and individuals reason to believe that they are fully accepted. It is essential that ethnic minorities, women, newcomers, the disabled, and so on—all feel that they count. We know how to fight that battle and should not let up.

Another step, equally critical, is to institutionalize arrangements for resolving disputes. Conflicting purposes and values are inevitable in our pluralistic society and part of the normal functioning of a healthy community. Indeed, groups that have been denied just treatment by the community find it necessary to precipitate conflict. But without processes for conflict resolution we can never achieve the "wholeness incorporating diversity" that we seek. Some systems for resolving disputes have been institutionalized over centuries. Our courts, our representative political institutions, and the economic marketplace resolve many conflicts. Some cities have community boards to deal with neighborhood disputes, commissions to work on racial harmony, or other instruments to diminish polarization.

Beyond that, there is an impressive array of measures that may be taken to resolve disputes. Every competent legislator knows the modes of building consensus and forming coalitions. Wise political leaders have learned the methods of collaboration and compromise.

The arts of reconciling conflicting purposes should be taught in every school and college in the world. Young potential leaders should be exposed to real-life situations—a political campaign, internship in a legislature or action in a community organization—where they learn the arts at first hand. The goal is not to abolish conflict, which is inevitable and even healthy, but to achieve constructive outcomes.

The third step is based on shared tasks. When individuals invest (time, energy, whatever) in their community, their bond with the community is strengthened. If they give something to (or give up something for) the community, they feel closer to it. Community problem-solving activities build community.

A healthy community will provide ample opportunities for the individual to participate in community efforts. Beginning early, boys and girls should take some responsibility for the well-being of any group they are in. This is a seemingly small step but without doubt the first step in responsible community participation, and for that matter the first step in leadership development. Through volunteer community service experiences outside of school, they will learn how the adult works and will have the experience of serving their society. Every organization serving the community should find ways to involve young people.

There should be an Experience Corps through which older citizens can engage in volunteer work. A Volunteer Technical Assistance Center should help every nonprofit institution in the community learn the rather complex art of using volunteers effectively.

4. Participation

A two-way flow of influence and communication is dictated by our value system. Our society requires a dispersed network of leaders spread through every segment of the organization and down through every level. Beyond this wide network of identified leaders, there will be, in a vital community, a large number of individuals voluntarily sharing those leadership tasks that lend themselves to sharing, for example, achieving a workable level of unity, motivating, explaining.

If the system under discussion is a community functioning politically, one would want to add that beyond this voluntary sharing of leadership tasks a very large number of people will be expected to participate in such matters as voting and attending town meetings.

There are those who are opposed to the very concept of "a leader"—and there is much in human experience that makes their attitude easy to understand. But leadership in the mode I've described is not the sort of coercive or exploitative process that we've seen so much of in human history.

For a city, perhaps the most important requirement for effective leadership is the continuous collaboration between city government and all the segments of private-sector leadership, profit and nonprofit. Private-sector groups are beginning to recognize that such participation is a positive duty.

The citizen voting or speaking out in public meetings is participating, but so are the parents who rear their children with a sense of community responsibility, and so is the teenager who volunteers to tutor disadvantaged children. The healthy community has many ways of saying to the individual, "You belong, you have a role to play, and the drama has meaning." It is this more than anything else that accounts for the sense of identity so characteristic of community members.

Steps Toward Solutions

Among the conditions that enhance the possibility of participation are the following:

A. A community culture that enables all members and all subgroups to feel accepted and confident that their needs will be considered.

B. Civic education as to how local government works and why it sometimes doesn't work.

C. Voter registration and "get out the vote" drives.

D. Strong and active neighborhood groups and civic associations.

E. Free and responsible media of communication.

F. An open and responsive political process—restoration of trust in government by making it worthy of trust!

G. A sound educational system that includes preparation for effective leadership and participation.

H. Avoidance of the delusion that experts and professionals will solve all problems—what some have called managerial liberalism—making citizen action necessary.

I. Forums in which community members can "work through" (to use Daniel Yankelovich's phrase) the key issues facing them. Yankelovich points out that the superficial poll responses that are labeled public opinion are not at all the same as public judgment, which can only result from public dialogue.

J. A strong tradition of voluntary public service.

Let me elaborate on "G" above: education for effective leadership and participation. The overwhelming emphasis in contemporary education on individual performance must be supplemented with education in the accomplishment of group purpose. Some of the new cooperative education programs achieve that result. At some point in high school and college, one or another form of community service or political internship is helpful.

Many other institutions in the community can help with the task of civic education. Any citizen group, any advisory commission, every civic task force is a potential training ground for leaders and community builders. In addition, the community should have one or another form of "community leadership program" of the sort sponsored by the National Association for Community Leadership or the American Leadership Forum. All segments of community leadership must be represented in such groups.

It would be wrong to conclude a discussion of participation without mentioning some of the complexities of the subject. First, participation is never total, and those who do participate are always a self-selected group. Some have a higher than average self-interest in participating, some have more of the energy that participation requires, some are more zealous (or dogmatic) on the issues, some thrive on emotional intensity and combative talk, some have more of the physical or psychological stamina required for interminable meetings. Whatever the basis of selection, the result is not a representative sample of the community.

Among those who do participate, there will be a small group of activists who come to dominate and a large number who play less effective (or down-right passive) roles. One cannot change that reality. One can design the system so that the small guiding group is required to act openly and is held firmly accountable by the others.

5. Affirmation

A healthy community reaffirms itself continuously. It builds its own morale. It may face up to its flaws and tolerate criticism, but basically it has confidence in itself. No group, no matter how well established, can take such affirmation entirely for granted. There are always young people to instruct and newcomers to welcome. Even a group with no history or tradition to build on can reaffirm its identity, its purposes, and its shared values. Individuals are generally members of more than one community and there are competing demands on them. The communities that survive the competition are likely to be those that press their claims.

In an earlier era, communities celebrated their beginnings, their roots. But in few American communities today can a majority, or even a sizable fraction of members, claim any link with the community's history. The story of most communities today is acceptance of wave upon wave of newcomers who over generations found a way of living with the culture, influencing it as they accommodated to it. The drama and pride of our communities has been the coming together of many cultures, with the consequent enrichment of all.

Steps Toward Solutions

Of course, a healthy community provides innumerable and ever-present affirmations of shared purpose just by being intact and vital. Everything from its nursery tales and its legendary figures to its structures of law and custom are forever conveying messages of instruction and reinforcement. Its history speaks, its symbols speak. It affirms the framework of meaning so important to community membership.

Normally, communities have ceremonies and celebrations to reaffirm the symbols of group identity, to recognize and reward exemplary members, to provide bonding experiences. In addition, there should be more formal measures to further civic education, not just in the schools and colleges but in the churches, youth organizations, and civic groups. It is everybody's business.

In thinking about the task of affirmation, we face the question of how far one carries a good thing before it becomes a bad thing. It is appropriate in a martial community such as the U.S. Marine Corps to pursue the matter somewhat obsessively. But for the normal community, excessive affirmation may create more pressure for conformity than is compatible with creativity.

6. Institutional Arrangements for Community Maintenance

Every community has institutional arrangements for group maintenance. In a city the most conspicuous arrangements are those we call government. In a nonprofit organization it is the board of trustees, the director and staff, and perhaps some volunteer committees. The forms are infinitely varied, and unwritten codes of conduct play their role.

There are marked variations from one community to the next in the extent to which the institutional arrangements are characterized by structure and control. We can't accept the extremes. Excessive community control does not accord with our ideal of individual freedom and responsibility. At the other extreme is a degree of anarchy that does not permit (or invite) the emergence of shared values, that tolerates a degree of disorder wholly incompatible with a sense of community.

Between the extremes we can tolerate considerable variation in the degree of structure and control.

In a democratic society, a high proportion of the population has some role in the maintenance system. In a town, for example, there are leaders in town government and in the private sector. There are lower level leaders in every segment of the community. And there are a considerable number of individuals throughout the system who "share leadership tasks" on their own initiative, working to maintain group motivation, to heal rifts, to do volunteer work, and the like. And then there are the many members who participate by voting, by setting an example of appropriate individual behavior, by nurturing younger members.

Steps Toward Solutions

Some of the writers who are most concerned about restoring a sense of community today are not inclined to pay much attention to government, but its role is critically important. If it doesn't work, it must be made to work. We cannot take it for granted. It has to be made an instrument of community and of participation, worthy of respect and trust. Politicians are much maligned, but the best of them, skilled in mediating among disparate groups, can make a significant contribution to community.

There must be continuous collaboration between local government and the private sector. There must be an infrastructure of neighborhood associations, churches, citizen groups, youth-serving organizations, and professional groups. Today some of these groups are genuinely interested in the community as a community, but most are highly specialized, each existing in its own little niche, rarely if ever thinking about the fate of the community as a whole. They must learn where their civic duty lies. They are an important part of the fabric of the community.

One of the most important functions in community maintenance is training and development of those who will ensure the continuity of maintenance. For this, the mingling of the generations is crucial. Young people should, from an early age, learn how their community functions and how it can be kept functioning.

CONCLUSION

Social theorists have pointed out that among the first acts of totalitarian dictators coming to power is to undermine the private associative links of the citizen, so there is nothing left but the state and a mass of separate individuals, easily dominated. Such theorists argue (correctly) that the close-in loyalties—to family, school, church, lodge, union, neighborhood, and community—are essential to the health of a free society. Not only do such loyalties make the rise of an absolutist state far more unlikely, but also they are teaching arenas for the arts of community that we need so desperately at national and world levels.

At first glance, it would seem that no other nation has, or could have, a richer diversity of associations than we do. We have taken pluralism to its limits. So what's the problem? Why aren't we in great shape?

The answer is that the conditions of contemporary life have leached out the ingredients of community from a great many of these potentially nurturing associations. How many congregations have we seen in which the element of community is so thinned out as to be nonfunctional? How many schools have we seen that might be splendid communities but in fact don't even approach that condition? How many neighborhoods might be coherent human settlements but are not?

I had occasion recently to spend considerable time with the local branch of a famous social service organization, committed in its public pronouncements to serve its clients humanely. I have reason to believe that the agency uses its funds carefully and provides its services dutifully. But the rich opportunities it has to provide an experience of community to clients who desperately need that experience are squandered. It is a station for the delivery of social services, but one might find more sense of community among the patrons of the nearest motel.

Another problem is that even for those of our associations that are in fact communities, there is often a reluctance to play their role in relation to the larger wholes of which they are a part. I know of one small business enterprise whose officers and employees constitute a satisfying little community, but they have little or no interest in the disintegrating city in which they are located.

Returning to a point made earlier, I think of community as a set of attributes that may or may not be present in a particular group or social system. I have tried to describe those attributes so that people can assess any particular institution or social system of which they are a part—school, congregation, village, work place, neighborhood, whatever—and judge whether it is in fact a community.

We must seek to regenerate the sense of community from the ground up. How can people work to make their metropolis a community when most of them have seldom experienced a sense of community in any familiar setting? Men and women who have come to understand, in their own intimate settings, the principles of "wholeness incorporating diversity," the arts of diminishing polarization, the meaning of teamwork and participation, will be strong allies in the effort to build elements of community into the metropolis, the nation, and the world.

It would be a grave mistake to imagine that, in a great burst of energy, we can rebuild our communities and then turn to other tasks. That assumes a degree of stability we once knew but may never see again in our lifetime. We can never stop rebuilding.

The communities we build today may eventually be eroded or torn apart by the crosscurrents of contemporary life. Then we rebuild. We can't know all the forms that community will take, but we know the values and the kinds of supporting structures we want to preserve. We are a community-building species. We might become remarkably ingenious at creating new forms of community for a swiftly changing world.

CHAPTER 17

Pluralism within Unity: A Communitarian Version of Multiculturalism

DIANE RAVITCH

One of the most fractious, divisive debates of the 1980s and 1990s centered on the word "multiculturalism." In the educational arena, the word became a red flag and a battle cry, a source of struggles in many school districts and college campuses over curricula and textbooks. The contentious issue that lay behind the arguments was the question of *whose* culture was to be taught in the classroom, or put another way, how should Americans define the "we" in "We the People"?

In the mid-1980s, the debate over multiculturalism was initially framed by those who hold extreme views. At one end were the proponents of cultural separatism, who gained press attention by attacking "Eurocentrism," disparaging American culture, and demanding separate and equal treatment for the study of their own (non-European, non-American) culture. At the other end of the debate were the monoculturalists, who insisted on a canonical rendering of European-American culture and resisted any retreat from "the great books" or what they understood as a traditional rendering of American history and literature.

The debate has raged most heatedly in higher education, where partisan scholars fight over the nature of the canon. But the debate has had its most serious effects in the schools, because there has been little or no intellectual capacity to resist the demands of extreme versions of multiculturalism. Thus, many school districts—and not only those with large enrollments of minority students in the inner city—have adopted a separatist version of multiculturalism, often with little discussion or reflection.

The schools, far more than the universities, are subject to fads and trends, and are far more likely than universities to jump onto the bandwagon of ill-

considered fashions. The university community is, after all, ultimately a community of scholars, and each scholar has considerable leeway to select his or
her readings, regardless of the views of the administration or even the department chair. In contrast, the politics of public schools predisposes them to
accept centrally determined curricula, regardless of the views of the teachers.
The central administration, at the state or district level, often selects the
textbooks and determines the curriculum; a determined interest group will
make more headway with the state or local superintendent than would be
possible on a college campus, where no one has the power to tell every
professor what to teach and what to believe.

At the school district level, the debate was decidedly one-sided. I am not
aware of any school district that aligned itself with the anti-multiculturalist position. Every recorded shift in curriculum and textbooks was toward more and
more multiculturalism in the schools. This happened with minimal discussion
about the available alternatives or about the potentially negative implications of
the separatist version of multiculturalism. Instead, in surprising numbers,
many school leaders accepted unquestioningly the proposition that children
must celebrate their cultural heritage or risk a devastating loss of self-esteem.

What I wish to suggest in these pages is that a communitarian perspective
on the debate would lead to a judgment that both warring camps are essentially flawed in their arguments. The separatists do not give us a vision on
which American society can build for the future; indeed, they give us a vision
for fragmentation and unending intergroup hostility. One has only to read
their texts and curriculum guidelines to see that they appeal not to an enlarged
and generous sense of community, but to prideful ethnocentrism and reaction-
ary separatism.

In their own way, the monoculturalists have been equally disappointing
because their arguments have ultimately been reflexive and unpersuasive.
Their appeal to the "great books" is essentially emotional, not rational; their
opposition to demands for the inclusion of works written by women and racial
minorities seems political and emotional, no less so than the arguments of
those who want writers included in the canon solely because of their color or
their gender. Why not include the work of W.E.B. DuBois or Virginia Woolf
or Toni Morrison? Why insist that it is unworthy to read Langston Hughes or
Claude McKay or James Weldon Johnson? Why not admit that the definition
of what is worth knowing changes in each generation? Why not accept the
burden of reading and rereading what may have been unjustly neglected
writers? My own sense is that the educational world is in a race against the
aliteracy and illiteracy of the electronic age; why should we feel threatened by
the books and stories of writers who have the potential to awaken children to
the beauty of words and well-expressed ideas? The monoculturalists seem to
suggest that Plato and Aristotle are being jettisoned for Zora Neale Hurston
and Charlotte Perkins Gilman; but in reality, students are scarcely reading
anything but the television schedule. To school teachers who struggle to get

students to read anything at all, the arguments by the monoculturalists are meaningless.

We must seek a way out of the sterile bipolarity of the discussion. The critical question that lies behind the debate, I believe, is the issue of American identity. Who are we as a people? Are we a people? How do we define ourselves as Americans? What role should the state play in advancing any particular definition of American identity? To help the discussion along toward a different angle of vision, I would like to offer several different theories about American identity, all well known, and consider how they connect to a communitarian vision of pluralism.

One definition of American identity is the idea of the *melting pot*. Since the 1960s, the melting pot has come to have negative connotations, but it was once considered a noble ideal, a vision of a society in which intermarriage would produce a new American people, unlike any other in the world. The melting pot as the symbol of American life is usually traced to a play of that title written by Israel Zangwill in 1908; in it, the hero gestures to Manhattan and says euphorically, "There she lies, the great Melting Pot—listen! Can't you hear the roaring and the bubbling? . . . Ah, what a stirring and a seething! Celt and Latin, Slav and Teuton, Greek and Syrian,—black and yellow—."[1]

But this notion of a melting pot—an amalgamation of different peoples into a new American people—long predates Zangwill. In the Revolutionary era, J. Hector St. John de Crèvecoeur saw the shaping of a new nationality: "I could point out to you a family whose grandfather was an Englishman, whose wife was Dutch, whose son married a French woman, and whose present four sons now have wives of four different nations. . . . Here individuals of all nations are melted into a new race of men."[2] He did not acknowledge that American Indians or Africans might become part of the new race, yet the logic for their inclusion was present.

Herman Melville wrote in 1849, "You can not spill a drop of American blood without spilling the blood of the whole world. On this Western hemisphere all tribes and people are forming into one federated Whole."[3] Ralph Waldo Emerson predicted the working of the melting pot, with a broader vision than that of Crèvecoeur. He wrote, "in this continent,—asylum of all nations—the energy of Irish, Germans, Swedes, Poles, and Cossacks, and all the European tribes—of the Africans, and of the Polynesians—will construct a new race, a new religion, a new state, a new literature."[4] Mid-twentieth-century ethnic leaders complained bitterly about the melting pot; complained that it was the result of an Anglo-American conspiracy to destroy their cultures, to deracinate them, and to strip them of their cultural vitality. Emerson reminds us that it was in its origins a generous, universal ideal, based on the hope that this land of minorities would eventually merge into a harmonious and vigorous whole.

Another definition of the American identity has been described as *Anglo-conformity*. Put simply, Anglo-conformists believe that the basic economic and political institutions in this country were modeled on English antecedents and that newcomers should embrace the nation's essentially Anglo-Saxon heritage. Milton M. Gordon's *Assimilation in American Life* describes this as "the most prevalent ideology of assimilation in America throughout the nation's history," one that came to be associated with pressures for the "Americanization" of immigrants. As Gordon shows, some version of Anglo-conformity animated nativist groups, but it also was expressed by many of the Founding Fathers. Both George Washington and Thomas Jefferson voiced concern about whether new immigrants would readily adapt to American institutions.

John Quincy Adams wrote about new immigrants:

> They come to a life of independence, but a life of labor—and, if they cannot accommodate themselves to the character, moral, political and physical, of this country with all its compensating balances of good and evil, the Atlantic is always open to them to return to the land of their nativity and their fathers. To one thing they must make up their minds, or they will be disappointed in every expectation of happiness as Americans. They must cast off the European skin, never to resume it. They must look forward to their posterity rather than backward to their ancestors; they must be sure that whatever their own feelings may be, those of their children will cling to the prejudices of this country.[5]

A third definition of American identity is captured by the term *cultural pluralism,* which is associated with the philosopher Horace Kallen, who first made the case against assimilation in 1915. Rejecting both the melting pot and Anglo-conformity, Kallen called for the creation of a federal system of cultural minorities, each preserving its ancestral culture, its religion, its institutions, and its language. He defended the right to be different and insisted that the nation would be best served by encouraging cultural diversity, even to the point of becoming a federation of nationalities. In one of his most memorable statements, Kallen wrote that "Men may change their clothes, their politics, their wives, their religions, their philosophies, to a greater or lesser extent; they cannot change their grandfathers."[6] Kallen used the metaphor of an orchestra to suggest the way that different ethnic, religious, and regional communities could relate to one another, each different but working together.

There are yet other metaphors that define American identity and how we relate to each other: American society as an ethnic and racial mosaic (which is similar in spirit to Kallen's definition of cultural pluralism); American society as a salad bowl, in which different cultures mix and mingle yet retain their distinctive flavors. And there are groups that insist on remaining out of the melting pot, out of the orchestra, and out of the salad bowl, like the Amish, Orthodox Jews, and Black Muslims.

Clearly, the question of American identity has been the subject of discussion throughout our history. How can we identify which of these definitions is correct? Is any correct?

I suggest that they are all true, to different degrees.

Although the metaphor of the melting pot is out of favor and has few open advocates, in reality the melting pot did work for millions of Americans. It remains a vibrant metaphor because it accurately depicts one version of reality. Many Americans *have* melted and are a blend of races, religions, and ethnic groups. There are many who cannot identify their ancestral culture because it is multitudinous. Intermarriage among racial and ethnic groups increases in each succeeding generation. Many people are black and white; Hispanic, black, and white; Irish and Italian and German and Polish. Many simply don't know how many ethnic strains flow through their blood. Yet we also know that the melting pot did not melt all Americans into a new race or a new people. Some people were "melted," but many were not.

What about Anglo-conformity? Like the melting pot, we must acknowledge that Anglo-conformity was a partial success. No matter how many diatribes are written against it, the fact remains that the United States is an English-speaking country. All of us are governed by a political system that was designed by men of British ancestry and by laws based largely on the common law of England. The men who wrote our basic law—the Constitution—were products of the European Enlightenment and American experience. No matter how many times the Constitution is amended (still a surprisingly rare phenomenon) and no matter how often the laws are revised, the continuity with Anglo-Saxon legal, political, and economic institutions remains powerful.

At the same time, cultural pluralism lives, indeed thrives, even though not in the distinct communities that Horace Kallen advocated. Some groups, such as the Amish and Orthodox Jews, have actively and successfully resisted assimilation. More typical is the experience of millions of Americans who have maintained a vibrant, powerful identification with their cultural heritage as Germans, Irish, Russians, Chinese, Africans, Latinos, Japanese, Koreans, Italians, and Jews, even though they do not necessarily live in culturally distinctive regions.

The key element in all this variation is noninterference by government. Individuals and groups are free to assimilate or to remain apart or to affiliate with people like themselves for purposes of cultural preservation. Or to do all of these things on alternate days or weeks. The choice is theirs.

As a nation of many cultures, we have learned from our history that we should not force individuals and groups of people against their will to assimilate and to abandon their traditions and group ways. We have also learned from our history that we should not force individuals and groups to live in segregated communities, apart from people who are different from them. Neither coerced assimilation nor coerced segregation is compatible with a democratic polity.

Perhaps we will learn in time that cultural pluralism should be neither prohibited nor promoted by government. Preserving ethnic traditions is the work of the family, the church, the community, social groups, and other voluntary organizations. When the ethnic community must rely on compulsory government programs in public schools to preserve its cultural heritage, one must wonder about the authenticity of the culture and its ability to survive absent the support of public institutions.

What, then, is multiculturalism in the United States today?

Unlike those who use the term *multiculturalism* as an epithet, I believe that American culture is inherently multicultural. I believe that we have a common culture that was shaped by American Indians, by Africans, and by the immigrants of many nations. Each generation has added its customs, its folkways, its celebrations, its foods, its music, and its reinterpretations of American culture.

Unlike those who use the term *multiculturalism* to promote programs of racial and ethnic separatism, I believe that multiculturalism refers to the mixing and mingling of different cultures and to the ways that different cultures influence one another. Multiculturalism in the United States refers to cultural syncretism. It is about Buddhists who enroll their children in Catholic schools because they share a sense of spiritual values. It is about the bagel stores in Manhattan owned by Puerto Ricans. It is about fast-food shops that sell tacos, pizza, bratwurst, and tropical ice cream at the same counter.

What, then, should we do in the public sphere? Certainly, we should recognize and celebrate the fact of our multiracial, multiethnic cultural heritage. It is appropriate, I think, to acknowledge the struggles of individuals from many different groups to build the legal and constitutional framework of a successful liberal democratic society. It is appropriate, too, to acknowledge the ingenuity and courage of pioneers in every field of endeavor who have developed the social, cultural, political, and economic institutions of our society.

But all of these celebrations and recognition of diversity should occur within the context of celebrating and recognizing the common bonds that made these accomplishments possible. In the past, we erred by ignoring our diverse cultural heritages while celebrating the common culture in which many Americans were not yet comfortable. Today, we make the reverse offer, celebrating diversity while ignoring any commonalities among us as Americans. Educators have gone overboard in canonizing diversity as an end in itself, oblivious of the painful lessons to be learned from societies like the former Yugoslavia that are being destroyed by social fragmentation and ethnic violence.

The current tendency in the public schools to promote ethnic pride and racial identification is dangerous to our social health. The creation of a peaceful multiracial, multiethnic society does not happen by accident. It occurs in some measure because of thoughtful cultivation of a sense of community. In a good society, people learn to think of themselves as citizens of the same nation, sharing a common fate. This sense of community creates bonds between people of different races, different religions, different social classes, different regions. When we learn to say, "Well, we may differ but we are all Americans," this is no trivial commitment. It is an acknowledgment of shared citizenship, of a readiness to stand together in time of peril and work together with people who are different from oneself.

The cult of ethnicity, as we learn again and again on the evening news, causes division, hatred, and suspicion. It dissolves the bonds of fellowship and citizenship in favor of blood ties. It is especially corrosive in a multiracial, multiethnic society like our own.

What we need, then, is pluralism with unity. We need to respect the diverse origins of our people while teaching and celebrating the liberal democratic tradition in which we all share. Ours is not simply a society in which a lot of different peoples are clustered. Ours is a democratic society that has institutionalized fundamental human rights and a system of justice. We have created a system dedicated to freedom and individual rights. This is no small achievement, and its survival is not automatic. Our society continues to be dependent on the intelligence and knowledgeable participation of its citizens.

To be a good society and a decent society, we must have a sense of shared citizenship. That sense of shared citizenship is the basis for communal responsibility. At present, it is threatened by the single-minded, unthinking cultivation of racialism and ethnicity. For this society to work, we must reach a point where people extend a helping hand to one another, without regard to the color of that hand and without regard to the cultural origins of the person who offers or needs a helping hand.

We have learned about the dangers of coerced assimilation and of coerced segregation. It is time now to recognize the dangers of multiculturalism untempered by a commitment to the common good. It is time now to value and nurture a healthy balance between cultural pluralism and the common good.

NOTES

1. Arthur Mann, *The One and the Many: Reflections on American Identity* (Chicago: University of Chicago Press, 1979), p. 99.
2. J. Hector St. John de Crèvecoeur, *Letters from an American Farmer*, quoted in Diane Ravitch, *The American Reader* (New York: HarperCollins, 1991), p. 34.
3. Herman Melville, *Redburn*, Chapter 33.
4. Joel Porte, ed., *Emerson in His Journals* (Cambridge, Mass., 1982), p. 347.
5. Milton M. Gordon, *Assimilation in American Life* (New York, 1964), p. 94.
6. Horace Kallen, *Culture and Democracy in the United States* (New York, 1924), p. 122.

CHAPTER 18

Mosaic of Hope: Ethnic Identities Clash with Student Idealism at a College

DENNIS FARNEY

Occidental College, like Thomas Jefferson's Monticello, surveys the world from high upon its hill. But Occidental gazes down on an America more diverse, more fantastic, than in any Jefferson dream or nightmare.

Jefferson feared that even a simple biracial America, white and black as equals, would not long endure. He advocated black freedom but remained paralyzed by its implications. "We have the wolf by the ears," he despaired of slavery, "and we can neither hold him, nor safely let him go."

Nearly two centuries later, the sprawling city below Occidental is an astonishing—and ultimately more hopeful—mosaic: black and white, brown and yellow, Latino and Korean and Chinese and Armenian, and more. Here, in the words of American Enterprise Institute scholar Michael Novak, is represented "the nervous system for the world"—the most diverse, the most encompassing society that history has ever known. And here, at continent's end, remain the ultimate American questions.

Can Americans live together? And, assuming that, can they create something grander, more noble, than the sum of their disparate parts? Can Americans create an American civilization?

This college, 15 miles from the fire-blackened heart of last April's [1992] riots, will be part of the success or part of the failure. For Occidental has been structured deliberately as Los Angeles was structured only accidentally: As an experiment in diversity.

Occidental, a prestigious private liberal arts college, was founded in 1887 to educate the white elite. One of its best-known graduates, class of '57, is Republican supply-sider Jack Kemp. Its very name bespeaks bone-white Greek temples and the accumulated weight of Western civilization. But in

1987 Occidental embarked on a bold new course. It went "multicultural," aggressively recruiting minority students and revamping its curriculum to give more emphasis to non-Western cultures. Today, more than 40 percent of its 1,650 students are minority. Occidental is reaching out for an emerging America—an America which, if present demographic trends continue, could cease to be majority-white around the middle of the twenty-first century.

The goal is "a community in which students may in some small measure experience a world that could be," says President John Brooks Slaughter, who is black. Anthropology Professor Mary Weismantel calls Occidental "a laboratory for the future of America."

It's an apt analogy. Here, in microcosm, are the conflicting forces of a new America-in-the-making: community versus fragmentation; trust versus mutual ethnic wariness. Here, too, an idealistic impulse is colliding with the most elemental force of the twentieth century. That force is ethnicity, the tinderbox for a century of civil wars, pogroms, and genocide.

"These tribal identities are not just quaint things—'Oh, how wonderful that we're all different,' " says Harvard history professor Stephen Thernstrom, editor of the *Harvard Encyclopedia of Ethnic Groups*. "They are why people are killing each other all over the world."

So perhaps it is not surprising that the Occidental experiment, while making progress, is proving more difficult than its architects anticipated. "We're diverse. We don't have community," concedes President Slaughter.

"We were expecting sort of a perfect salad," says David Axeen, the dean of faculty. "That's not happening."

A perfect salad: Out of diverse ingredients, a whole. A lofty vision—but in retrospect, says President Slaughter, an overly "romantic" one.

It's not enough, he says, to simply throw diverse people together. It's not enough "to walk away from here saying, 'Oh yeah, I had a black friend.' That's not multiculturalism. . . . What we're talking about is difficult to achieve: A sense that everyone can share common goals, that people can be expected to shed their personal ambitions for the commonweal."

A visitor here does observe many friendships that cross racial and ethnic lines. There is tolerance—and, for many, something that transcends tolerance: caring. "Because of Oxy," says Sophie Martin, a white theater major from the New York suburbs, "it's impossible for me not to care."

And yet. . . . And yet the Occident experiment is colliding with an instinct embedded in the human heart—an instinct, ultimately, to cluster with one's own kind. "Our student union is virtually segregated," observed a group of Constitutional Law II students in a class paper. At lunch time, whites tend to congregate with whites, blacks with blacks, Asians with Asians, Latinos with Latinos.

Out of the grassy Quad and in the residence halls, the pattern persists. Ethnic groups not only clump together but also exert peer pressure against members who too eagerly move beyond their confines. An Asian American who too obviously embraces Anglo culture risks being labeled a "Twinkie"—

yellow on the outside but white on the inside. An ancient force remains at work, reflects junior Chris Rand: "that natural feeling . . . that tribal phenomenon."

That force can erupt in ugly ways. In recent weeks the campus has been troubled by a rash of hate graffiti. Swastikas have been scrawled on the doorways of Jewish students; racial slurs have defaced residence hall walls. Although hardly unique here, the incidents stand out starkly against Occidental's lofty aspirations. They also dramatize one of the most heated debates within academia: Does multiculturalism bring Americans together—or push them apart?

DEEPENING DIVISIONS

"Multiculturalism is another name for social justice," argues Eric Newhall, an Occidental English professor and a driving force behind the experiment here. But critics see it differently. They argue that academic multiculturalism, by definition, emphasizes the very racial and ethnic differences it seeks to bridge—deepens the very divisions it seeks to heal.

"Multiculturalism is a good thing when people live it. It's a destructive thing when it becomes an ideology," concludes Joel Kotkin, an author and a student of ethnicity with the Center for the New West. Ironically, he asserts, that ideology is more likely to flourish inside the classroom than outside. "Intellectuals and advocates have an interest in *maintaining* differences."

Historian Arthur M. Schlesinger Jr., author of *The Disuniting of America*, shares similar concerns. He spoke on campus last year and came away feeling that Occidental is "striking a good balance." But he cautions that multiculturalism can easily degenerate into "feel-good history" that distorts the past to boost ethnic self-esteem. Or into "political correctness" that suffocates intellectual debate. Or into teaching that depreciates the Western traditions that, for better or for worse, lie at the heart of the American experience.

At bottom, he warned in his speech here, a growing "cult of ethnicity" threatens the pivotal idea "that has thus far managed to keep American society whole." That idea is that Americans are—must be—one people, indivisible.

"WHAT IS THE AMERICAN?"

Assimilation has been America's genius and its triumph. Two centuries ago a French immigrant who gave himself the extravagant name of J. Hector St. John de Crèvecoeur asked a question that resonates even today: "What then is the American, this new man?" And answered himself: "Here individuals of all nations are melted into a new race."

But in a modern nation precariously balancing its ethnic heritages against its search for community, how much assimilation constitutes "good enough"? Integration as defined in the 1960s, with minority cultures melting into a dominant white culture? Or something different?

Here at Occidental, as in the city and nation beyond, one senses that the answer is going to be something different. And, just possibly, something better: richer, less homogenized, more vibrant. But this assumes a great deal. It assumes that Americans can transcend the racism and the nihilism that erupted in riots last April after a suburban Los Angeles jury acquitted white police officers of beating Rodney King, a black man.

Those riots sobered Occidental. They tore at its students.

Yuri White, Korean-born but reared in picket-fence America, saw her mother's clothing store looted, then burned. Now her anger has hardened against a "system" she sees as pitting minority against minority. She looks back on her picket-fence days as on a distant world. "I'm against everything I once lived."

Luz Torres saw the flames come within blocks of her family's home. And then—so quickly, it seemed—the attention of the city and the nation moved on to other things. "Is it forgotten already?" she asks.

Sheli Henderson, a black sophomore who dreams of becoming a U.S. senator, rushed to the First African Methodist Church and was trapped there for hours by the violence raging all around. The acquittals of the white police officers in the first trial deepened her conviction that racial prejudices are woven into the very fabric of American society. "We won't see it," she says when asked to imagine a considerably more tolerant America. "Our kids won't."

HOPE AMID THE FLAMES

But some salvaged hope from the worst of times. Angel Cervantes, a campus militant for Latino causes, went down into the riot zone with Geoff McNeely, an Anglo football player for the Occidental Tigers. What lingers in Angel's memory are the fire-lit intersections where ordinary citizens of all races risked their lives to direct traffic. "What I saw that night was true multiculturalism," he says.

When it was all over, Aileen Cho, American-born of Korean immigrants, wrote a poem. It depicted an Asian-American woman and African-American man, abruptly estranged in an America that had brought them together:

> *I tried to read his face,*
> *my narrow eyes narrowing*
> *while people who looked like him*
> *hit people who looked like me*
> *on the screen . . .*

This college, like the United States itself, is a web of subcultures. Each subculture is a code, as intricate as DNA, prescribing not only how to act but also how to perceive. Students here aren't passively absorbing some monolithic American culture. Out of their multiple perceptions, they are redefining the American culture. They do so against the backdrop of a nation amid its most sweeping demographic transformation in three-quarters of a century.

The bedrock fact is that America's white majority is shrinking, both in relative size and in relative importance.

Los Angeles County, in exaggerated form, prefigures a changing America. There are more Hispanics in the county, some 3.4 million, than there are people in Iowa. There are more Asians, over 900,000, than there are people in Montana. Together, blacks (some 935,000), Hispanics, and Asians constitute 59 percent of the population. "The term 'minority' is becoming increasingly obsolete," concludes demographer Peter Morrison of Rand Corporation.

The state of California is on a similar track. In 1986, the state's demographic research unit estimated that California would have a "minority majority" by the year 2007. Two years later the unit revised the date downward, to 2003. Now fresh data indicate the year could be as early as 1996.

THE GREAT REALIGNMENT

The United States is moving toward a "minority majority," too. Current Census Bureau projections, assume this could well occur around the middle of the next century. However, changes in the mix of immigrants—currently heavily minority—or changes in relative fertility levels could delay the event by decades. Some skeptics, including Harvard's Mr. Thernstrom, question whether it will occur at all. In any event, Hispanics are expected to supplant African Americans as the nation's largest minority group by the year 2015.

This great realignment, unimaginable in almost any other nation on earth, will affect every aspect of American society. But how profoundly? That depends heavily on the engine of American assimilation. In his Occidental speech last year, Arthur Schlesinger warned that the engine could falter amid an upsurge of ethnicity:

> In a nation marked by an even stranger mixture of blood than Crèvecoeur had known, his celebrated question . . . is asked once more, with a new passion—and with a new answer. Today many Americans disavow the historic goal of "a new race of man." . . . A cult of ethnicity has arisen . . . to denounce the idea of a melting pot, to challenge the concept of "one people" and to protect, promote and perpetuate separate ethnic and racial communities.

But there are other views, and more sanguine. Harvard's Mr. Thernstrom notes that there were similar alarms, even fears of "race suicide," when America opened its doors to a surge of eastern and southern Europeans early in this century. "One worrier," he has written, "calculated that after 200 years 1,000 Harvard men would have left only 50 descendants, while 1,000 Romanian immigrants would have produced 100,000."

It isn't working out that way. Birth rates among those immigrant groups moderated, but more important, the immigrants assimilated. "The capacity to Americanize immigrants and to enlarge the meaning of America is unprecedented in history," agrees scholar Michael Novak. "Why do people think it's going to stop now?"

GRADING AMERICA

Enlarging the meaning of America: that is the work in progress on this hilltop campus. It is an old task, as old as America is old. And yet it is as fresh and new as the voices of the students here. And what they say, however haltingly, is this:

America is not about genetics. America is about ideas, the enduring ideas of freedom and opportunity.

America *"connects* you, right away," says senior Angelica Salas, who was smuggled into this country—twice—from her native Mexico. "You are connected by these ideas."

America is not about divisions. America is about transcending divisions.

Sophomore Chris Coker—white, fraternity man, and Young Republican— says classroom discussions here have sometimes made him feel like "the white oppressor," personally responsible for history's ancient wrongs. Nevertheless, he recently ventured into potentially hostile territory, a Latino group headed by Angel Cervantes. He was consciously reaching out, and there came a moment when it appeared he had failed: Someone, he recalls, talked of "kicking some white ass." But the outburst was greeted by embarrassed silence. And afterward, members of the group came up to apologize.

America, in the last analysis, is not about the past. For as Thomas Jefferson insisted, "the earth belongs to the living, and not to the dead." America is about the future.

That future, unknowable, is the subject when a visitor joins an Occidental discussion class entitled "The American Dream." The students, as diverse as their America is diverse, are gathered around a double conference table. And their visitor asks: Suppose they were to grade the American civilization, grade it just as their professor grades them? How would they grade America?

It is freshman Jona Goong, a Hawaiian of Chinese ancestry, who says it best.

"If I were to grade America," she says softly, "I would give it an incomplete."

CHAPTER 19

A Mandate for Liberty: Requiring Education-Based Community Service

BENJAMIN R. BARBER

The extraordinary rise in American interest in community service has inspired widespread participation by the nation's young in service programs. It has also provoked a profound and telling debate about the relationship of service to voluntarism on the one hand, and to civic education and citizenship on the other. Two complementary approaches to service have emerged that are mutually supportive but also in a certain tension with one another. The first aims at attracting young volunteers, particularly students, out of the classroom and into service projects as part of a strategy designed to strengthen altruism, philanthropy, individualism, and self-reliance. The second is concerned with integrating service into the classroom and into academic curricula in hopes of making civic education and social responsibility core subjects of high school and university education.

Underlying these two complementary approaches are conflicting, though not altogether incompatible, views of the real aim of student community service programs. The differences are exemplified by the issue of whether education-based service programs should be voluntary or mandatory. If the aim of service is the encouragement of voluntarism and a spirit of altruism—if service is seen as a supererogatory trait of otherwise self-regarding individuals—then clearly it cannot be mandated or required. To speak of coercing voluntarism is to speak in oxymorons and hardly makes pedagogical sense. But if service is understood as a dimension of citizenship education and civic responsibility in which individuals learn the meaning of social interdependence and become empowered in the "liberal arts"—literally, the acts of liberty—then to require service is to do no more in this domain than is done in curricular decisions generally.

As it turns out, the educational justification for requiring courses essential to the development of democratic citizens is a very old one. America's colleges and common schools were founded in part to assure the civic education of the young—to foster competent citizenship and to nourish the arts of democracy. Civic and moral responsibility were goals of both colleges organized around a religious mission and secular land-grant colleges. The premise was that democratic skills must be acquired. We think of ourselves as "born free," but we are, in truth, born weak and dependent and acquire equality as a concomitant of our citizenship. Liberty is learned: it is a product rather than the cause of our civic work as citizens.

When we coerce behavior, we impose beliefs heteronomously. When we require a certain pedagogy, we aim at empowering the person and thus at cultivating autonomy. Those most in need of training in the democratic arts of citizenship are, in fact, least likely to volunteer. Complacency, ignorance of interdependence, apathy, and an inability to see the relationship between self-interest and broader community interests are not only the targets of civic education: they are obstacles to it, attitudes that dispose individuals against it. The problem to be remedied is here the impediment to the remedy. Education is the exercise of authority—legitimate coercion—in the name of freedom: the empowerment and liberation of the pupil. To make people serve others may produce desirable behavior, but it does not create responsible and autonomous individuals. To make people participate in educational curricula that can empower them, however, does create such individuals.

In most volunteer service programs, those involved have already learned a good deal about the civic significance of service. Students who opt to take courses incorporating service have often done extensive volunteer service prior to enrollment. Such programs reach and help students who have already taken the first and probably most significant step toward an understanding of the responsibilities of social membership. They provide useful outlets for the expression of a disposition that has already been formed. But that preponderant majority of young people that has no sense of the meaning of citizenship, no conception of civic responsibility, is, by definition, going to remain entirely untouched by volunteer programs.

Thinking that the national problem of civic apathy can be cured by encouraging voluntarism is like thinking that illiteracy can be remedied by distributing books on the importance of reading. What young people require in order to volunteer their participation in education-based community service courses are the very skills and understandings that these courses are designed to provide.

There are, of course, problems with mandating education of any kind, but most educators agree that an effective education cannot be left entirely to the discretion of pupils, and schools and universities require a great many things of students—things less important than the skills necessary to preserve American freedoms. It is the nature of pedagogical authority that it exercises some coercion in the name of liberation. Civic empowerment and the exercise of liberty are simply too important to be treated as extracurricular electives.

This account of education-based service as integral to liberal education in a democracy and, thus, as an appropriate subject for mandatory educational curricula points to a larger issue: the decoupling of rights and responsibilities in the United States. We live at a time when our government has to compete with industry and the private sector to attract servicemen and women to the military, when individuals regard themselves almost exclusively as private persons with responsibilities only to family and job, with endless rights against an alien government, of which they see themselves, at best, as no more than watchdogs and clients, and at worst, as adversaries or victims. The idea of service to country or an obligation to the institutions by which rights and liberty are maintained has fairly vanished. "We the People" have severed our connections with "It" the state or "They" the bureaucrats and politicans who run it. If we posit a problem of governance, it is always framed in the language of leadership—as if the preservation of democracy were merely a matter of assuring adequate leadership, surrogates who do our civic duties for us. Our solution to problems in democracy is to blame our representatives. Throw the rascals out, or place limits on the terms they can serve. Our own complicity in the health of our system is forgotten, and so we take the first fatal step in the undoing of the democratic state.

Civic education rooted in service learning can be a powerful response to civic scapegoatism and the bad habits of representative democracy (deference to authority, blaming deputies for the vices of their electors). When students use experience in the community as a basis for critical reflection in the classroom and turn classroom reflection into a tool to examine the nature of democratic communities and the role of the citizen in them, there is an opportunity to teach liberty, to uncover the interdependence of self and other, to expose the intimate linkage between rights and responsibilities. Education-based community service programs empower students even as they teach them. They bring lessons of service into the classroom even as they bring the lessons of the classroom out into the community. A number of institutions around the country have been experimenting with programs; a few have even envisioned mandatory curricula. Many others, including Stanford University, Spelman College, Baylor University, Providence College, Brown University, Notre Dame, the University of Minnesota, and Harvard University, are beginning to explore the educational possibilities of service learning as a significant element in liberal education.

Rutgers University has tried to offer pedagogical leadership to sister institutions. In the spring of 1988, the late Rutgers President Edward Bloustein gave a commencement address in which he called for a mandatory program of citizen education and community service as a graduation requirement for all students at the State University of New Jersey. In the academic year 1988–

1989, I chaired a Committee on Education for Civic Leadership charged with exploring the president's idea and trying to develop a program through which it could be realized. We began with nine governing principles—the foundation of the practical programs—which continue to govern the development of the Rutgers program following the tragic death of President Bloustein in 1989:

> That to teach the art of citizenship and responsibility is to practice it: so that teaching in this domain must be about acting and doing as well as about listening and learning, but must also afford an opportunity for reflecting on and discussing what is being done. In practical terms, this means that community service can be an instrument of education only when it is connected to an academic learning experience in a classroom setting. But the corollary is also true, that civic education can only be effective when it encompasses experiential learning of the kind offered by community service or other similar forms of group activity.

> That the crucial democratic relationship between rights and responsibilities, which have too often been divorced in our society, can only be made visible in a setting of experiential learning where academic discussion is linked to practical activity. In other words, learning about the relationship between civic responsibility and civic rights means exercising the rights and duties of membership in an actual community, whether the community is a classroom, a group project or community service team, or the university/college community at large.

> That antisocial, discriminatory, and other forms of selfish and abusive or addictive behavior are often a symptom of the breakdown of civic community—both local and societal. This suggests that to remedy many of the problems of alienation and disaffection of the young requires the reconstruction of the civic community, something that a program of civic education based on experiential learning and community service may therefore be better able to accomplish than problem-by-problem piecemeal solutions pursued in isolation from underlying causes.

> That respect for the full diversity and plurality of American life is possible only when students have an opportunity to interact outside of the classroom in ways that are, however, the subject of scrutiny and open discussion in the classroom. An experiential learning process that includes both classroom learning and group work outside the classroom has the greatest likelihood of impacting on student ignorance, intolerance, and prejudice.

> That membership in a community entails responsibilities and duties that are likely to be felt as binding only to the degree individuals feel empowered in the community. As a consequence, empowerment ought to be a significant dimension of education for civic responsibility, particularly in

the planning process to establish civic education and community service programs.

That civic education is experiential learning, and community service must not discriminate among economic or other classes of Americans. If equal respect and equal rights are two keys to citizenship in a democracy, then a civic education program must assure that no one is forced to participate merely because he or she is economically disadvantaged, and no one is exempted from service merely because that individual is economically privileged.

That civic education should be communal as well as community-based. If citizen education and experiential learning of the kind offered by community service are to be a lesson in community, the ideal learning unit is not the individual but the small team, where people work together and learn together, experiencing what it means to become a small community together. Thus, civic education programs should be built around teams (of say five or ten or twenty) rather than around individuals.

The point of any community service element of civic education must be to teach citizenship, not charity. If education is aimed at creating citizens, then it will be important to let the young see that service is not just about altruism or charity, or a matter of those who are well off helping those who are not. It is serving the public interest, which is the same thing as serving enlightened self-interest. Young people serve themselves as members of the community by serving a public good that is also their own. The responsible citizen finally serves liberty.

Civic education needs to be regarded as an integral part of liberal education and thus should both be mandatory and receive academic credit. Because citizenship is an acquired art, and because those least likely to be spirited citizens or volunteers in their local or national community are most in need of civic training, an adequate program of citizenship training with an opportunity for service needs to be mandatory. There are certain things a democracy simply must teach, employing its full authority to do so: citizenship is first among them.

The program we developed on the foundation of these principles has been endorsed by representatives of the student body and by the Board of Governors. From 1990 through 1994 the program has offered more than a thousand students in a variety of majors, departments, and schools, over twenty-four different service learning courses. Since the program's inception, more than 100,000 hours of community service have been completed, and the program has become a model for colleges and universities around the nation. The original plan, much modified by subsequent practice, called for:

A *mandatory civic education course* will be organized around (though not limited to) a classroom course with an academic syllabus, but also including a strong and innovative experiential learning focus utilizing group projects. A primary vehicle for these projects will be community service, as one of a number of experiential learning options; while the course will be mandatory, students will be free to choose community service or nonservice projects as their experiential learning group project. The required course will be buttressed by a program of incentives encouraging students to continue to participate in community service throughout their academic careers at Rutgers.

Course content will be broad and varied, but should guarantee some coverage of vital civic issues and questions, including the following:

1. The nature of the social or civic bond; social contract, legitimacy, authority, freedom, constitutionalism—the key concepts of political community.
2. The meaning of citizenship—representation versus participation, passive versus active forms of civic life; citizenship and service.
3. The university community; its structure and governance; the role of students, faculty, and administrators; questions of empowerment.
4. The place of ethnicity, religion, race, class, gender, and sexual orientation in a community: does equality mean abolishing differences? Or learning to respect and celebrate diversity and inclusiveness? How does a community deal with differences of the kind represented by the dis-equalizing effects of power and wealth?
5. The nature of service: differences between charity and social responsibility; between rights and needs or desires. What is the relationship between community service and citizenship? Can service be mandatory? Does a state have the right to mandate the training of citizens or does this violate freedom?
6. The nature of leadership in a democracy: are there special features to democratic leadership? Do strong leaders create weak followers? What is the relationship between leadership and equality?
7. Cooperation and competition: models of community interaction: how do private and public interests relate in a community?
8. The character of civic communities, educational, local, regional, and national. What is the difference between society and the state? Is America a "community"? Is Rutgers a community? Do its several campuses (Camden, Newark, New Brunswick) constitute a community? What is the relationship between them and the communities in which they are located? What are the real issues of these communities— issues such as sexual harassment, suicide, date rape, homophobia, racism, and distrust of authority?

A *supervisory board* will oversee the entire program, including its design and development, its standards, and its operation. The Board will be composed of students, faculty, community, and administrators who will act as the sole authority for the civic education program and who will also supervise the planning and implementation process in the transitional period. The Board will work with an *academic oversight committee*, a senior faculty committee responsible for academic design and for ongoing supervision over and review of course materials. This committee will work closely with community representatives and School of Social Work experts to assure quality control over community service and other group projects. Course section will be taught by a combination of volunteers from faculty, graduate students, and more senior students who have graduated from the program and wish to make seminar leadership part of their continuing service.

Variations on the basic model will be encouraged within the basic course design, with ample room for significant variations. Individual colleges, schools, and departments will be encouraged to develop their own versions of the course to suit the particular needs of their students and the civic issues particular to their disciplines or areas. The Senior Academic Committee and the Supervisory Board will assure standards by examining and approving proposed variations on the basic course. Thus, the Engineering School might wish to develop a program around "the responsibilities of scientists," the Mason Gross School for the Arts might wish to pioneer community service options focusing on students performing in and bringing arts education to schools and senior centers in the community, or Douglass College might want to capitalize on its long-standing commitment to encouraging women to become active leaders by developing its own appropriate course variation.

Experiential learning is crucial to the program, for the key difference between the program offered here and traditional civic education approaches is the focus on learning outside the classroom, integrated into the classroom. Students will utilize group projects in community service and in other extra-seminar group activities as the basis for reading and reflecting on course material. Experiential learning permits students to apply classroom learning to the real world and to subject real-world experience to classroom examination. To plan adequately for an experiential learning focus and to assure that projects are pedagogically sound and responsible to the communities they may engage, particular attention will be given to its design in the planning phase.

The team approach is a special feature of the Rutgers proposal. All experiential learning projects will be group projects in which individuals learn in concert with others and experience community in part by practicing community during the learning process. We urge special attention be given to the role of groups or teams in the design both of the classroom format and the experiential learning component of the basic course.

Community service is only one among the several options for experiential learning, but it will clearly be the choice of a majority of students and is, in fact, the centerpiece of the Rutgers program. For we believe that community service, when related to citizenship and social responsibility in a disciplined pedagogical setting, is the most powerful form of experiential learning. As such, it is central to our conception of the civic education process.

An incentive program for continuing service is built into the Rutgers project because our object is to instill in students a spirit of citizenship that is enduring. It is thus vital that the program, though it is centered on the freshman year course, not be limited to that initial experience, and that there be opportunities for ongoing service and participation throughout the four years of college.

Oversight and review are regarded as ongoing responsibilities of the program. In order to assure flexibility, adaptability to changing conditions, ongoing excellence, and the test of standards, every element in the program will be subjected to regular review and revision by the faculty and the student body, as represented on the Supervisory Board, the Academic Oversight Committee, and the Administration. This process of review will be mandated and scheduled on a regular basis, so that it will not come to depend on the vagaries of goodwill.

This model plan has evolved into a more flexible and varied practice at Rutgers, but is offered here in its original form to suggest the power of certain formative principles.

In 1993, President Clinton visited and endorsed the program and later that year introduced legislation creating a Corporation for National and Community Service, which was passed and funded by Congress. The new corporation will fund tens of thousands of "Americorps" volunteers who will do a year or more of citizen service in return for education vouchers and a minimum wage stipend. Much, then, has been accomplished in the last few years, but not yet enough.

In a vigorous democracy capable of withstanding the challenges of a complex, often undemocratic, interdependent world, creating new generations of citizens is not a discretionary activity. Freedom is a hothouse plant that flourishes only when it is carefully tended. It is, as Rousseau once reminded us, a food easy to eat but hard to digest, and it has remained undigested or been regurgitated more often than it has been assimilated by our democratic body politic. Without active citizens who see in service not the altruism of charity but the necessity of taking responsibility for the authority on which liberty depends, no democracy can function properly or, in the long run, even survive.

National service is not merely a good idea, or, as William Buckley has suggested in his book endorsing a service requirement, a way to repay the debt owed our "patrimony." It is an indispensable prerequisite of citizenship and thus a condition for democracy's preservation. Democracy does not just "deserve" our gratitude: it demands our participation as a price of survival.

The Rutgers program and others like it offer a model that integrates liberal teaching, experiential learning, community service, and citizen education. It also suggests a legislative strategy for establishing a national service requirement without raising up yet one more elephantine national bureaucracy. Require service of all Americans through federal guidelines, but permit the requirement to be implemented through service learning programs housed in schools, universities, and, for those not in the school system, other local institutions. Using the nation's schools and colleges as laboratories of citizenship and service might at once offer an attractive way to develop civic service opportunities for all Americans and to help educate Americans in the indispensable obligations of the democratic citizen. This would not only serve democracy, but could also restore to our educational institutions a sense of mission they have long lacked.

CHAPTER 20

Crossing the Tracks:
A Lesson in Public Service

SUZANNE GOLDSMITH

One of the arguments most commonly given in favor of national service programs—programs that would enroll large numbers of young people to do community service—is that service has a transformative effect, that it has the power to change lives. We are worried about the next generation of Americans, with their guns and their drugs and their sex and their suicide and their seeming lack of respect for anything and anyone, and we want to believe that there is a program out there that would reform them, that would make them see the light.

Democratic presidential candidate Bill Clinton evoked this hope in an early campaign debate when, asked about furloughs for convicted felons, he answered with an anecdote about a young man who had abandoned a life of juvenile delinquency after joining a nine-month national service program in Boston called City Year. Clinton wasn't saying we should send all felons out into the community to work in child-care centers, but he was revealing a basic assumption about service. It has the Power to Save: the answer to the Youth Problem.

NOT A QUICK FIX

This is a dangerous belief. To dream of a quick fix for the sociopathic tendencies that seem to be growing more and more prevalent among youth is to turn our backs on the real causes of problems that begin in early childhood, or even in utero. But more specifically, as someone who believes that national service is a good idea, I see this belief as a threat to a legitimate program with positive benefits. If we set up saving souls as the goal of national service, we are setting the program up for failure.

I spent nine months in City Year last year as a participant–observer, working alongside the young corps members as part of my research for a book about national service. City Year recruits youths aged 17 to 22, gives them uniforms, pays them a stipend of $100 a week, and at the end of nine months, awards a cash grant of $5,000, which is tied to enrollment in higher or continuing education, or to the pursuit of other mutually-agreed-upon post-service goals. I knew the young man Clinton was speaking about, and I believe his story is true. I also knew some of the others who were not transformed—like Charles, a member of my team. Charles (a pseudonym) was 21 and he came to City Year straight from jail. His rap sheet included everything from drug possession to car theft. Nevertheless, he was charming and handsome, and at times he worked very hard. At other times he not only shirked his duties but made it nearly impossible for anyone else to work. During our meetings, he laughed at odd moments, cursed aloud, and fell asleep. He stole people's lunch money, a bus pass, gloves, and a radio. When we were placed as classroom aides in a public school, he bullied the students and slept in class. By the time he was fired, he had claimed almost $2,000 in stipend payments and had nearly driven others on the team to quit in frustration. Later, he came back and assaulted a teammate in front of children at an after-school program run by the corps.

Another of my teammates failed even more dramatically. Richie (also a pseudonym) had all the cards stacked against him. He was abandoned by his mother at 3, and his father went to jail for murder when Richie was 11. He spent his teen years in a whirlwind tour of Massachusetts' group homes and juvenile-detention facilities. But in City Year, Richie showed promise. At the school where we served, the children loved and revered him, and he offered them real thoughtfulness and caring. For a while, Richie did appear transformed; he held his head high when he walked around that school. Other things started to go right for him. He earned a high school equivalency degree. He went back to live with his grandparents. He talked about college and becoming a lawyer, like City Year's directors. He was earnest, smart, and likable, so much so that we all overlooked his shortcomings—lateness, poor attendance, and a general sloppiness that set in late in the year and grew worse as graduation neared.

Six weeks before graduation, he wrote this: "The biggest lesson I have learned this year is a personal one. I have learned how to complete something. Before this year I had never completed anything in my life. I always found a way out and that doesn't get you anywhere."

Richie didn't graduate, however. A week after writing those words, he disappeared under suspicion of stealing a CD player, a camera, a VCR, and a stereo from a teammate who had given him a key so he could crash at her apartment. Though she was hurt and angry, she still wanted to help him—but nobody could find him. He turned up a couple of months later in the hospital, his body bruised and broken after he had rolled a car over at 100 miles an hour on a highway exit ramp.

National service will not change criminals into angels, nor will it save those who are in desperate need. That's not what we should expect. That's not what should be promised.

THE BUSH PLAN

George Bush had his own set of goals for national service. He tried to put his own monogram on the idea back in 1989 by creating, for the first time, a White House Office of National Service. His goal was to boost the volunteer sector. "If you have a hammer, find a nail," he said. "If you know how to read, find someone who can't. If you're not in trouble, seek out someone who is. Because everywhere there is a need in America, there is a way to fill it. . . . There is no problem in America that is not being solved somewhere." Fine words. But how did Bush expect to accomplish this? With press releases and cheery pats on the back, it appears. The White House Office of National Service gave out "Points of Light" awards to innovative and committed volunteers. But it offered no money and no national plan.

According to Bush, government money and leadership were not needed. When he signed the National and Community Service Act of 1990, which in the summer of 1991 awarded $63 million in grants to states for a full-time youth corps, school- and college-based service, and other community service programs, he did it with reluctance, noting that "Although the use of financial incentives may be appropriate in some circumstances, I have reservations about the wisdom of employing 'paid volunteers' to the extent contemplated by S. 1430."

NOT A FREE LUNCH

Research shows that national service participants could indeed fill a good many of our nation's pressing needs. A Ford Foundation study found 3.5 million openings nationwide for unskilled youth volunteers in education, health, child care, conservation, criminal justice, and other service fields. My experience supports the capacity of youth volunteers for real, important work. During my nine months in City Year, my team did the following:

- Painted and repaired a dilapidated greenhouse at a mental hospital to give patients in locked wards a place for controlled, satisfying outdoor activity.
- Rebuilt a community garden and playground that had been claimed by drug dealers who terrified the neighbors.
- Worked in an overcrowded elementary school, helping out with everything from tutoring to crowd control.

- Gutted and began rehabilitation work on an old house that now provides communal living for people who were homeless.
- Organized a community clean-up in the bankrupt city of Chelsea, bringing neighbors together to improve communities that the government had abandoned.

Other City Year teams created after-school programs for latchkey kids; cleaned apartments for, and visited with, elderly homebound people; gave drug awareness and violence prevention programs in schools; and organized a recycling drive. All this was done with just seventy-two kids.

The projects were sponsored by existing social service agencies. There is little question that the work is out there to be done by anyone who has the initiative to get involved. But without pay, who can really afford to dedicate weeks at a time to such demanding projects? Only those with leisure time and disposable income. When President Bush talked about national service, he was talking about the Junior League's style of volunteering, not the kind of gritty, no-thanks work we performed.

City Year is many things, but it is not the Junior League. Instead, my City Year team was a diverse group of youths—black, white, Hispanic, Asian, rich, poor, dropout, college-bound; a Skidmore graduate and a Job Corps graduate; an aspiring diplomat and a convicted drug dealer.

Most of them would not have been able to join without the financial incentives City Year allowed. With supervision and overhead, the total cost came to roughly $20,000 per corps member. That money came from corporate sponsors like Reebok and the Bank of Boston, from individual donations, and from foundations. But three years after City Year began, it is no longer the glamorous new kid in Boston, and corporate seed money has begun to dry up. City Year's founders have had to knock on Congress's door. To sustain the program over the long haul, government funds will be needed. Happily, the new Commission on National Service named City Year a model program and awarded it $7 million of federal money over two years to allow it to expand. National service can accomplish a lot. But make no mistake, it is not a free lunch.

BEYOND THE MELTING POT

Beyond the value of the services that can be performed by its participants, there is a potential benefit that makes national service more than worth the cost.

We live in a society that is highly segregated—by class, by income, by ethnicity, by education. We pay lip service to the melting-pot ideal, and we identify our exclusive neighborhoods by euphemism ("inner city," "suburb"). But the lines are as clear as day, and we all know it. Inequality of opportunity, lack of understanding, lack of compassion, lack of ambition—all are fostered by this segregation. And it hurts us all, whether we are on the right or the wrong side of the tracks. We all live with the fear of crossing those boundaries because to cross them would bring certain rejection. And our social institutions— churches, public and private schools, colleges, the work place—do little to help us try. They give us very few opportunities to connect, as equals, with those who are different from ourselves. There is no place where we can experiment safely with crossing social barriers.

For the young people on my team, City Year was a chance to break through this American version of economic and cultural apartheid. It was a place where each of us, no matter what his skin color, gender, SAT score, social class, cultural background, or likability quotient, had something to offer, and where everyone could offer it together; a place where we all learned to cooperate because we had to cooperate to get things done. The success of each project depended, to a large extent, on trust. Are you going to get up on a ladder to paint the ceiling if you don't trust the guy below? Are you going to hold the stake steady if you don't trust the guy holding the sledgehammer? Are you going to get up and perform before a group of people if you don't trust those performing with you not to embarrass you or let you down? Are you going to go to work in a dangerous neighborhood if you don't trust your teammates to stick together and look out for you?

PRACTICING VALUES

Success also depended on learning to develop and enforce a code of conduct. I learned that lesson before going to City Year, when I supervised my own team of youth volunteers in New York's City Volunteer Corps. My team held a tribunal to consider the case of a girl on the team who was stealing candy for the candy drive at the school where we were working. Despite warnings from her friends, she had continued to steal. When she refused to acknowledge wrongdoing, they voted to cast her out. Everybody liked her, but she was destroying the team's credibility in the school. One of the basic characteristics of community, that elusive thing so many people are talking about these days, is a sense of shared values. We are (rightly, I think) hesitant about teaching values didactically in schools. Values are something that should emerge organically from a sense of shared interests. The teams in City Year, in the City Volunteer Corps, and in other youth service corps around the country (of which scores have emerged in recent years) are mini-communities where values become real and where they can be practiced.

Adding merit to a program like City Year is the fact that the team includes all kinds of people, not just one's own kind. Thus, one is forced to realize that shared interests are not necessarily based on race, or class, or culture. For what good is it to talk about community, if what we are talking about is not one community of people together, but isolated, homogeneous communities, one pitted against the other?

NOT THE ELEVEN O'CLOCK NEWS

One sad but instructive story from my team says volumes about the real lessons that can be taken from an experience like City Year.

Tyrone was somewhat remote and introspective, and since he was with us only a month, I didn't get to know him all that well. But I have some hoarded images: Tyrone sick with a cold but still working hard, shoveling dirt with a drop of sparkling mucus clinging to the tip of his nose. Or shouting angrily at a bus driver who had closed the door before a dawdling teammate could get on. Tyrone had drive and discipline, as well as a finely honed sense of righteousness.

I knew that he was 21 and had done two years in the Job Corps, and that he was working toward a high school equivalency degree. Some of the others on the team also knew that he was using part of his City Year stipend to help his mother pay the rent. And that he had a 4-year-old son.

Four weeks after City Year began, Tyrone was killed outside his home in one of Boston's poor black neighborhoods by a person with swift feet and a gun. We still don't know who shot Tyrone, or why, and it seemed the police did very little to find out. But we know how it felt to lose him.

There were 149 murders in Boston in 1990. Sixty-two percent of the victims were black or Hispanic males; one-third were between the ages of 19 and 24. The only one that got significant press and police attention was an aberration: the murder of Carol Stuart, a white woman from the suburbs who was shot in her car while leaving a birthing class in a hospital on the edge of the ghetto. Boston's attention—and the nation's—was riveted as the story unfolded. It turned out that her husband had killed her. In contrast, outside of the minority community, those many young male victims whose blood washed the streets in 1990 were quickly forgotten, if noticed at all—except for Tyrone. Because of his network of City Year friends and acquaintances, Tyrone's death touched hundreds of communities, from the ghetto to wealthy suburbs to corporate sponsors. For some of his friends, Tyrone was yet another on a long list of lost friends and acquaintances. For others, he was the very first victim of inner-city violence to be more than a sensational headline or a grainy newspaper photo. Tyrone was real to us: we knew the sound of his laughter, the timbre of his voice, the way he walked, what he ate for lunch. When he died, we cared. And now, when we read in the paper about another young male getting shot—whether the shooting occurs two blocks or two miles from our homes—we can no longer quickly turn the page, relieved that we are not part of that world. We know that we are.

CHAPTER 21

Between the State and Market: Voluntarism and the Difference It Makes

ROBERT WUTHNOW

When politicians call for more of the needs of society to be met by volunteers, it is easy to be cynical. Are they not simply proposing "band-aid" solutions? Are they failing to address the real issues, relying instead on warm feelings generated by the few heroic volunteers who make headlines running soup kitchens and participating in Special Olympics? When professional athletes and rock stars raise money for their favorite charities, it is also easy to be cynical. Are they not making token gestures, gaining more in publicity than their donations are worth? And when multinational corporations call on their employees to spend an hour a month cleaning up the park, or when the head of a prominent charity is accused of fattening his own pocketbook, it is again easy to be cynical. Like any institution, voluntarism is subject to abuse. It can be manipulated by government, by business or the mass media, and by its own leaders. Its ability to heal social ills is limited. Indeed, a minor industry has now arisen among academics and social policy experts who are willing to lift their voices against the voluntary sector. Writes one such critic: "From the charities fleecing the state and the public, to the champagne fund-raisers charged off to Uncle Sam, to the corporations developing ever more ways of getting tax deductions for having their trash hauled away free of charge, the fix is in."[1]

But voluntarism is a fundamental feature of American life. Civic associations have proliferated, as have special interest groups and religious organizations, and larger umbrella organizations have emerged to coordinate welfare programs, youth initiatives, overseas relief, lobbying, and a host of other activities. At present, most studies show that at least a third of the adult population claims to be involved in some form of charitable or social service activity at any given time. Slightly more than this are involved if all types of volunteer organizations are taken into account, and a majority donate money to support religious, educational, community, artistic, musical, and other voluntary institutions.[2]

Despite the cynicism it sometimes generates,[3] voluntarism is thus a vibrant aspect of American society. It is one of the primary bases from which communitarian thinking emerges and in which this conception of society is put into practice. It commands vast resources, not only in the time and money it is capable of eliciting from volunteers, but also in its all-encompassing institutional structure. Nonprofit organizations function in nearly all segments of society, providing services in areas as diverse as health care and child care, publishing and gerontology, prayer services and arts administration.[4] They are organized at the national and international level, and yet many of them also have grassroots affiliates, chapters, and local support groups that extend deeply into neighborhoods, families, and ethnic groups.[5] They have gained legal protection that permits them to operate with relative autonomy from government and in ways that offer freedom from markets. Indeed, a communitarian vision of American democracy depends greatly on maintaining the vitality of these organizations and in fostering their distinct contribution to society, relative to that of political institutions and for-profit economic institutions.[6]

Although voluntary associations are at present strong in the United States, a conception of society emphasizing the voluntary sector suggests normatively that associations must also remain strong for the health of our society. Tocqueville's warnings of a century and a half ago still ring true: that a democratic society leaves its citizens "independent and feeble" unless they "learn voluntarily to help one another."[7] These associations stand between the self-interested individual, on the other hand, and the state, on the other hand, providing a place in which moral obligations can be cultivated, a way in which citizens can do things for themselves, and a shield against the atomizing effects of market relations and the totalizing effects of central government. Indeed, as Tocqueville suggests, without them, "civilization itself would be endangered."[8]

THE MORAL DIMENSION[9]

One important reason voluntary institutions are vital to a communitarian society is that they reinforce basic human values that cannot be encouraged directly by political and economic institutions. They may, in fact, preserve values that are in danger of being undermined by these other institutions. For example, religious organizations are by far the most common type of voluntary association in the United States, and these organizations (despite secularizing trends working against them) still speak for values such as worship, reverence of the supernatural, forgiveness, and humility. None of these values is likely to be regarded as a valuable goal of political or economic action, and indeed, many of them may be at odds with the norms of efficiency, self-reliance, assertiveness, and competitiveness promulgated in these other institutional spheres.

This moral dimension is variously considered to consist of virtues such as cooperation, "we-ness," altruism, social relationships as ends in themselves, intimacy for its own sake, and such moral absolutes as integrity and honesty, or the love of beauty and truth. It is the case, of course, that governments and business firms sometimes encourage the moral dimension because governance or business depends on it. Voluntary organizations, in contrast, can form around the promulgation of moral values themselves. Churches can argue sincerely that love of neighbor is an ultimate value, fraternal associations can bring people together for the purpose of simply bringing them together, and arts organizations can assert that aesthetic values are worth preserving for their own sake.

Voluntary institutions also have the capacity to maintain values that may be questionable to a democracy and yet, in broader terms, are part of what democracies themselves are supposed to ensure. Particularisms, such as ethnocentrism, prejudice, localism, and fundamentalism, are perhaps the key example. Many such particularisms are, in fact, reinforced by voluntary institutions. They span a wide range of causes and concerns, from the Ku Klux Klan and neo-fascist organizations, to black nationalist or Islamic antidefamation societies, to fundamentalist churches that seek to proselytize their neighbors, to local-pride organizations and booster clubs. These associations deliberately give special privileges to members who hold particularistic values. In effect, they do "discriminate" on the basis of religion, creed, racial or ethnic origin, gender, or sexual preference.

In comparison, political entities are prevented from discriminating in these ways, having to abide by universalistic standards as well. Businesses are often constrained to respect such standards, too, but are compelled even more strongly by market forces to make profitable choices. Thus, a business may specialize in selling Nazi memorabilia but may find it more profitable to add peace buttons and environmentalist T-shirts to its stock as well. Voluntary institutions are thus the primary context in which genuine particularism can be nurtured, and in so doing, these settings give richness and texture to society. They are sometimes engaged, as Gilles Kepel observes of fundamentalist movements, in a "logic of conflict" that seeks to "reconquer the world" from the forces of secularism evident in all modern institutions.[10] They maintain the distinct heritage of ethnic groups, for example, thereby preventing these traditions from sliding into bland concerns about universally applicable rights and responsibilities. They ensure that genuine diversity is upheld in a society that gives lip service to multiculturalism, but in the very act of doing so may, as Louis Menand suggests, be on the verge of realizing that "real diversity has disappeared."[11]

The special advantage voluntary institutions have in fostering moral values is that they do not have to put a price on these values and they do not have to be concerned about what is in the interest of the larger public. They do not have to withstand competitive market pressures or tests of majority rule, legislative appeal, or procedural correctness. Compared with market firms, they can thus labor in values that are difficult or impossible to price.[12] As Alan Wolfe observes, the moral codes of voluntary associations and of markets may even be quite different. "One," he suggests, "is based on sacrifice and puts the interest of the collective before that of the individual [while] the other is rooted in distrust and pleasure maximization."[13] Compared with political entities, voluntary associations can emphasize values that may challenge present interpretations of laws (or the Constitution) or values that policymakers themselves cannot claim to understand.[14] Voluntary associations are thus the appropriate venue in which to emphasize the priceless, the transcendent, the holy, and even the ephemeral, the whimsical, the idiosyncratic, and the idiotic. They are the place to be creative, to be inefficient, and to be impractical. In short, they uphold values that may run against the grain and yet be a vital expression of the human spirit.

CURBING PRIVATIZATION

A second contribution of voluntary institutions is to encourage citizens to take a more active role in public affairs. The prospect of increasing privatization is as real as it is frightening.[15] Feeling that they cannot make much of a difference in public life, individuals turn their attention toward their own interests. Rather than voting, they work on hobbies; rather than taking an active interest in the well-being of their communities, they focus on working harder to advance the interests of themselves and their families. Not only do they retreat behaviorally from public life, they also retreat psychologically. They feel alienated from large, impersonal institutions. They feel that all that really matters is what matters to *me*. And they think the best measure of truth is what *feels* right, and the best sign of civic responsibility is to let everyone else alone.[16] Individual autonomy thus comes to mean, as Thomas Luckmann has observed, "the absence of external restraints and traditional taboos in the private search for identity."[17]

Voluntary institutions help to curb these kinds of privatization in a number of ways. They do so by providing information about the public roles that individuals can play and by empowering them through collective experiences. Feeling that a woman should have a right to choose whether to have an abortion, for example, may result in a purely private, relativistic view that says, in effect, keep your mouth shut and don't bother anyone else, but in the context of a voluntary association it may encourage an individual to sign a petition, work at a local health clinic, donate money to keep that health clinic in business, or take part in a local demonstration. Voluntary associations also curb privatization simply by giving individuals an opportunity to discuss what were formerly their own private opinions. Self-help groups, for example, empower people by creating occasions for them to discuss their fears, thereby enabling them to move beyond these fears. They may also provide support, encouragement, and mutual bonds of accountability necessary to recover from addictions or other personal dysfunctions.[18] Religious organizations increasingly provide similar experiences, encouraging believers to talk about their faith and to think of ways in which to put their faith into practice.

It is perhaps paradoxical that participation in voluntary associations often derives from a sense of alienation from public institutions and yet results in greater involvement in these institutions. In studying volunteers, for example, I found that a great number enjoyed their volunteer work because it was more personal, permitted greater freedom, and allowed them to be "themselves" more so than the businesses for which they worked.[19] They also felt they were making a difference, whereas political institutions seemed too bureaucratic and inefficient. Many of them shared a distinctly personalistic orientation toward social problems, for example, arguing that the best approach was to do something yourself rather than worrying about the larger problem. They were, in this sense, privatized or individualistic in the ways that many critics of voluntary institutions have suggested. And yet their voluntary participation led them to realize that there were larger problems, that it was necessary to band together with other volunteers or to lobby for political change, and in many cases resulted in their becoming more interested in community affairs, more likely to vote, and more involved in a wider range of public institutions.

THE DE-MASSING OF SOCIETY

A third contribution of voluntary institutions is to shield individuals from the effects of mass culture. This contribution is not unlike that of curbing privatization. But the danger of mass culture is somewhat different from the danger of privatization. Privatization means that each individual turns increasingly inward toward the self, personal interests, and family, simply becoming disinterested in larger social institutions. In the process, each individual may become more and more distinct, making any kind of value consensus in the society less and less likely. The specter of mass culture, in contrast, is that everyone becomes increasingly alike.[20] Rather than genuinely retreating from public life, individuals cease participating in it actively, but are nevertheless the passive recipients of its influences. They may feel alienated from large institutions, but they remain absorbed by the messages transmitted by them, for example, following the personal lives of public figures with interest and avidly consuming news, television programming, and advertising. In the extreme, they become increasingly subject to manipulation by the mass media, by corporate advertising, or by authoritarian political leaders. As William Kornhauser has observed, "Mass standards are supported by organizations that treat people as members of an undifferentiated (mass) audience or market. They . . . sustain the mass audience required for commercial success by the mass media of communication, or for political success by the mass party.[21]

Voluntary associations provide a buffer between individuals and these mass influences. They do so in at least two ways. One is simply by diverting attention toward other issues and needs. For example, a person who sits at home every evening watching television may think a great deal about which brand of beer tastes best, but a person who spends those same evenings volunteering at a shelter for abused women is likely to become preoccupied with more pressing concerns. The other way is by filtering the messages received from the mass media. Participating in an African-American community association, for example, can provide a chance for citizens to say, yes, the federal government's new health policies may be fine, but what are their implications for our community? An association of this kind can provide a forum for discussing the news, for bringing in pieces of information not provided by the mass media, for confronting local or national leaders directly, and for considering what actions should be taken.

Paradoxically, mass society generally means greater emphasis on the individual—not in its individual uniqueness and therefore in the collective diversity of individuals, but in the individual as the basic unit of society, the ultimate locus of responsibility.[22] Thus, mass advertising focuses on the individual consumer, appealing to personal tastes, mass government focuses on the individual voter and (more importantly) the individual taxpayer, and mass business focuses on the individual employee as a repository of skills, seller of same, and keeper of resumes. Mass society individuates the individual as a means of control, finding it easier to manipulate these small, relatively powerless units than having to deal with, say, consumer protection groups, taxpayer organizations, political interest groups, or organized labor. The danger of mass society is thus that the individual becomes weaker relative to large-scale institutions and, in the process, communities of individuals become increasingly fragmented into atomized units.

Voluntary organizations are the antidote to this process. They forge bonds among individuals on the basis of common interests. Most consumer protection groups, taxpayer organizations, political interest groups, and labor organizations are, in fact, voluntary organizations. They depend mainly on volunteers and are formally organized as nonprofit entities. They transform an individualistic mass society into a communitarian society both by bringing people together in face-to-face contact and by convincing government and business that it is in fact advantageous to bargain with these collective entities rather than dealing only with atomized individuals.[23] The United States has thus far been spared the worst excesses of mass society because churches, unions, and citizens groups of all kinds have proven effective in dealing with government and business.

AGAINST THE POLITICIZATION OF EVERYTHING

Voluntary institutions also provide individuals and groups with ways of doing things that do not depend on government. By empowering people at the local level, they permit action to be mobilized, not simply for the purpose of influencing government, but to make government programs less vital to the overall functioning of society. Voluntary associations are thus a barrier against the type of society, described some years ago by Robert Nisbet, in which "the basic needs for education, recreation, welfare, economic production, distribution, and consumption, health, spiritual and physical, and all other services . . . are made aspects of the administration structure of political government."[24]

Some discussions of voluntary organizations emphasize only their potential for aggregating the special interests of individuals and presenting them to government agencies for action. These views have been especially prominent among social scientists since the 1960s. Taking the civil rights movement, the anti-Vietnam War movement, and the feminist movement as implicit models, they assume that the only real game in town is political action. The point of voluntary associations is thus to engage in what Craig Jenkins and others have termed "nonprofit advocacy."[25] That is, the voluntary sector brings pressure to bear on the state which, in turn, uses its enormous power to create a better society. The growing penetration of the state (including law) into all realms of life makes these views tenable; at the same time, this penetration is also encouraged by these views. But voluntary associations do a great deal more for society than simply organize citizens to bring pressure on the state.

They are themselves an effective means of fulfilling social functions, often more effective means, in fact, than government. Recent discussions of a federally organized national service program for youth provide an example. Some estimates suggest that such a program would provide tuition grants for as many as 25,000 young people in return for "voluntary" service to their communities over some specified period of time. Critics point out that a program of this magnitude would cost more than government might be able to convince taxpayers to support and would likely result in the usual administrative top-heaviness and inefficiency associated with federal programs. Even supporters point out that such a program would be little more than an increment to the vast amount of volunteer activity in which American youth are already engaged through their churches, scouting organizations, and other nonprofit agencies.[26] Millions of young people are already involved, and they are effective at peer counseling, tutoring, substance abuse and alcoholism prevention, feeding the homeless, assisting the physically challenged, and a host of other activities because they are truly volunteering, are working in their own communities, and are organized by nonprofit agencies in these same communities.

The work of religious organizations provides another example. Social scientists, schooled to believe that political policy is the ultimate goal of all research, often fail to understand why any of their number would deign to study such arcane topics as churches and synagogues. Yet these organizations are major suppliers of social services. They channel vast sums of money, as well as equivalents in volunteer time, to the sick and the needy among their own congregants and in their communities, staff nursery schools and day-care centers, provide transportation for the elderly, supply emergency relief to members on a kind of mutual-aid-society basis, offer counseling, host recovery programs, and support hospital and prison chaplains.[27] They also remain one of the strongest sources of altruistic values and of beliefs about neighborly love, courage, conviction, forgiveness, healing, stewardship, and social justice, all of which serve as powerful motivators for individual members to become involved in other forms of community service as well as informal acts of kindness.[28] Government could never fulfill those functions. Indeed, societies in which government has tried to control religion too closely have generally seen only a reduction in the strength of religion.

A communitarian democracy is one in which government has a place, promoting social programs that require universal involvement, maintaining standards of fairness and equity, protecting national security, stimulating economic growth, and engaging in redistributive policies aimed at countering the worst excesses of market-driven economics. But a communitarian democracy must also be one in which the politicization of everything is itself curbed. Most people, judging from opinion polls, believe this, of course, and yet they also believe that the best counter to government is an unregulated market system that supposedly generates economic growth sufficient to benefit everyone. What communitarians must emphasize more effectively is that three parties are required in any balanced society, not just two, the third being voluntary associations. Only these can deal with many of the needs generated by a complex society.

PRESSURES FROM GOVERNMENT AND MARKETS

The voluntary sector has remained strong in the United States, and yet it is subject to increasing pressures from government and from market-oriented firms.[29] Part of the pressure comes from public expectations themselves. Government is expected to do everything but at a minimal price. Litigation increases, and so do taxes, the number of government employees, the number of bills and laws, and the realms of personal and public life subject to government regulations. Markets also penetrate an increasing array of activities, from motherhood (paid surrogate mothers and for-profit day-care centers) to apple pies. More and more of life can be priced and sold, not only the time one spends at work, but also the relationships between parents and children, the household services that people used to provide for themselves, and the ways in which they spend their leisure time. Regulations and markets expand because they are attractive, preventing homes from burning down because of inadequate safety standards, for example, or permitting busy people to cook and clean more efficiently. But regulations and markets also threaten the viability of voluntary institutions.

The most direct threat to voluntary institutions comes from direct intervention in their activities by government and for-profit business itself. As much as half of all the funding for nonprofit organizations in the United States now comes directly from government, meaning that these organizations are no longer truly "charitable" or "voluntary" and that government can dictate more closely what they do. Government funding for "meals on wheels" programs, for example, makes it possible for government to regulate not only the quality of food served but also who the recipients should be. The line between nonprofit and for-profit organizations has also become blurred. Some of the nonprofits, for example, depend almost entirely on quarterly earnings of the for-profits. And in many cases, nonprofit board members consist overwhelmingly of corporate executives.

A second kind of threat comes from government and business competition. Government, for example, might not intervene directly in the affairs of a private, church-related college (although there are many forms of direct intervention in practice). Government does, however, run public-funded colleges and universities in most of the same communities as these colleges. Church-related colleges must therefore keep expenses down to competitive levels and find ways to emulate the science, music, or athletic programs of their secular counterparts. For-profit businesses have also become competitors of voluntary associations, hospitals being one of the chief examples in recent years. Lawsuits brought by for-profit weight-loss programs against the YMCA for providing free exercise classes, or competition between national, for-profit day-care chains and nurseries provided by local churches are other examples.

In addition, government and business threaten voluntary associations by promulgating norms and expectations that gradually influence the functioning of these associations as well. Many nonprofit agencies, for example, compete with one another as if they were for-profit firms, struggling to expand their "market share" and attract more "customers." Churches increasingly compete with one another to see who can grow larger and therefore provide more sophisticated or luxurious programming. Nonprofit adminstrators are encouraged to be "entrepreneurial" by their corporate board members. Norms of efficiency also become more prevalent, as do standards of rationality, bureaucratic procedure, and goal-oriented planning. Thus, a Rotary Club picnic can be evaluated more on these criteria than simply being valued because it allows volunteers to have fun together.

The sheer size or overall strength of the voluntary sector, therefore, is not an infallible measure of its health. The United States still devotes more hours and money to volunteer associations than do most other advanced industrial societies. Yet there are pressures in the United States that threaten to transform the quality of voluntary institutions in ways that are already evident in these other societies. Germany, Sweden, and Japan, for example, all have larger voluntary sectors than many Americans realize. Yet a neighborhood basketball team in Germany or Sweden is likely to be organized by the government, and "voluntary donations" to the Boy Scouts in Japan are likely to be the result of a formal arrangement between business leaders and government officials. Without vigilance, the same could become true in the United States.

KEEPING THE VOLUNTARY SECTOR STRONG

Ordinary citizens, policymakers, and business leaders must all recognize the vital role played by voluntary institutions and do their part to keep these institutions strong. Ordinary citizens can support voluntary associations most directly by donating time and money. In doing so, they must also consider carefully their own motives and expectations. Voluntary associations can play a useful social role by supplying needed services. But their role is also to cultivate virtue. Volunteer service performed strictly for self-interested reasons may be less than ideal. Altruism, compassion, and community itself are values that need to be included.[30] Policymakers can help preserve voluntary associations by acknowledging their importance alongside government and by working closely with them in providing social services.[31] Policymakers also need to respect the autonomy of these associations. Business leaders can play a similar role by continuing to support them financially and by encouraging employees to donate time, and also by recognizing that voluntary associations should not operate by the same norms as for-profit firms.

Students of communitarian thought must do their part as well. Communitarianism should not be understood strictly as a political philosophy, that is, as a theory of government that encourages political leaders to promote cooperation and to respect the traditions of communities, rather than focusing entirely on utilitarian conceptions of rights and freedoms. More importantly, it should be a *social* theory that recognizes the importance of both governmental and nongovernmental ways in which community values can be nurtured, and that acknowledges the special role of voluntary institutions. In modern societies, communities still exist in the form of kin groups, neighborhoods, and villages, but they are increasingly intentional or purposive entities that depend on formal organization. Voluntary associations are to a considerable degree the contemporary counterpart of naturally occurring, ascriptive communities in traditional societies.

As such, voluntary associations provide community, and yet foster communal bonds that are both limited and precarious. They are limited because they generally do not span entire lifetimes, do not forge significant bonds of financial obligation among their members, can easily be broken as people move to new geographic areas, and in fact may involve their members for no more than a few hours a month. They function well *because* they are limited in these ways. They allow modular, plastic commitments to occur within the spaces available in our highly scheduled lives. They are, however, precarious for the same reasons. They can become so modular that commitment itself is virtually meaningless. They can provide token ways of fulfilling moral obligations, but require little in the way of genuine involvement or personal sacrifice. Even when commitment is minimal they can also generate personal strains because they are artificial, tacked onto the rest of life, rather than being an integral part of other institutions. They can require participants to make difficult decisions, for example, about whether to spend time volunteering or whether to devote time to one's family and work—because the one does not necessarily complement the other or have close, obvious links to it.

Thus, greater attention needs to be devoted to the cultural assumptions underlying voluntary institutions rather than only to the services provided by these institutions. Voluntarism may be a way to deliver goods and services to the needy or to patrons of the arts. But it is also a way to stir up fundamental questions about how to live and about how to create a good society in which to live. Voluntary associations provide crucibles in which different values can be entertained than on the political stage or in the corporate board room. The very fact that the values are different, and therefore jar a person into making difficult choices, is important. Voluntary institutions do not provide easy solutions to society's problems, but they do evoke tough questions.

NOTES

1. Theresa Funiciello, *Tyranny of Kindness: Dismantling the Welfare System to End Poverty in America* (New York: Atlantic Monthly Press, 1993), p. xvii.
2. For a statistical overview, see Virginia A. Hodgkinson and Murray S. Weitzman, *Giving and Volunteering in the United States: Findings from a National Survey* (Washington, D.C.: Independent Sector, 1992).
3. Some figures from my own research on cynicism about voluntary institutions are presented in Robert Wuthnow, "Giving and Caring in the 1990s," *Second Opinion*, (January 1993), pp. 18, 69–80.
4. Walter W. Powell, ed., *The Nonprofit Sector: A Research Handbook* (New Haven, Conn.: Yale University Press, 1987).
5. The local activities of voluntary institutions are considered in Robert Wuthnow,

Sharing the Journey: Support Groups and America's New Quest for Community (New York: Free Press, 1994).

6. The "three-sector" model of society implied in this statement is elaborated in Helmut K. Anheier and Wolfgang Seibel, eds., *The Third Sector: Comparative Studies of Nonprofit Organizations* (Berlin: DeGruyter, 1990); Jon Van Til, *Mapping the Third Sector: Voluntarism in a Changing Social Economy* (New York: The Foundation Center, 1988); and Robert Wuthnow, ed., *Between States and Markets: The Voluntary Sector in Comparative Perspective* (Princeton, NJ: Princeton University Press, 1991).

7. Alexis de Tocqueville, *Democracy in America* (New York: Vintage, 1945 [1835]), p. 115.

8. Ibid.

9. For the context of this discussion, see Amitai Etzioni, *The Moral Dimension* (New York: Free Press, 1988), and Amitai Etzioni, *The Spirit of Community: Rights, Responsibilities, and the Communitarian Agenda* (New York: Crown, 1993), especially Chapter 1.

10. Gilles Kepel, *The Revenge of God* (London: Polity Press, 1994), p. 203.

11. Louis Menand, "Multicultural Awareness," *Times Literary Supplement* (October 30, 1992), pp. 3–4.

12. Burton A. Weisbrod, *The Nonprofit Economy* (Cambridge, Mass.: Harvard University Press, 1988).

13. Alan Wolfe, *Whose Keeper? Social Science and Moral Obligation* (Berkeley: University of California Press, 1989), p. 87.

14. Jennifer R. Wolch, *The Shadow State: Government and Voluntary Sector in Transition* (New York: The Foundation Center, 1990).

15. On privatization, see Jürgen Habermas, *Legitimation Crisis* (Boston: Beacon Press, 1976), and Robert N. Bellah et al., *Habits of the Heart: Individualism and Commitment in American Life* (Berkeley: University of California Press, 1985).

16. The various meanings of privatization are reviewed in Robert Wuthnow, *The Struggle for America's Soul* (Grand Rapids, Mich.: Eerdmans, 1989), Chapter 5.

17. Thomas Luckmann, *The Invisible Religion* (London: Macmillan, 1967), p. 110.

18. Wuthnow, *Sharing the Journey*, Chapter 11.

19. Wuthnow, *Acts of Compassion: Caring for Others and Helping Ourselves* (Princeton, NJ: Princeton University Press, 1991).

20. Among the many discussions of mass society and mass culture, my favorite still is William Kornhauser, *The Politics of Mass Society* (New York: Free Press, 1959).

21. Ibid., p. 104.

22. The classic statement of this argument is Reinhard Bendix, *Nation-Building and Citizenship: Studies of Our Changing Social Order* (Berkeley: University of California Press, 1977), Part one.

23. This, of course, is a restatement of the argument about voluntary associations in Tocqueville, *Democracy in America*, especially pp. 99–171.

24. Robert A. Nisbet, *The Quest for Community* (New York: Oxford University Press, 1953), p. 282.

25. J. Craig Jenkins, "Nonprofit Organizations and Policy Advocacy," in Walter W. Powell, ed., *The Nonprofit Sector* (New Haven, Conn.: Yale University Press, 1987), chapter 17.

26. Virginia A. Hodgkinson and Murray S. Weitzman, *Volunteering and Giving among American Teenagers 12 to 17 Years of Age: Findings from a National Survey* (Washington, D.C.: Independent Sector, 1992).
27. Virginia A. Hodgkinson, *From Belief to Commitment* (Washington, D.C.: Independent Sector, 1990).
28. Wuthnow, *Acts of Compassion*, Chapter 5.
29. Many of these pressures are reviewed in David Harrington Watt, "United States: Cultural Challenges to the Voluntary Sector," in Robert Wuthnow, ed., *Between States and Markets*, Chapter 9.
30. Wuthnow, "Altruism and Sociological Theory," *Social Service Review* (September 1993), pp. 87–110.
31. For a parallel argument, see David Osborne and Ted Gaebler, *Reinventing Government* (Reading, Mass.: Addison-Wesley, 1992), especially Chapter 2.

PART IV

Shoring Up Communities

We need to know much more about shoring up communities, from finding new ways of protecting public spaces (from parks to palaces, the places where communities happen) to making spaces more community friendly. The selections here are but teasers and tasters for a subject that requires much more exploration, study, and, above all, social action.

In Fred Siegel's view, public spaces have been lost to the menace of modern-day urban America, depriving the country of one of its richest resources. A set of utopian ideas stressing the primacy of individual rights, he suggests, has brought on this crisis by encouraging the disastrous decriminalization of public drinking and other minor "victimless" offenses, and the deinstitutionalization of the mentally ill.

Getting cops out of their cruisers and onto their feet to cultivate a relationship with their community may not be the hoped-for panacea. However, as Brian Forst shows, it is a step in the right direction of bringing government and the community closer together, and it may serve to curb crime to some extent. Other devices to this effect were discussed earlier in Chapter 7 when Roger Conner explored the issues that arise around roadblocks to stop drug traffic. A report concerning walled-off communities raises both the specter of even more isolated communities and hopes for safe neighborhoods that have a clearly defined sense of identity.

Communities are often frequently embodied in institutions ranging from local schools to local hospitals. Economic pressures often encourage smaller groups and associations to merge into larger ones. However, as the case studies by Ina Jaffe (for National Public Radio), Elizabeth Ginsburg, and Lisa Belkin illustrate, the social costs may outweigh the economic gains. To be sure, one cannot assume that all local institutions can or must be maintained despite the cost. When one examines the closing of local institutions from a communitarian viewpoint, however, both considerations should be given ample attention.

CHAPTER 22

The Loss of Public Space

FRED SIEGEL

We have come to the end of our national romance with cities and the public spaces that define them. At their best our cities have been engines of innovation, their streets settings for the creative disorder which has inspired our artists as much as our economists. For many people, the public character of their private selves was revealed in the pleasure they took in being described as "streetwise." But the streets, which were once the very depiction of democracy and inspired our largely urban common culture, now too often induce fear as even the most innocent of experiences become fraught with potential danger. It was surely a milestone of decline when some cities had to give up their long-standing campaigns to teach children to "cross at the green, not in between," because the corners were dominated by drug dealers. "Cities," says Mayor Michael White of Cleveland, "are becoming a code name for a lot of things:. . . [for] crumbling neighborhoods, for crime, for everything that America has moved away from."

What unnerves most city dwellers, however, is not crime per se but rather the sense of menace and disorder which pervades day-to-day life: the gang of toughs hanging out on the corner exacting their daily tribute in the coin of humiliation; the "street tax" paid to drunk and drug-ridden panhandlers; the "squeegee" men shaking down the motorist waiting for a light; the threats and hostile gestures of the mentally ill making their home in the parks; the provocations of pushers and prostitutes plying their "trade" with impunity; and the "trash storms," the swirling masses of garbage left by peddlers, panhandlers, and open-air drug bazaars on uncleaned streets. These are the visible signs of cities out of control, cities, regardless of their economic health, that can't protect either their space or citizens. "When you take your child to a public playground and find a mental patient has been using the sandbox as a toilet," writes liberal columnist Lars-Erik Nelson, "it's normal to say, 'Enough, I'm leaving.' "

Nelson is by no means alone. Recent polls show that 43 percent of residents in Boston, 48 percent in Los Angeles, and 60 percent in New York would like to leave the city. A 1989 Gallup poll found that only 19 percent of the country wanted to live in cities.

Fearing the return of nineteenth-century urban conditions, the better off, particularly families, flee, sorting themselves into suburbs and leaving cities to the poor, those most in need of public space. They move into areas organized by homeowners' associations, private governments that stand beyond the reach of cities and their experiments in civil liberties. Thirty million Americans belong to such community associations, 80 percent of which administer territory as well as buildings. In return for the bastion such communities erect against the pathologies of the metropolis, residents agree to a "covenanted conformity" dictating everything from the size of their mailboxes to the type and number of visitors permitted. These shadow cities generally establish "one-dollar one-vote governments" that re-create the preindustrial world of power to the property holders.

Even those who remain in the cities migrate away from the problems they associate with disordered public space. Oscar Newman's "defensible space principles," which William H. Whyte has decried as "the fortressing of America," are now so fundamental to design that they are sometimes written into zoning regulations. Cities that revitalize their downtowns are creating controlled spaces deliberately separated from the street. MCA, [the Motion Picture Corporation of America] for example, built City Walk, a 100 million square foot shopping and entertainment center in the ethnically mixed, middle-class San Fernando Valley. Billed as "an exact replica of Venice Beach and Sunset Boulevard" minus the menace, graffiti, and homelessness, the mall tries to re-create the variety and unexpected pleasure of street life before "the fall."

From Los Angeles to Chicago to Miami, communities are trying to achieve some small measure of the security that even poor neighborhoods once took for granted and that now comes only with "private police" and "covenanted communities." Those who can't or won't leave are increasingly turning public space into a potent political issue.

Recent elections in San Francisco and Los Angeles revolved around public space and safety. San Francisco Mayor Art Agnos was defeated in 1991 by relatively unknown challenger Frank Jordan, who campaigned against the growth of graffiti, trash, and aggressive panhandling. Jordan, a former police chief, criticized Agnos for allowing homeless encampments in the parks, and he proposed that the homeless be put to work cleaning off graffiti. In 1992 San Franciscans approved Proposition J, a ballot initiative prohibiting "harassing or hounding acts in connection with soliciting money or any other valuable thing."

The 1993 Los Angeles mayoral race cut to the underlying assumptions behind the politics of public space. In a race without an incumbent, maverick Republican Richard Riordan campaigned against disorder, using a mailer with an unflattering picture of a homeless man on the front and proposals on panhandling and graffiti within. Democratic candidate Michael Woo responded that the urge for order was a disguised call for conformity: "my goal has never been to turn Hollywood Boulevard into an antiseptic, artificially sanitized area. . . . Hollywood Boulevard will be an exciting, diverse and exotic place. Homeowners will see kids with ghetto blasters. . . . I don't want to drive out the eccentric and interesting people, who are no harm to anyone else. I want to encourage real street life on Hollywood Boulevard." Although Los Angeles is overwhelmingly Democratic, twice as many voters thought graffiti should be a new mayor's first priority as thought health care or the environment should, and Woo thus lost by seven points to Riordan. People prefer not to choose between the antiseptic and the antisocial, but our contemporary cities often force them to.

How can we explain the unparalleled social breakdown of public space during a period of both peace and prosperity? Poverty per se is not a good answer. New York, as Senator Daniel Patrick Moynihan points out, was a far poorer but far more tranquil city fifty years ago. The breakdown has proceeded apace regardless of the phase of the business cycle. Nor is it primarily a matter of Reagan–Bush policies. New York, for instance, boomed in the 1980s, and minority income grew even as the breakdown continued unabated. In his justly acclaimed article for *The American Scholar,* "Defining Deviance Down,"[1] Senator Moynihan uses Durkheimian functionalism to describe the mechanisms of accommodation to growing levels of violence and pathology. We can as a society, he argues, accept only so much deviance. The excess gets defined away until the pathological is routinely accepted as unavoidable—at least for those who can't or don't flee. But except for a reference to family disintegration, important as that is, he doesn't explain the source of the breakdown in public conduct.

Over the past quarter century a great experiment has been carried out in what Herbert Marcuse described as "radical desublimation." In this experiment zealous reformers of various stripes have tried to dissolve the tension between individual desire and communal conscience by solely favoring desire on the grounds that it would move us "beyond all known standards . . . to a species with a new name, that shall not dare define itself as man." In that new and higher state there would be no need for individuals to engage in either self-control or social coordination since, much in the manner of the free market for goods and services, the free market in morals would produce growth, albeit of the personal and self-expressive kind.

But there is no such thing as a self-regulating market in morals: instead of reaching an equilibrium in behavior we now have a downward spiral. An unparalleled set of utopian policies has produced the unprecedented dystopia of day-to-day city life. Particularly damaging, besides the deinstitutionalization of the mentally ill, was the attempt to turn public drinking and drug use into victimless crimes.

VICTIMLESS CRIME

Jane Jacobs, whose 1961 book *The Death and Life of Great American Cities*[2] set the terms of how public space has been discussed ever since, argued that "lowly, unpurposeful and random as they may appear, sidewalk contacts are the small change from which a city's wealth of public life may grow." "The tolerance, the room for great difference among neighbors," she went on, ". . . . are possible and normal only when the streets of great cities have built-in equipment allowing strangers to dwell in peace together on civilized but essentially dignified and reserved terms."

In the late 1960s and early 1970s, some of the "built-in equipment" was systematically dismantled. The movement to decriminalize what were known as victimless crimes—crimes in which none of the consenting adults directly involved has either cause or desire to press for legal action—was caught up in a new Vietnam-era version of the old argument that "you can't legislate morality." The moral authority of American institutions and the force of conventional norms were shattered by the cultural conflicts that broke out over Vietnam and racial injustice. Traditional authority and conventional morality were equated with authoritarianism or worse.

The need for a modicum of order, for instance, became entangled with the need to redress racial wrongs. Too often the discretionary authority to police public drunkenness or loitering has been used to harass racial and sexual minorities. In *Coates v. Cincinnati*, for instance, the U.S. Supreme Court struck down a loitering statute of long-standing provenance typical of other cities. The Court argued that it was unconstitutional to outlaw "loiterers," who by congregating might "annoy" others, because enforcement "may entirely depend on whether or not a policeman is annoyed." The statute, the justices concluded, was an "invitation to [racially] discriminatory enforcement."

The argument for "victimless crimes" has a venerable pedigree. Jeremy Bentham, one of the founding fathers of modern liberalism, had in the early nineteenth century described drunkenness and fornication as "imaginary offenses," "acts which produce no real evil but which prejudice, mistake, or the aesthetic principle have caused to be regarded as offenses." The more immediate motivation came from reformers like anthropologist Ruth Benedict who had an enormous influence on post–World War II liberalism. "Abnormals," she wrote, "are those who are not supported by the institutions of their civilization." A wiser and more mature society, she argued, would incorporate the widest range of personality types possible by becoming less judgmental, less willing to treat different types of behavior as deviant or shameful. Benedict's call was taken up by "Situationists" of the 1950s, social scientists who argued that invidious distinctions were often made based on a misunderstanding of how marginalized people, often racial minorities, were forced by their circumstances into less than admirable actions. Going a step further, others used labeling theory to claim that "criminal laws, by definition create criminals."

Edwin Schur, the leading proponent of decriminalizing "victimless crimes," spoke for many of his fellow sociologists, then at the peak of their since-shattered self-confidence, when he argued that social science research demanded reform. "As empirical data and realistic analysis replace misinformation and stereotyped thinking," he wrote, "neither the long-standing existence of a criminal statute nor a majority adherence to the norms and values it seeks to uphold is likely to be accepted as sufficient justification for maintaining it." "Past support for these laws," he insisted, rested on hypocritical moralizing, "misinformation . . . and . . . unsubstantiated assertions of the 'horrible consequences' likely to follow from decriminalization."[3]

Then in an argument parallel to that of the anti-anticommunists, Schur turned the tables on the proponents of "traditional morality" by arguing that the cure was worse than the disease. "Proscribed behaviors [don't] necessarily constitute social problems," he argued. Rather, "It is the proposed 'solution,' that is the gist of the problem." "Social problems," he went on, "are simply conditions about which influential segments of the society"—the uptight white middle class—believe "something ought to be done."[4] The problem, it seemed, was less in the inherent actions deemed criminal than in the constricted morality of those white "squares" who attempted to impose their values on others through police action by complaining about the "harm" being done.

The intellectual bullets first forged by the anthropologists and then the sociologists were fired by the police chiefs and legal reformers. Policing vice, they argued with considerable evidence, was inherently corrupting, while maintaining civility by arresting drunks and crazies was derided as social work as opposed to "real" police work. By decriminalizing vice and other minor offenses to civility, a mésalliance of police chiefs and law professors argued, the police would be freed up to concentrate on major crime. The 1967 Task Force Report of the President's Commission on Law Enforcement and Administration of Justice captures what shortly became the conventional wisdom of numerous books, articles, and reports. "Only when the load of law enforcement has been lightened by stripping away those responsibilities for which it is not suited," they said, "will we begin to make the criminal law a more effective instrument of social protection."

What went wrong? First off, the reformers straining to be "hip" often trivialized the collateral consequences of the behavior they wanted decriminalized. "That prostitution tends to encourage derivative kinds of criminal activity can hardly be denied," wrote sociologist Gilbert Geis, "any more than it can be denied that kissing may lead to illegitimate births."[5] In the reformers' ideological calculations, there were only individual rights and state power. It was as if an economist wrote about commercial interactions of a chemical company without considering the externalities like pollution.

In New York City, where decriminalization was carried the furthest, not even running a red light was considered criminal. In New York, where 3

percent of the people hit by cars are already lying in the road, traffic tickets
were "defined downward" in an effort to unclog the courts. Even serious traffic
violations became merely civil offenses so that no warrants were issued. Fully
one-quarter of the citations are ignored, inviting, says Deputy Chief Thomas
Selvaggi, "contempt for the law."

In practice, as George Kelling has demonstrated again and again, "victimless" disorders can soon flood a neighborhood with serious, "victimizing
crime." There is, as the New York Transit police learned under Chief Bill
Bratton, a "seamless web," an inextricable interconnection between low-level
disorder like fare beating and violent crime. Roughly two of thirteen fare
beaters, Bratton points out, have outstanding warrants, often for felonies. The
decriminalizers got it backwards: by refusing to police small disorders we
didn't free up the cops; rather, we imprisoned the public at great cost to the
vitality of our streets and cities.

DEINSTITUTIONALIZATION

When New York Governor Mario Cuomo was asked recently about the problems of violent mental patients on the streets of New York City, his answer, in
the words of Lars-Erik Nelson, was that "it's not true. . . . Or if it is true, it's
not his fault, he's powerless." Or in Cuomo's own words: "The Constitution
says you cannot lock up a person just because he's a nuisance, urinating in the
street." How about changing the law? Cuomo says "Can't be done." He explains, "Suppose you had a law you could lock up anyone who is endangering
his health. I could come to you and say you're drinking, you're smoking, I've
got to lock you up." The slippery slope, it seems, slides in only one direction.
In legal terms, Cuomo is arguing that the patient's liberty interest must be
paramount.

How did we come to this pass? Erving Goffman[6] argued that mental
hospitals were responsible for most of the symptoms of their patients. He
argued further that he knew of no supposedly psychotic misconduct that could
not be precisely matched in everyday life by the conduct of persons who are
not psychologically ill.

Several years ago, in the "Billy Boggs" affair, in which a homeless schizo-
phrenic in New York City fought for her right to live and defecate on the
streets, the American Civil Liberties Union (ACLU) played the Goffmanesque
game. Did Billy Boggs urinate on the sidewalk? So did cabdrivers. Did she
tear up or burn the money she had begged? This was a symbolic gesture
similar to the burning of draft cards during Vietnam. And on it went. Billy
Boggs, whose real name was Joyce Brown and who had grown up in a loving
family and received social security checks she never bothered to collect, was
described by her NYCLU attorneys as a "political prisoner," a victim of social

indifference and Reagan's housing policies. Far from insane, she "sounded," said her attorney Robert Levy, "like a member of the board of the Civil Liberties Union."

Freed from the "clutches" of New York City hospitals, wined, dined, and reclothed at Bloomingdales, she was hustled on to talk shows and the Ivy League lecture circuit, exploited to score legal and public relations points. When the spotlight faded, however, she was within weeks back on the streets screaming, defecating, and destroying herself. In a series of publicized incidents she was arrested for fighting, harassing passersby, and using hard drugs. As former civil rights hero Charles Morgan put it, the ACLUers had become "ideologues frozen in time." The fight for deinstitutionalization initially aimed to free those people who, made passive by many years of often unjust and unnecessary incarceration, posed little threat to society. Following this victory, however, the newly established community care system failed to continue providing calming psychotropic drugs and other types of assistance, and many of the mentally ill were moved from the back wards to the back alleys and eventually to the main streets.

For civil libertarians devoted to the abstract concept of freedom, this wasn't neccessarily the problem with the new system. Paul Friedman, an early director of the NYCLU Mental Health Law Project, worried that "because the deprivation of liberty is less in community based treatment than in total institutionalization . . . the resistance against state intrusion will be less and the lives of many more people may be ultimately interfered with."[7] The project's founder, Bruce Ennis, asserted: "I'm simply a civil libertarian, and in my view you don't lock people up because they've got a problem." "It's never been very important to me," he went on, "if there is or is not mental illness. My response would be the same." "Lawyers," he said, "are doing what they think is right in terms of civil rights, whether it's good for the patients or not."[8] This mix of principled ignorance and militant nonconsequentialism was one thing when the first deinstitutionalized populations were released into the streets, but quite another when some of those patients, as well as those never institutionalized in the first place, increasingly became addicted to alcohol and drugs.

The full meaning of this militantly nonconsequentialist perspective was made manifest in the Larry Hogue case. In and out of mental institutions and generously provided for with a $3,000 monthly V.A. check, Larry Hogue began in the mid-1980s to terrorize parts of Manhattan's liberal Upper West Side. As Robert Spoor of the New York State Office of Mental Health notes, "The charges against Hogue have always been misdemeanors." Arrested more than forty times, he has never been convicted of a felony. He has, however, chased people down the street with a club, threatening to murder them; set numerous fires, including fires under cars; repeatedly strewn garbage all over sidewalks; defecated in the back seat of a car after first threatening to kill its owner and then breaking into the auto by smashing part of a marble bench into the auto's window; masturbated in front of children; lunged at terrified women with a knife; and has run about screaming, with burning newspapers in hand.

Local community groups made a concerted effort to see Hogue incarcerated or institutionalized. But under current mental health law, people like Hogue can be institutionalized only as long as they present an immediate threat to themselves and others. The staff at Manhattan State Hospital told community leaders that "Hogue is more violent than you think," but that they were "unable to hold him because of his rights." The official story of Hogue is that, while it is true that he behaves wildly when on the crack he buys with his V.A. check, he's perfectly fine when off drugs, so that the mental health authorities have no recourse but to release him. Researcher Heather MacDonald, however, has discovered part of the reason why he's so quickly released is that mental health authorities can't control him either; so they want to get rid of him as quickly as possible. According to Dr. Michael Pawel, a psychiatrist who has treated Hogue, no one wants to deal with an unruly patient who isn't going to get better and ruins their statistics, as is typical of *dual diagnosis* patients—patients afflicted by a combination of mental illness, drugs, or drink.

The public is now well aware of the high percentage of ex-mental patients addicted to drugs, but less aware of the impact of alcohol as well. At about the same time that mental patients were being released in large numbers during the early 1970s, cities took Bentham's advice and began treating intoxication as a public health issue instead of a criminal problem. But in a parallel with deinstitutionalization, the promise to build public detoxification facilities was never carried out. The upshot, as demonstrated in a Wesley Skogan study of public disorder in forty neighborhoods, is that public drinking is the most persistent problem.[9]

As early as the late 1970s, Martin Begun of the New York City Department of Mental Health, Mental Retardation and Alcoholism Services, warned of the impending collision between the different versions of moral deregulation. "Two-thirds of the mentally ill" in New York City, he noted in 1993, "are addicted to drugs or alcohol." "We are operating," he explains, "with a mental health system created in the 1960s and 1970s on the basis of assumptions that are no longer applicable in the 1990s."[10]

WHAT CAN BE DONE?

Limited Institutionalization

Upon learning that Larry Hogue was about to be released once again, a New York panhandler who had been intimidated by him responded, "We'd all be better off if he were committed." He's right. We should institutionalize the most dangerous of our mentally ill, often drug-dependent, homeless. Taking away someone's liberty is a very serious matter that should be done only with reluctance and caution. But there are some cases where both the patient and the society would benefit. For the most seriously sick, notes psychiatrist E. Fuller Torrey, the right to be psychotic is "is an illusory freedom, a cruel hoax perpetrated on those who cannot think clearly by those who will not think clearly."[11]

Carefully Tailored Anti-begging Ordinances

We can pass laws targeted not at panhandling per se, which the courts have tended to define as free speech, but at restrictions of time, manner, and place. Carefully crafted laws restricting aggressive panhandling, where the action overwhelms the words, are on the books in eleven cities, including Cincinnati and Seattle, and are likely to withstand legal challenge. Passed because aggressive panhandlers were driving people from the downtown streets, Seattle's law prohibits "intimidation" and "obstruction." Similarly, restrictions on begging in front of ATM machines and in confined spaces like subways and buses have also been upheld. Modern anti-begging laws, says Rob Teir of the American Alliance for Rights and Responsibilities [AARR], are aimed at specific harmful conduct, not at an individual's status.

BIDs and Decentralized Public Space Management

Business Improvement Districts (BIDs) are localized self-assessing tax districts designed to reclaim public space from the sense of menace that drives shoppers and eventually store owners and citizens to the suburban malls. BIDs sweep the streets, augment police patrols, upgrade transportation, and generally promote downtowns. Thirty-eight states have passed enabling legislation, and there are about 1,000 BIDs in the United States. Philadelphia's Center City BID is credited with erasing the image of the downtown as "Filthadelphia," home to "trash storms." The Louisville BID has successfully promoted the kind of sidewalk sales, trolley transport, and security that have made the downtown more attractive.

A nongovernmental variant of public space management is offered by consulting firms for "sick spaces," like the Project for Public Space. Traditionally, architects have approached the design of plazas as an aesthetic exercise. The Project associates instead approach the problem anthropologically, with an eye toward how the space can be made hospitable. For example, movable chairs in public areas facilitate conversation and cordiality in a way that fixed park benches do not. The Project's microscopic methods have succeeded in reviving a number of "dead" or drug-ridden spaces, such as Bryant Park in midtown Manhattan.

Community Cops, Courts, and Prosecutors

Community policing is now so popular and widespread as to require little comment. George Kelling and James Q. Wilson's argument[12] that low-level disorder, such as "the appearance of un-fixed broken windows," encourages "higher" order problems has gained wide acceptance.

Less well accepted are the attempts to supplement community policing with community courts and community prosecution teams. Both are aimed at giving neighborhoods some say in how they are to be policed. At some point this kind of localism may prove threatening to civil liberties. For now it is forcing police departments and judges to set their priorities in a less bureaucratic manner, such as when community organizations in the Bronx pressured the police and judges to look upon the prostitution that was destroying their neighborhood as something more than a "victimless crime."

There is, it is true, no going back to an older concept of community that was too often racially exclusive, but there is growing support for a reassertion of common standards of public behavior. And "unlike previous calls for public order," says Rob Teir, "which often came from racially homogeneous upper classes, current demands for public civility come from people of all races" wanting to walk streets or ride buses without feeling under constant siege by others asserting their "right to be offensive." Teir's point is sustained by Antonio Pagan, a Puerto Rican city councilman representing the Lower East Side of Manhattan. "The people asking for the laws to be enforced," he says, "are the minorities themselves." Pagan is disdainful of the constant attempts to "cheapen the discussion" by references to racially discriminatory enforcement in the past. Civil libertarians, he argues, "try to turn it into a black/white issue to avoid the issue" of the social breakdown afflicting our neighborhoods.

The transformation Pagan represents is encapsulated in the story of an African-American tenant activist: Mrs. Jones (a pseudonym) has lived in Red Hook Houses, the single biggest public housing project in New York, for thirty-six years. She and her husband raised six children there. When they first arrived, there were five dollar fines for small violations of project rules. Minor vandalism, littering, loitering, keeping dogs in apartments, playing on the grass when it was being grown—all brought fines. But the absence of due process recourse gave management enormous discretionary authority that it sometimes abused. Like many tenants, she resented the arbitrary authority by which these fines were sometimes imposed by the white manager.

As a tenant leader, she fought to strip the manager of his authority to levy fines, something she now regrets. Those small rules she says once set the tone for projects are now being overwhelmed by crime and violence. Much else has happened to drive the breakdown, but the revival, she argues, has to begin by restoring the standards of behavior she and her neighbors, their teenagers excepted, all share. She now mourns the loss of legitimate authority. She says she never wanted to undermine authority in general, just its racially arbitrary forms.

Her conclusions, I would suggest, are shared by an overwhelming majority of urbanites who recognize that the very heterogeneity of city life imposes "a premium on moral reliability" and a longing to see a new ideal of urbanity emerge.

NOTES

1. Moynihan, Patrick. "Defining Deviance Down," *The American Scholar*, Vol. 62, Winter 1993.
2. Jacobs, Jane. *The Death and Life of Great American Cities*, New York: Random House, 1961.
3. Bedau, Hugo Adam and Schur, Edwin. *Victimless Crimes: Two Sides of a Controversy.* Englewood Cliffs, NJ: Prentice Hall, 1972.
4. Bedau and Schur, Ibid.
5. Geis, Gilbert. *Not the Law's Business?: An Examination of Homosexuality, Abortion, Prostitution, Narcotics and Gambling in the United States*, Washington, D.C.: National Institute of Mental Health, Center for Study of Crime and Delinquency, 1969.
6. Goffman, Erving. *Asylums*, New York: Doubleday, 1961.
7. Friedman is quoted in Issac, Rael Jean and Armat, Virginia. *Madness in the Streets: How Psychiatry and the Law Abandoned the Mentally Ill*. New York: Free Press, 1990.
8. Ennis, Ibid.
9. Skogan, Wesley. *Disorder and Decline: Crime and the Spiral of Decay in American Neighborhoods.* New York: Free Press, 1990.
10. Begun, Martin, et al. "Deinstitutionalizing the Mentally Ill," *City Journal*, Spring 1993.
11. Torrey, E. Fuller. *Nowhere to Go: The Tragic Odyssey of the Homeless Mentally Ill.* New York: Harper and Row, 1988.
12. Kelling, George and Wilson, James Q. "Broken Windows," *The Atlantic*, March 1988.

CHAPTER 23

Community Policing

BRIAN FORST

Taking police out of their patrol cars and putting them back on the street has become the subject of increasing interest among public officials across the country. Throughout the 1980s, community policing materialized in a variety of forms: foot patrols in Flint [Michigan], Newark, and Baltimore; neighborhood "mini-precinct" stations in Houston; and specially assigned community police officers, with decentralized authority and neighborhood meetings in most of these and in other cities, including Miami, New Haven, Portland, Pasadena, and St. Petersburg. By 1993 more than 400 cities had adopted some form of community policing.

In 1990 David Dinkins, then mayor of New York City, announced that the city would adopt community policing as its "dominant operational philosophy." Perhaps the most telling endorsement of community policing came from the Warren Christopher Commission in the wake of the beating of Rodney King and the ensuing riots in Los Angeles. While the performance of police forces in urban areas came under national scrutiny, the Commission's evaluation of the Los Angeles Police Department (LAPD) prescribed community policing as the way to realign its discredited force with the community it serves.

WHAT IS COMMUNITY POLICING?

Community policing represents a significant departure from the "professional" model that has characterized policing since the 1950s. The professional model emphasizes police responsibility for crime control and views citizens primarily as victims, witnesses, or offenders—not as partners. Professional policing stresses adherence to rules, features a centralized bureaucracy, and places emphasis on rapid response to calls and the effective handling of individual incidents. Police officers cruise neighborhoods in patrol cars and are alerted to crimes and problem situations by means of centrally dispatched radio messages. For this reason, the approach has earned the unofficial title of "911 policing."

This model lost its support as large segments of the public expressed resentment because of what they considered police insensitivity, a concern aggravated by the distance that developed between the police and the public. Because most American cities experienced an increase in visible street crime in the 1980s, police departments drew fire for offering what many saw as quick-fix or token solutions: for instance, shows of force in highly publicized drug sweeps or lectures to school children on the hazards of drug abuse. Many maintain that crime cannot be effectively dealt with if such programs are grounded in elitist notions that place the police above large segments of the community. Assessing community–police relations following the Los Angeles riots, the Governor's Commission report summed up the rage the nation felt over the beating of Rodney King: "There is much deep-seated hostility, mistrust and suspicion in this relationship, and it cries out for a change in the old ways of doing business."

Community policing, in contrast, aims to strengthen officer–community relations to prevent crime. This model shifts authority from the supervisory hierarchy to officers on the beat. By building bridges to the community— through door-to-door contacts, foot patrols, and the establishment of accessible neighborhood precincts—officers encourage residents and commercial tenants to cooperate with them on matters of community concern, and establish the foundations for a working relationship. For example, in Takoma Park, Maryland, an officer's typical day might include meeting with neighborhood groups, planning crime prevention strategies with residents, and circulating newsletters with updates on crime patterns and solutions. Partnership is the core of this new approach: The safety of the community is the responsibility of both the police and the citizens. Criminologists Jerome Skolnick and David Bayley see the distinction between the two models as a matter of carrots and sticks: "The emphasis on community policing is toward soliciting, enlisting, inviting, and encouraging, while in traditional policing it is toward warning, threatening, forcing, and hurting."

In addition, community policing requires a change in focus—from a preoccupation with arrests and crime rates to a concern for the living conditions of the community. Under the professional model, the basic mission of policing is crime control through law enforcement, and success is defined in terms of crime and arrest statistics. Noncrime-related tasks such as reducing street disorder were considered "social work," and such neglected problems contributed to the decline of some inner-city neighborhoods. Community relations is often seen as a side-issue—a matter of public image and damage control. In contrast, the community-policing approach recognizes that a department's effectiveness depends on the officers' commitment to the community and respect for all of its members—perhaps even the offenders. A growing cadre of advocates of community policing, including Lee P. Brown, U.S. drug czar and former chief of three major police departments (New York, Houston, and Atlanta), and David Couper, chief of the Madison, Wisconsin, Police Department, interpret the mission of policing even more broadly: improving the vitality of the community.

DECENTRALIZATION VERSUS ACCOUNTABILITY

Shifting responsibility and authority from a centralized bureaucracy to a cop on the beat gives officers the opportunity to invent creative solutions to varying community problems. Community police officers in New York, for example, have dealt with a wide range of concerns: in Brooklyn, Officer Randy Mazzone worked with residents to seal abandoned buildings in order to reduce drug trafficking and related crimes; and in Manhattan, Officer Carl DeFazio organized tenants of an apartment building to help bring about the arrest and incarceration of a landlord who had intimidated them with pit bulls and weapons. Other officers have established evening basketball games to keep kids off the street, fixed street lights, and towed abandoned cars to create an environment that is less conducive to crime.

Yet to many, the idea of decentralization competes with the idea of police accountability. Critics of this approach point to the demise of the cop-on-the-beat style of policing that had been the standard mode of municipal policing until the 1950s. The unaccountability and corruption associated with these foot patrols contributed in large part to their discontinuance. Proponents of community policing, on the other hand, argue that the increased visibility and higher degree of accountability involved in this updated form of decentralization would make corruption a problem of the past.

One should not underestimate the difficulty of implementing the changes that community policing entails. It is not simply a matter of getting officers out of their patrol cars or adding sections on community policing to the academy's training manuals, but in trying to change the way officers, citizens, and social workers see their roles in maintaining safety. Community policing holds that citizens are no less responsible for their safety than police officers; each neighborhood should be more self-reliant in ensuring its own safety. "If citizens don't do more for themselves and social agencies don't pick up the slack, it will be difficult to do community policing with the current resources," explains Robert Trojanowicz, director of the National Center for Community Policing. Whether and how it is possible to bring about such attitudinal changes remain to be seen.

DOES IT REDUCE CRIME?

Another common concern of critics is whether community policing substantially reduces crime. Does an officer's concern about abandoned cars, poor lighting, and the welfare of the residents in his or her beat come at the expense of crime control? A recent survey of residents of Madison, Wisconsin, conducted by Mary Ann Wycoff of the Police Foundation, suggests that it does not. Following an experimental period of community policing, these residents perceived robberies and burglaries to be less of a problem than they had been under conventional policing. Yet is this enhanced feeling of security backed by a decrease in crime statistics?

Police Foundation researchers found that these beliefs had modest empirical support. In areas patrolled by community police officers in Newark in 1985, researchers found a decline in Part I crime rates (the aggregate of homocide, rape, robbery, aggravated assault, burglary, larceny, motor vehicle theft, and arson) and in personal crime rates, but not in control areas. And a recent LAPD study on the Foothill Division of Los Angeles found that burglaries and rapes had dropped in the 18 months the community policing program there had been in effect.

Although conclusive evidence of a significant decrease in crime due to community policing is yet to come, the benefits such a program brings the community extend beyond crime statistics. Almost every study on community policing has shown that residents feel a heightened sense of security. Their living conditions improve, whether owing to decreased drug traffic and sealed abandoned buildings, or to the ousting of a bully landlord. Most of all, the rapport between the community and its officer is strengthened. This is not a benefit easily measured by statistics.

A BRIDGE TO THE COMMUNITY

Officer Joe Balles of the Madison, Wisconsin, Police Department is a case in point. One of the many 1980s converts to the principles of community policing, Officer Balles volunteered for one of the department's ten community policing assignments in 1989. Although Madison is largely an upper-middle-class university town, many of its residents live in low-income apartments that are common to Chicago, Milwaukee, and other urban centers in the Midwest. Officer Balles's beat is such a neighborhood—a six-block apartment complex that houses some 2,500 people, about 55 percent low-income blacks. The crime rate in this complex is substantially higher than that for Madison as a whole. Eight people were shot there in 1991, and one was killed; burglaries and robberies occur far more frequently there than in most other neighborhoods of the city.

Officer Balles operates out of a converted apartment space in the complex. He spends much of his time walking his beat and much of the rest of the time chatting with residents in his office. Once a month he convenes a meeting with rental property managers, owners, and the building inspector to exchange information about crime and crime-related conditions in the neighborhood. When a problem such as an abandoned car or inadequate lighting surfaces, Balles tries to find a solution from the managers and owners, or from the city. If the city bureaucracy is unresponsive to a public works problem, a story about the problem is likely to turn up in the newspaper or on television. Officer Balles, in short, takes on problems that conventional patrol officers do not.

In turn, the bonds developed with the community benefit Balles's work in ways that would not necessarily happen if he were a conventional patrol officer. In June and July of 1991, Racine and Milwaukee were experiencing a wave of armed robberies by a 29-year-old man recently released from prison. When the man showed up at a relative's apartment in Balles's beat, Balles received a discreet call from the relative, with whom Balles had previously developed a close relationship. The offender was arrested, and the one-man crime wave was ended.

It is incidents like this that have made community policing a growing trend in police departments nationwide. As then-New York City Police Commissioner Lee Brown stated in a 1991 *Harvard Business Review* interview: "The better your relationship with the people, the more information you'll get." And as one resident in Southeast Washington, D.C., reports of her neighborhood's community policing efforts, the approach benefits both sides of the partnership. "United by the purpose of improving the quality of life in our neighborhood, we became a community." Indeed, although studies do not yet conclusively prove that community policing reduces crime, it helps bring officers and community members closer together and reduces resentment, a worthy end in itself.

CHAPTER 24

L.A. Gated Communities

NATIONAL PUBLIC RADIO

Robert Siegel: This is "All Things Considered." I'm Robert Siegel.

Ten years from now, the shape of Los Angeles will reflect what happens to thirty-five documents that are sitting now in a file cabinet in the city's Department of Public Works. They are applications from neighborhood associations that want to turn their communities into gated enclaves by fencing off the streets that connect them with the rest of the city. All these applications have come in over the last five years. During that time, the crime rate in the city has risen by about 14 percent. There is opposition to barricades. Critics argue that after the riots, the city is at a turning point and that walling off neighborhoods one from the other will destroy what fragile sense of community remains. NPR's Ina Jaffe reports on the trend toward barricades that's taking root in Los Angeles.

Ina Jaffe: Isolation is already a feature of many Los Angeles neighborhoods. They're perched on hilltops or cut off from the city by canyons or the ubiquitous freeways. But the increase in crime here and the increase in fear have created a sudden demand for even greater seclusion. This is seen not only in the surge of applications for closing off public streets but in the trend for brand-new housing tracts to be designed from the ground up as gated compounds. One real estate analyst said that these days, new tract homes are hard to sell unless they're behind gates, and the most upscale of these communities have guards as well.

(Sound of gate opening)

Unidentified Guard: Yes?

Jaffe: Hi, I'm here to see Beverly Gold.

Guard: Your name?

Jaffe: Ina Jaffe.

A thousand feet above the Pacific Ocean, surrounded by scrub-covered hills, are a few dozen mansions known collectively as Ridgeview Country

Estates. A guard controls the electric gates that keep out whatever curiosity seekers manage to find their way this far up the canyon.

Beverly Gold, her husband Barry, and their son, Adam, moved here four years ago when the development was brand new.

Beverly Gold (**Ridgeview Country Estates**): The guardhouse wasn't even in place when we bought, so I had no idea how much I was going to enjoy it. But we knew that it was going to be here, and it was a factor. I mean, it just made it that much more exciting knowing that, oh—I mean, not only does it give you security but it also—there's a certain amount of prestige that goes with it, too.

Jaffe: Security and prestige. Nobody understands better than Beverly Gold what that can do for property values. She's a real estate agent for another hilltop enclave nearby.

Beverly Gold: And we've just released 40 lots, guard-gated, that we haven't even started advertising yet, and I already have four reservations. There's definitely a need and a want for guard-gated areas, so those properties will sell quicker than properties that are non-gated.

Jaffe: The Golds' current house, like the two they lived in previously, is in the town of Pacific Palisades, best known as the place where Ronald and Nancy Reagan lived before they moved into the White House. The Golds' son, Adam, has spent all of his 11 years in this community, but he says the new house is his favorite.

Adam Gold: I used to be scared of stuff a long time ago.

Jaffe: Yeah.

Adam: Well, here you can't get scared of anything because there are gates and stuff so . . .

Jaffe: What kind of stuff did you get scared of?

Adam: Just like burglars—cat burglars.

Jaffe: Cat burglars?

Beverly Gold: Been watching a lot of movies. We get a lot of cat burglars in Palisades. No, I don't think so.

Jaffe: Was your house ever burgled?

Adam: No.

Beverly Gold: But Adam feels so secure that he begs us to let him stay home alone. If we go out to dinner, we say, "Come on, Adam. Let's go out to dinner." He says, "No, you go. I'll just stay here."

Jaffe: Would you want to stay home alone if it wasn't gated?

Adam: Probably not.

Jaffe: Do you think there's a big difference between having a gate with a guard or just having a gate?

Adam: I think there's a difference because when there's a guard, he protects the gate. They all have .357 Magnums.

Jaffe: Beverly Gold and her husband Barry also find the high level of security comforting. That was especially true during the riots.

Beverly Gold: I felt insulated up here. I felt that nothing can touch me.

Jaffe: How about you?

Barry Gold (**Ridgeview Country Estates**): To me, the riots weren't as significant as the fact that we've simply had an increase—a dramatic increase—in crime. So living in a guard-gated community gives you a certain amount of security that you wouldn't otherwise have.

Beverly Gold: It's sad that it has to be done, but that's definitely going to be the trend. There's so much negative publicity about our crime here now—gang shootings, drive-bys—that people are fearful. And being in real estate, I see a lot of people leaving LA because of it. They don't leave because of earthquakes. They leave because of crime.

Jaffe: Security does not come cheap. The homeowners of Ridgeview Country Estates each pay about $360 a month for the guards at the end of their street, but then this is a city where those who can afford it expect to pay for their own protection. The most common lawn ornament in affluent neighborhoods is a sign with a logo of a private security service and the warning: armed guard response. According to Mark Baldassare, head of the Department of Urban Planning at the University of California at Irvine, this is not really a new phenomenon but the revival of an old one.

Mark Baldassare (**University of California at Irvine**): Cities were developed around the concept of walls to defend those with the wealth from those who don't have the wealth. A very small group of people lived in the walled cities in preindustrial times. And if you go back to the nineteenth century, you go back to a period in which the wealthy hired their own police forces and paid for their own private services before we had the widescale use of city services and before people became interested in the idea of city government handling these issues.

Jaffe: But it's no longer just the wealthy who are willing to pay for extra security. The neighborhood of Athens Heights is solidly middle class, an island of quiet streets lined with palm trees and single-family homes surrounded by a much grittier section of south Los Angeles. Henry King and his wife have lived in this mostly African-American community for nearly three decades and raised five children here. About ten years ago, burglars broke into their home. The way they left it told Henry King that crime in Los Angeles had taken a malicious new twist.

Henry King: The things that they stole weren't really too bad, but the damage that they did on the inside, like painting graffiti, the piano that you saw all painted, the lamps were painted, the shades on the lamps—the chandeliers were painted, the pictures on the mantel board were painted, all of the mirrors were painted . . .

Jaffe: With graffiti.

King: With graffiti, yes. I guess gang signs, so forth and so on. It—it was really debilitating, so I—it was something that I didn't want to happen again.

Jaffe: Did your burglar bars that are on the front door go up shortly after that?

King: The next day.

Jaffe: Henry King stands in front of his house and points out which of his neighbors have also put up burglar bars, which have tried electric fences or alarms. But six years ago, the residents of Athens Heights decided that more drastic measures were necessary and sought permission from the city to barricade almost all of the streets leading into their neighborhood.

King: Hoover and El Segundo, Hoover and 120th, 125th and Vermont, 126th and Vermont, 127th and Vermont . . .

Jaffe: Eventually, there could be ten gates in all, with only a single open street leading into Athens Heights. Right now, most of the barricades are temporary wooden partitions. The only permanent fence, wrought iron and 7 feet high, is at the end of Henry King's street, blocking an intersection with one of the busiest thoroughfares in Los Angeles. The fence has been there less than a year. The gang members have already anointed it with spray paint.

King: That will be down very shortly to—to paint it out—perhaps by the weekend.

Jaffe: Crime in Athens Heights has gone down since the barricades were installed, but Henry King feels that peace has been won at some cost. The wide streets, the gracious front lawns with their neat, colorful gardens were something that King took pleasure in sharing with passersby. He misses seeing those unknown neighbors, especially the youngest of them.

King: As far as the children going back and forth to school, the way that they now have to go—a lot of graffiti that they see, and I think if they walked through here, they would see a lot of beauty instead. I feel that and it's regrettable that they're now precluded from seeing that, and there's nothing like a child—seeing a child growing up and going to school from elementary, and then after about twelve years, you no longer see that child, then you know something has happened. Either they've gone on to adulthood or they've gone on to college perhaps. Hopefully, one of these days, we'll be able to allow the children to return.

Jaffe: If those who gate themselves in have regrets, that's nothing compared to the feelings of some of those who are locked out. Across town, John Jay lives a steep quarter mile above tough and tacky Hollywood Boulevard and just a few yards outside of a gate leading to the narrow, leafy streets at the top of the hill. That gate, he says, sends a wrong message to the neighborhood.

John Jay (**Citizens Against Gated Enclaves**): It says "stay out," and it also says, "We are the wealthy, and you guys are not, and this gate shall establish the difference."

Jaffe: For now, the gate remains open. Jay and his neighbors have formed a group called Citizens Against Gated Enclaves or CAGE, and they've sued the homeowners at the top of the hill. State law prohibits the placing of barriers on public streets, says Jay. Also, residents of his block could find themselves completely stranded if a moving van or a garbage truck blocked the bottom of the hill and the gate closed off the top.

Jay: That's one of the points that upsets everybody, because they do technically remain as public streets, and we, as the public, continue to pay for them through our taxes, and we should be able to walk on those streets. They are our streets.

Jaffe: Some city officials are now trying to resolve this growing conflict between public access and private safety. In the past, requests to close off streets were fairly rare, so they were judged on a case-by-case basis, and there have never been any formal criteria for saying yes or no. Rita Walters, a member of the City Council from South Central Los Angeles, says [that] with nearly three dozen applications pending, the city must now set rules. She would like to find a way to reverse the trend.

Rita Walters (**City Council**): If you're willing to pay the money it takes to wall off your community, to pay for private security, why not be willing to pay for an extra measure of tax that may not be as much, that will benefit the city as a whole, and then you don't have to have these guards and walls and what have you. But it's like people who will complain about the public school system—won't vote for a bond issue for a public school but will pay to send their kids to private school. When you wall off one neighborhood, what about the next one? Does the crime then move to the next neighborhood? Then do you wall that off? At what point does this, carried to its logical extension, stop?

Jaffe: It has not stopped with the wealthy or even the middle class. One of LA's newest gated enclaves is Marvista Gardens, a public housing project on the West Side. A complex of two-story barrackslike apartment buildings spread across forty-three grassy acres. A couple of city streets used to run through here. Now the project's completely enclosed by a steel fence with the look of more fashionable wrought iron. There's just one way in and the same way out, with a security guard watching who comes and goes.

Lyndon Cullen (**Housing Authority Officer**): We used to have in the front here, in this parking lot and the parking lot on the side, a lot of drug dealing, and putting the fence up has driven all this out of here. They used to have open-air sales right in the front here.

Jaffe: Lyndon Cullen is one of two housing authority officers who patrol Marvista Gardens in the evening. The fence and the extra security were paid for by a grant from the federal antidrug program. Cullen says that unlike residents of affluent neighborhoods, the tenants of Marvista Gardens did not at first view the fence as a status symbol.

Cullen: Thought they were being fenced in, made sort of like a cage that they couldn't go out into the community and, you know, things like that. The—someone felt, well, they really didn't have a say in it, whether it was going to go up or not. But once it's—it's been up, I would say 90 percent of the people here like it.

Jaffe: The fence may have added to the stigma of living in public housing, says resident Anna Castillo, but she knows the project's middle-class neighbors have never had a high opinion of Marvista Gardens.

Anna Castillo (**Resident, Marvista Gardens**): They say the—that's a zoo. They say it's a zoo—keep the people inside there.

Jaffe: But Castillo says that Marvista Gardens was a really nice place ten years ago when she first came to live here. So when she heard about the fence, she was all for it. Her only complaint, she says, is that it hasn't worked well enough.

Castillo: I thought it would keep more—most of the dru—drug—the drug traffic out. It seems like it—it's still coming in though.

Jaffe: Can you see any difference at all?

Castillo: Yeah, I can see—there is a big difference. There's no more like drive-by shootings because they can't come—they can't—there's only one way out. That's the good thing about it. There has been no more drive-by shootings.

Jaffe: There's still a lot of drug dealing that goes on here. You were telling me that you heard people the other night until 3:00 in the morning.

Castillo: Until 3:00 in the morning. All—all—all us neighbors were all up until about 3:00—3:30 in the morning. Didn't get no sleep or anything—loud music, gang members fighting outside your window.

Jaffe: Is that every night or just occasionally?

Castillo: Almost every night.

Jaffe: Fence or no fence, the drug dealers—the guys, she calls them—still determine much the way Anna Castillo lives her life. The guys are the reason she still takes her 15-year-old daughter to school every morning and picks her up in the afternoon. The guys are the ones she watches for every minute she's home, staring through windows doubly veiled with blue lace curtains and venetian blinds. Without warning, she rises from her kitchen chair and tiptoes to the living room window.

Castillo: See, they're all walking around now.

Jaffe: Are those the guys that hang out here?

Castillo: One of them is. Where did he go?

Jaffe: He's walking—one of them's walking down toward the cars away from the building.

Castillo: They're all walking. It must be the police that they got scared of . . .

Jaffe: The fence around Marvista Gardens may not have brought Anna Castillo peace and safety, but she finally has hope that it will, which may be ultimately what all these enclaves offer: the hope that behind the gates, it's still possible to live in the mythical Los Angeles; the sun-drenched land of promise where the citizens are less violent, less desperate, and less divided by race, by money, and by walls.

In Los Angeles, I'm Ina Jaffe.

Robert Siegel, host: For Mike Davis, the gated community is just one device by which Los Angeles controls the space that used to be public and free. Davis teaches urban theory at the Southern California Institute of Architecture. In his book, *City of Quartz*, he describes Los Angeles as "a place designed to control the mobility of inner-city youth, a city hostile to and hardened against its own poor." The images, he cites in evidence, include a public library that looks like a fort, complete with a police lookout turret, and a bum-proof bench.

Mike Davis (Southern California Institute of Architecture): This is a barrel-shaped bus bench ingeniously designed to prevent anyone from sleeping or relaxing on it. And it's a part of a kind of spatial schizophrenia where on one side of Hill Street, which is the great economic class divide in downtown LA, the city's spending millions of dollars to create luxurious public environments for tourists and businessmen, places where you're invited to relax and take a nap. While south of Hill Street, in the traditional downtown skid row area, you have nothing but a set of deterrents to taking a nap or relaxing or hanging around. So on one hand, we're fortifying a city against the poor while at the same time we're using tax dollars to subsidize pseudo-public spaces for tourists and managers.

Siegel: In Los Angeles, I gather, there also is a park where people who sleep out in it, who are either homeless or vagrant or whatever, might be interrupted at random intervals in the middle of the night by sprinklers which are designed primarily to—to awake them and interrupt their sleep.

Davis: Yeah. And this has been so popular that it's been adopted by a number of local businesses that have sprinklers now outside on their walls which go on at random times to discourage anyone from sleeping on the adjacent sidewalk. So what we're, in fact, creating here is not just spatial apartheid but different classes of citizenship where the—the poor and the homeless, who have the greatest need for the use of the commons, the public space, are prevented from so doing and, in fact, are increasingly warehoused in—in—in a totally hostile militarized spatial environment.

Siegel: The—the Los Angeles that you describe is one where the spaces that used to be public spaces and that as—as you describe architectural and planning critics have—have said that some of those public urban spaces were, in fact, designed to take the edge off social and class conflict where people could congregate and socialize—those spaces are getting smaller and more hostile, and there's not much left of the city anymore, if I read you right.

Davis: No, there isn't. Or rather the city becomes each day more recogniz-
ably a colonial city—a city like you find left in Africa where the—the
white raj, the white colonial class lived in a fortified separated part of
town, and the rest of the city was the—the casbah, the indigenous quarter. And—and these, of course, spatial relations that cut across the entire
grain of American democratic precedent in the use of public space and in
the understanding what our cities should be.

Siegel: Why is Los Angeles so special in this regard, or is it? Is it simply that
you live and write about Los Angeles? Or is it that Los Angeles's history
is—is unique?

Davis: No, Los Angeles's history isn't unique, but it does, in some ways,
present the future to other American cities. First of all, because of what
people in this city have always denied but now can scarcely escape from
admitting, which is Los Angeles has a consistent history of—of racism and
dealing with the problems of racial injustice by dealing with the symptoms
and not with the causes. And secondly because this is a—this is a city
which has always had a kind of dialectical tension between its urban
spaces and the suburban desire to live in some thicket of privacy on a—on
a hillside or along a beach. There's always been a tension in the city
between the private and public realm, probably, you know, more so than
in any other great American city.

Siegel: Architect Mike Davis wrote *City of Quartz* and spoke to us from Los
Angeles.

CHAPTER 25

This Town Will Die
without Our School

ELIZABETH GINSBURG

This Union County borough is a self-contained place. Most of its 7,574 residents are employed nearby and shop in the strip of stores along Kenilworth Boulevard. "It's the kind of town where you're born, you go to school, get married, raise a family, and die," said Janet Glynos, a Kenilworth native.

Now, forces inside and outside the community have combined to endanger its way of life. Since 1970, the population has declined by almost 1,600 people. A new shopping center and supermarket are going up on one end of town, threatening the downtown businesses. And David Brearley Regional High School, which Charles Vitale, a former school board president, calls "the social and civic hub of the town," is scheduled to be closed at the end of the 1993 school year.

The threatened closing of the school and dispatch of its students to another school in the regional district reflects concerns that are felt in many parts of the state where enrollments have been falling and school costs skyrocketing. The pressure to save money by merging school districts, for example, inspired the recent enactment of state legislation to provide incentives for such "regionalization."

But the prospect of losing their high school has led many of Brearley's parents to mount an intense campaign to save the school. In the process, they have sued the school district. They have also inspired a bill now before the State Legislature that would actually make it easier to dissolve existing regional districts and permit member schools, like Brearley, to go their own ways.

Ever since the 1930s, Kenilworth and the nearby towns of Berkeley Heights, Clark, Garwood, Mountainside, and Springfield have been linked by participation in Union County Regional High School District No. 1. The district's four high schools are supervised by a district board and superintendent.

Socially and economically, Kenilworth and Garwood, whose students also attend Brearley, have little in common with the four other towns in the school district. Kenilworth has a median family income of $45,774, whereas the wealthiest of the district's towns, Mountainside, has a median family income of $80,699. About 9 percent of Kenilworth's residents are college graduates, as opposed to about 33 percent in Berkeley Heights and Mountainside, and 27 percent in Springfield.

"We're blue-collar people," said Mrs. Glynos, one of the leaders of S.O.S. (Save Our School). She characterizes Kenilworth as a town of small family-owned businesses, where houses are passed down from parents to their grown children.

Over the last twenty years, enrollment in the four regional high schools has gone from a high of 5,798 in 1972–1973 to the current enrollment of 2,163. The yearly average cost per pupil rose from just over $3,000 in 1980–1981 to about $15,000 in 1992–1993.

In the spring of 1990 and again in 1991, voters rejected the district's school budget proposals. After the budget defeats, the board began to examine ways of cutting costs, including the closing of one or more of the four schools, and in September 1991 the Brearley parents organized to fight such a move. "We didn't want to see it happen to anyone," Mrs. Glynos said.

In the spring of 1992, S.O.S. campaigned on behalf of the district school budget in the belief, Mrs. Glynos said, that Dr. Donald Merachnik, the district superintendent, had promised that Brearley would stay open if the budget was accepted. (Tom Long, the spokesman for the district, denies that any such promise was given.)

Among the voters the organization pursued were the borough's elderly residents. Charles Vitale, who is now president of the Kenilworth Senior Citizens, said that by far the majority of elderly residents supported the idea of keeping the local school open.

"Our taxes will go up anyway," he said, adding that the members of his group had backed S.O.S. because Brearley is such an integral part of the close-knit community's way of life.

The 1992 school budget was passed. Then, in October of that year, Dr. Merachnik presented a 27-page report that recommended, among other things, that Brearley High School's 400 students be "reassigned" to Jonathan Dayton High School in Springfield. The Brearley building would then be leased, the report said, possibly to another district, with its classrooms, auditorium, and playing fields to remain available, if possible, to the Kenilworth community.

In November, the district board voted to carry out Dr. Merachnik's recommendations. Only the board representatives from Kenilworth and Garwood voted against the proposal.

"WE WERE DEVASTATED"

"We were devastated by the decision," said Linda McMenamin, president of the Brearley High School Parent-Teacher Association. Mrs. McMenamin also said she thought the Kenilworth school had been "targeted" for closing because Kenilworth and Garwood are the least affluent of the six towns.

The day after the November board vote, S.O.S. hired a lawyer, Robert P. Glickman, a former New Jersey Superior Court administration law judge, who sued the regional district in Superior Court to stop the closing. He charged that the decision to close Brearley was "capricious" and made without sufficient time for the board to study alternative solutions.

While Mr. Glickman prepared for trial, S.O.S. began enlisting community support and sponsoring cake sales and auctions to raise money for legal expenses.

The trial last month produced a cavalcade of lawyers and expert witnesses and boxes of documents. Experts on both sides testified on the physical condition of all four buildings, the economic and educational advantages and disadvantages of high schools with 400 students (like Brearley) or 800 students (the approximate number of students in the three remaining high schools after the closing of Brearley), and the effect that Brearley's closing would have on Kenilworth property values. As of June 2, no decision had been rendered.

SCHOOL BUDGET REJECTED

Although only Kenilworth and Garwood face school closings, voters in all six of the district's towns rejected the proposed 1993 school budget because of the growing school costs.

There is also substantial support in several of the towns for Assembly Bill No. 2294, introduced in February. Sponsored by Union County legislators, the bill would permit the dissolving of a regional district with an average per-pupil cost of $15,000 or more a year if approved by the majority of the member towns. Current law requires a unanimous vote. A companion bill has been introduced in the State Senate. S.O.S. has lobbied for the bill with an extensive letter-writing campaign.

If the parents' organization succeeds in its effort to prevent the closing of Brearley, Mrs. Glynos says, the goal will be to remove the school from the regional district and to enrich its course offerings by making arrangements with neighboring educational institutions like Union County College.

But the central issue for her and other members of S.O.S. is to save Brearley and its special relationship to Kenilworth. "This town will die without our school," Mrs. McMenamin said.

CHAPTER 26

Where Necessity
Ends for Hospital Care

LISA BELKIN

The Julia L. Butterfield Hospital, which sits on the outskirts of this tiny town, is not much to look at. Its melon and gray facade is hardly beautiful. There are cracks in the tiles on the upstairs halls. Although the emergency room was renovated last year, the X-ray machine dates back four decades, and the ventilation system is almost as old.

For years the 2,200 residents of Cold Spring have seen the hospital as evidence that they have a basic right to immediate and total health care. Reluctantly, others came to a different conclusion: that the price of keeping the hospital open—$2 million to save thirty-five beds—is too high.

The difference in views illustrates a central question of the current health care debate: where is the line between medical necessity and economic luxury? Across the United States, 642 hospitals have closed since 1980, forcing patients to drive extra miles to deliver their babies, recover from their illnesses, and have their surgeries. The next-closest hospital to Cold Spring is about 20 miles away. How far is too far? How much is too much? Does the right to health care include the right to a community hospital?

"The current economics of health care don't allow a community hospital in every town," said Donna Gaidamak, a spokeswoman for the association.

Butterfield Hospital was founded in 1925 in a bequest left in the will of its namesake, a wealthy local woman whose son had died in childhood after a fall from a horse. If only there had been a hospital nearby, Mrs. Butterfield believed, her little boy might have been saved.

The institution has been on financially shaky ground from its first year of operation, when it had a deficit of $1,500. Since then, there have been economically good years mixed with the bad ones, but national trends were not in Butterfield's favor.

The cost of providing health care coupled with a push by insurance companies to reduce the length of each hospital stay has strained small hospitals to
the breaking point. Since 1980, 404 hospitals have entered merger agreements with neighboring institutions. More than half of those mergers took
place in the last five years.

"A small place like this can't keep up with technology," said Marcel Mar-
tino, chief executive officer of Butterfield. "Our radiology equipment is thirty,
forty years old, we can't get parts. We can't expand our physician base, because doctors want to work with larger hospitals. People feel secure knowing
we're here, but they don't really want to come here, either. They want to go
where the doctors are and the technology is. Most people in the community
have never been inside."

UNABLE TO MEET PAYROLL

Ten years ago, Butterfield nearly merged with Vassar Brothers Hospital in
Poughkeepsie, 20 miles north of Cold Spring, which is 55 miles north of
New York City, but the agreement fell through in its final stages. Five years
ago the hospital was scheduled to be closed, but another small hospital
in Beacon closed first, and the New York State Department of Health urged
that Butterfield remain open so that the area would not lose two hospitals
at once.

The latest threat to Butterfield began in March of [   ] when the board
of trustees found itself unable to meet the hospital payroll. The board turned
to the Hudson Valley Hospital Center, which had formerly been the Peekskill
Community Hospital. Hudson Valley took control of Butterfield in exchange
for an infusion of $500,000 to meet immediate expenses and allow the hospital
credit with which to buy medical supplies.

Shortly after Hudson Valley took charge, it announced that it would close
Butterfield's thirty-five beds on July 1, when the building would be turned
into a nursing home. The Butterfield emergency room would remain open for
as long as possible, Hudson Valley said, but if the economics proved impossible, it too would be closed. All patients from Cold Spring would have to travel
18 miles to Hudson Valley's 114-bed hospital for care.

In response to that announcement, the governing boards of Cold Spring
and neighboring Nelsonville formed the Joint Commission for Butterfield Hospital to find alternatives to Hudson Valley's plans. The group found another
hospital—St. Luke's Community Medical Center, across the Hudson River in
Newburgh, New York—which was willing to consider running the hospital
and keeping the beds open.

ANOTHER OPTION PURSUED

Hudson Valley, in turn, said it would relinquish control of Butterfield if it could recoup the $500,000 already spent to acquire the hospital, and if there was evidence that the community had raised an additional $1.5 million toward an operating endowment.

The Joint Commission set out to meet that challenge.

"We should do what people do in Mudpuddle, Utah," said Jacqueline Lofaro, a commission member whose elderly parents are regular users of Butterfield. "Make quilts, bake cakes—it seems like an awfully cheap price for a hospital."

To their surprise, members of the commission found that others in the community did not share their optimism. Business is slow in the antique shops and cafes that are the primary livelihood here, since the flood of weekend tourists ebbed with the recession. Raising the equivalent of $1,000 per person, some residents said, was simply not possible.

"This community cannot raise this kind of money," said Katherine O'Donnell, owner of the Main Street Cafe, where the conversation over eggs and muffins is often about health care. "You have to sell a lot of cupcakes to raise $1.5 million. These are working people."

The commission said the money could be found—in time. But time was the one thing it did not have.

"We'd gone as far as we could go," said Ms. Lofaro. "But we just couldn't meet the July 1 deadline."

And so the cost of health care in Cold Spring will change soon.

"That's a price of living away from everything," said Shawn Luther, who grew up in Nelsonville and is working at the Hudson Land Company real estate office before he leaves for college in the fall. "You have to drive 15 minutes for shopping. You have to drive 15 minutes for everything. Now you have to drive that far to the hospital. At least it isn't further."

PART V

Toward a Responsive Society

How do we ensure that communities will be governed in line with the values of their members and not those of a local despot, an oligarchy, or some other unrepresentative group? Robert Dahl points to the limits of the democratic approach in answering this question, citing the increased scale and complexity of the political arena and the glut of information reaching the public. He suggests that transferring authority to smaller government units, creating assemblies of ordinary citizens, and fostering mutual understanding will enhance citizen participation in public life. Whatever position one takes on this issue, no communitarian approach is complete without a conception of the polity of the community.

The editor argues that much of the governance in our society, and ideally more so, takes place in institutions other than the state, such as hospitals, schools, churches, ethnic and neighborhood associations, labor unions, and scores of others. We are members of these organizations or groups, and we must ensure that they will be responsive to the whole community, not merely to the government.

As the competition between communism and capitalism has come to a close, a new rivalry has emerged between factions of capitalism itself. The individualist British-American system has faced off against the more communitarian German and Japanese economies. Lester Thurow examines the variant forms of capitalism in terms of economies, government, and history, and postulates what the future may hold. The result of this nascent rivalry, he suggests, is that America will no longer be capable of forcing the world to play by her rules.

David Osborne highlights a new trend that transcends the age-old debate concerning the relative merits of the private market versus a system based on government intervention. He sees greater value in government—private-sector cooperation and in reinventing the government to be run more like a consumer-oriented private enterprise. Although there is still room for disagreement within the parameters of this new approach to governance, its underlying assumptions could revitalize the way we solve society's problems.

CHAPTER 27

Participation and the Problem
of Civic Understanding

ROBERT DAHL

The difficulties citizens in democratic countries now face in making political decisions have become serious enough to require a systematic search for new solutions. I want to explain why and suggest several ways of improving citizens' competence that are worth exploring further.

1. STANDARDS: THE CLASSICAL GOOD CITIZEN

What do we consider adequate standards for citizen competence? A traditional answer is to say that in a good polity the rulers should possess both knowledge of the "public good" and a robust and sustained desire to achieve it; that is, they should possess the quality traditionally called civic virtue. For rulers to possess both knowledge and "virtue" in turn presupposes that they have the opportunities and incentives to acquire the necessary knowledge and the predispositions to act steadily on the basis of that knowledge.

A committed democrat might object that if we accept knowledge and virtue as standards for rulers, we must necessarily commit ourselves to rule by an elite—like Plato's aristocratic Guardians, a Confucian bureaucracy, a Leninist vanguard party, a technocracy, and so on. Lest the argument that follows be misinterpreted, let me say as emphatically as possible that the idea of rule by a minority of Guardians who are supposed to possess exceptional knowledge and virtue is, I believe, deeply flawed both morally and empirically. But to make that case would deflect us from the problem that we democrats need to confront.[1] Consequently, I am going to assume that in a democratic system, as in any other, it is reasonable to ask that the rulers—the citizens—be politically competent; that is, they should possess adequate knowledge of what they want their government to achieve, and a predisposition to act in ways intended to bring it about.

Even this formulation, however, immediately suggests a deep and difficult problem. Whose or what interests or good do we expect our citizens to seek?[2] The most usual answers fall roughly into two categories, which might be called, respectively, the broad or classical view and the narrow or modern view. The broad view is that citizens should seek the good of some larger collectivity of which they are a part: the *polis;* the good of all; the general good; the public interest; the general welfare; the interests of their class, country, people, and so on.

Applying this view to the modern democratic citizen often produces a portrait like this: The good citizen is highly concerned about public affairs and political life; well informed about issues and, where these are relevant choices, candidates and parties; engaged often with fellow citizens in deliberations on public matters; an active participant in efforts to influence governmental decisions by voting, communicating views to public officials, attending political meetings, and the like; and in all these activities strongly motivated by a desire to foster the public good or general welfare.

It would be hard to find an observer familiar with modern political life who would contend that many citizens in democratic countries actually measure up to this idealized portrait. Most citizens, indeed, appear to fall far short of it. Moreover, when applied to the citizen of a modern democratic country one potentially lethal weakness in the classical view is immediately apparent: it took for granted that the citizen was a member of a single monistic polity. Today, however, innumerable communities exist to which a citizen might be attached, ranging from one's city to humankind. This multiplicity of communities, attachments, and loyalties is particularly extensive in our modern and postmodern world. Thus, the classical view provides no answer to the question: assuming that citizens ought to seek the "public good," of *which* public should they seek the good?[3]

2. THE GOOD CITIZEN AS RATIONAL EGOIST

A much narrower view, one more consistent with modern egoism and individualism, is that each citizen should (or in some versions, as an empirical matter does) seek to foster the interests or good of oneself, stretching "self," perhaps, to include other persons with whom one closely identifies, such as family and friends. According to one common version of the narrow view, the "public" good consists, then, of the total of all the individual interests, which have to be summed up, aggregated, or integrated according to a justifiable rule or principle like majority rule.[4]

The narrow view shares much with the spirit and substance of the classical view. For example, it allows for the possibility that individuals may have an interest in protecting or advancing the ends of a larger community. Indeed, common observation indicates that they almost certainly will at times. Because of the importance of political life, they would also feel a high level of concern with public matters, actively engage in political affairs, deliberate extensively with fellow citizens, strive to acquire adequate knowledge, and be strongly predisposed to participate as fully as possible in political life.

If we adopt three reasonable assumptions, however, the narrow view makes substantially lighter demands on citizens and therefore on civic education: It is easier for citizens to acquire an adequate understanding of their own interests than of the general good. Their incentives for acting to achieve their own interests are likely to be much stronger than their incentives for striving to achieve the good of a more inclusive group. And if citizens understand their own interests, then their natural egoism ensures that they also have sufficiently strong incentives to seek these interests.

Given these assumptions, the problem of competence is reduced to a problem of knowledge, not of incentives, predispositions, or civic virtue. On the broad view, this happy coincidence of knowledge and incentives does not exist. For even if citizens know what would be in the general interest, they may lack strong incentives to seek it. Knowledge of what is in the best interests of "all" is one thing; acting to achieve it is quite another. What is more, if some citizens believe that their own interests conflict with the general good, then their incentives to achieve the general good will be drastically weakened. Given a conflict between their own interests and the public good, evidently civic virtue would require them to act altruistically. One who believes that people do sometimes act altruistically might reasonably conclude nonetheless that incentives for acting altruistically are in general considerably weaker than incentives for acting in a more self-interested way.

3. NOT GOOD BUT GOOD ENOUGH: THE ADEQUATE CITIZEN

After an accumulation of more than four decades of studies of political participation, one is forced to conclude that, although either the classical view or the narrower modern view of the citizen as the active rational egoist might serve as ideals, neither can be taken as a satisfactory *description* of the average citizen in democratic countries. Although there are variations among democratic countries (notably on turnout in elections), the evidence seems to show that in all democratic countries the average citizen falls far short of the standards of the good citizen as portrayed in either the classical or modern version. Only a minority of citizens are deeply interested in politics, and, except for voting, even fewer are actively engaged in political life, whether by attempting to persuade others to vote for a candidate, working for a political party, attending political meetings and rallies, or joining political organizations. And the average citizen's knowledge of political issues and candidates is pretty skimpy.

Faced with the evidence now available, suppose that we lower our sights somewhat by aiming for the *good enough* or *adequate* citizen. We replace the loftier idea of goodness, so to speak, with the more down-to-earth conception of adequacy. But what is a good-enough citizen? Suppose we agree that an adequate citizen would possess sufficiently strong incentives to acquire some undefined minimal level of knowledge of the citizen's own interests and of the political choices most likely to advance them (or least likely to damage them); and to induce the citizen to act with the intention of carrying out these choices in political life.

Do the practices and institutions of modern democratic countries tend to produce the good-enough citizen? The evidence suggests to me that they do not. Consequently, a challenge confronts us democrats. Unless we are prepared to accept a considerable depreciation in the value of democracy, we need to discover genuinely feasible ways of raising citizen competence.

4. THE CONVENTIONAL SOLUTION OF MODERN DEMOCRACIES

The general solution to the problem of citizen competence in modern democratic countries appears to me to be something like this: Most citizens receive a level of formal education sufficient to ensure political literacy. Their political understanding is further increased by the widespread availability of relevant and low-cost information supplied by the media and political leaders competing for office and organized in political parties. In their adversarial competition for votes, leaders are compelled to supply information on which citizens can make informed judgments about the policies, programs, and proposals of parties and elected leaders, as well as the trustworthiness, honesty, ability, and other relevant personal or organizational characteristics of political leaders. Armed with information of this kind, citizens may hold elected officials or parties accountable in a succeeding election. Because political leaders know they will be held accountable, they have strong incentives for following through on their campaign commitments.

That there is a good measure of truth in this portrayal probably no one would deny. It is more valid as a description of accountability over the long run than over the short run. In periods as short as the interval between elections that most abstract models of voting choice assume, accountability is often weak. But over a series of elections, persistent stability or sizable changes in public opinion are more or less mirrored in stability and change in leaders' policies and proposals.

It would be misleading to assume that voters' choices in elections necessarily reflect informed opinions about specific policies. However, we can reasonably interpret elections as aggregations of voters' judgments about the performance of the parties or leaders in power, which voters appraise in light of their judgments about the recent, current, and expected future situation of themselves and others with whose well-being they are concerned. Voters do not need detailed information about specific policies to conclude that things are not going well and to place the blame on the government. Political competition induces political leaders to respond to such moods. In the medium term, political leaders and government policies tend to persist if voters are more or less contented, and they tend to change when discontent grows. At a minimum, in democratic countries over the medium run of several elections, political leaders and government policies are not imposed against the clear preferences of a majority of voters.

5. THREE DEVELOPMENTS THAT THREATEN THE CONVENTIONAL SOLUTION

Three interrelated developments cast doubt on the continuing adequacy of the conventional solution.

Changes in Scale   Actions that significantly affect the lives of people are made over larger and larger areas that include more and more people within their boundaries. For citizens in democratic countries to gain influence over these increasingly remote actions often requires shifting controls away from smaller to larger political units. It may even require that new and much larger associations be created, as with the European Community and its own expanding boundaries.

This is not to say that an increase in the territorial scale of governments is inevitable, a universal trend, or by any means irreversible. Witness the creation of regional governments in Italy, the increased authority of local powers in Belgium and France, the strength of movements for devolution or independence in Quebec and Scotland, not to mention the dramatic breakup of the central state in the Soviet Union and Yugoslavia. The point is, however, that when a government cannot significantly influence actors who greatly and persistently affect the lives of its citizens, but act outside its boundaries, one solution is to shift decisions away from the existing governmental unit to some larger and more inclusive unit, whether a territorial government in the conventional sense, an association of governments bound by treaty arrangements, or what not.

Complexity   The average level of formal education has risen in all democratic countries, and probably it will continue to rise. If the cognitive difficulty of public matters were more or less static, the increase in levels of education could be chalked up as a net gain for civic competence. The problem is, however, that the difficulty of understanding public affairs has also increased and may have outstripped the gains from higher levels of education.

The major cause of increased cognitive difficulty is that public matters have become more complex. Although the idea of increasing (or decreasing) complexity is difficult to make precise, it could be shown more rigorously than I shall attempt here that over the course of the last half century or so in every democratic country the number of different matters relevant to politics, government, and the state has increased, to the point, indeed, where literally no single person can be expert in them all—in more than a few, in fact.

Cognitive difficulty is increased not just by the sheer number but also by the *internal* complexity of issues and policies within a given domain. Moreover, the diversity of considerations that bear on policy decisions, whether in a broad domain (like foreign affairs) or in a narrower field within that domain (foreign economic aid, for example), makes it difficult or impossible to generalize usefully for judgments about policy A to judgments about policy B. Then too, policies change over time, and they change at different rates in different spheres of policy, sometimes slowly and incrementally, sometimes abruptly and dramatically. Finally, policy decisions ordinarily require judgments about tradeoffs—how much of x we shall give up to yield more of y. Not only are these judgments fraught with uncertainty, but also, in important (though not all) respects, they are not strictly empirical in character: for example, how much should we pay in higher gasoline taxes in order to reduce consumption and thus pollution?

Ironically, the sheer complexity of public affairs means that experts are generally no more competent over a range of policies than ordinary citizens. Indeed, they are likely to be even less competent. Their narrowness of outlook, understanding, and values; their idiosyncratic biases reflecting their own field of specialization; their unwarranted confidence in the applicability of a theory, model, or style of thinking that is at best valid only under certain very limited conditions; their all-too-human tendency to force highly complex phenomena to fit the Procrustean bed of a highly specialized framework; their blindness to the impact of their own ideology on their analysis; their unwillingness or inability to recognize the limits of their own expertise—these qualities often drastically impair the judgments of experts.

Communications   As everyone knows, the social and technical framework of human communication in advanced countries has undergone extraordinary changes during this century: telephone, radio, television, interactive television, fax, opinion surveys almost instantaneous with events, focus groups, techniques by which advertisers, politicians, political advisers, and others can make sophisticated analyses of public responses and strategies for manipulating it, and so on and so on.

It is surely the case that with changes in the technology of communications the sheer amount of available information about political matters, at all levels of complexity, has increased enormously in democratic countries in this century. It is also true, no doubt, that the increasing supply has been accompanied by lower costs to consumers of information. To this extent, political information may be more widely available than ever before.

Nevertheless, an increased availability of information does not necessarily lead to greater competence or heightened understanding: as we have just seen, scale, complexity, and the greater quantity of information itself impose ever stronger demands on the capacities of citizens.

6. SOME CONSEQUENCES

The consequences for citizen competence of changes in scale, complexity, and communications technology are several.

Need for Theoretical Understanding The *effects* of remote decisions may be directly experienced, as is the case when decisions in Tokyo that produce a more competitive automobile result indirectly in the layoff of automobile workers in Turin or Detroit. But for *understanding* causes and making competent judgments about possible policies for controlling or remedying the effects, direct experience is a poor guide. Insofar as understanding is possible within the limits of existing knowledge, to apprehend the causal connection between remote events and immediate experience would require citizens to search for and understand reliable and theoretically relevant information that simply cannot be gained entirely from direct experience, if it can be gained at all. To the extent that citizens can no longer depend on direct experience to provide most of what is required for competent judgments about public affairs and must rely instead on indirect theoretical constructs, however crude these may be, the *costs* of gaining relevant information also rise, often perhaps to levels beyond the reach of ordinary citizens.

In one respect, however, citizens could be fully as competent as experts or leaders, if not more so. I say *could* be, not *are*, because to become so would require some institutional innovations. What I have in mind is the complexity arising from the fact that, as I said a moment ago, virtually all policy decisions require judgments about *tradeoffs*. Later on, I want to mention a promising innovation for appraising tradeoffs, which at the very least deserves some systematic experimentation.

Egoism, Altruism, and Conflicts of Interest.[5] When the population and territory of a political unit greatly increase, several interrelated changes take place that drastically reduce the prospects for the practice of civic virtue among the citizens of the larger unit. First, the larger a collectivity, the more likely it is to contain diversities and as a consequence conflicts of interest. Moreover, as the number of persons increases, knowledge of "the public good" necessarily becomes more theoretical and less practical. For any citizen to know all the other citizens concretely becomes more and more difficult. Beyond some limit—a limit that on the scale of a country, let alone a transnational entity like

NATO or the EC, is infinitesimally small—concrete knowledge of others is flatly impossible. Beyond infinitesimally small limits, then, the "community" is no longer a body of concrete human beings actually known to one another, much less an association of friends; it is an aggregate of distant persons called class, nation, ethnic group, country, humanity, or what not. How is a citizen to apprehend the interests of the people who comprise aggregates like these?

It follows that, as the number of persons in the aggregate increases, valid knowledge of what the common interest or the general good might be in specific situations must necessarily depend less and less on one's own direct experience, and more and more on images and abstractions.

What is more, as diversities show up, cleavages develop, and political conflicts appear, differences between the general good and the perceived interests of oneself or one's group become an increasingly common feature of political life. From Aristotle onward, it has been commonly assumed that a predisposition for acting justly toward others could be adequately supported by strong habits and social ties that promote *empathic understanding*, acquired through love, affection, friendship, neighborliness, and the like. Empathic understanding means putting oneself in the other's shoes, sensing how the other sees, experiences, and interprets the world. Given sufficiently powerful feelings of empathic understanding, civic virtue blends imperceptibly with egoism and may be sustained even if one's egoistic interests occasionally take a few hard knocks.

What is remarkable about the affective bonds that promote empathic understanding, however, is the extent to which they depend on intimacy and direct relationships, which in turn can exist only within small-scale groups. Thus, the large scale of modern and postmodern societies poses both cognitive and affective obstacles to acquiring predispositions toward civic virtue.

Discussion and Deliberation   As the scale of a political association increases, the number of fellow citizens with whom one can directly engage in discussion and deliberation necessarily constitutes a smaller proportion of all citizens. Moreover, because of the greater complexity of public issues, the level of competence that a group of average citizens can achieve merely by deliberating among themselves is severely limited. Consequently, if deliberation is to enhance the competence of citizens and not merely ratify prevailing opinion, it will need the participation of experts. Here again, the institutions of democratic countries seem to me inadequate.

The Weakness of Trustworthy Surrogates   No one can know enough to make a fully informed judgment on every issue one confronts. In order to arrive at judgments about most matters, everyone must necessarily rely on trusted surrogates. A *trusted* surrogate, however, may not be a *trustworthy* surrogate: that is, one who justifies the trust. If citizens could confidently depend on trustworthy surrogates, some of the obstacles to civic competence imposed by changes in complexity, scale, and communications technology would be less formidable.

7. SOME POSSIBILITIES[6]

Giving Authority to Smaller Units Within Larger Units   In thinking about the impact of increased scale, we need to distinguish between an increase in the territorial scale of a *problem*—sources of pollution, for example—and an increase in the territorial scale of *government* with authority to address the problem. To be sure, the first generally creates some justification for the second. But surely it does not follow that a *single* territorial government should always be endowed with authority sufficient for the task. *The task might sometimes be better left to smaller territorial governments.*[7]

Citizen Assemblies as Trustworthy Surrogates   Several writers have argued that assemblies of randomly selected citizens engaged in deliberation, reflection, and recommendation would constitute important institutions for civic participation and for the enhanced competence of the participants. But it is also important to emphasize that citizen assemblies could serve as trustworthy surrogates for the preponderant majority of citizens who would not participate in the assemblies. Randomly selected citizen assemblies need not replace legislatures; instead, they could provide what opinion surveys cannot: judgments arrived at by a body of well-informed citizens after deliberation assisted by experts.

How to Make Theoretically Relevant Information More Accessible   By means of telecommunications, the knowledge and skills of scholars and specialists could be made readily accessible to citizens at varying levels of cognitive difficulty. Although the question of how to organize this effort is formidable, a solution that might be widely applied in decisions requiring highly technical knowledge would be for citizen assemblies to screen and select experts whom they could trust to participate in their behalf. In effect, the citizen assembly would identify a trusted surrogate.

Telecommunications and Citizen Participation   Some writers have explored ways of using interactive television as a means of deliberation, discussion, and communication among citizens and between citizens and officials.[8] These possibilities surely deserve further investigation and experimentation.

Empathic Understanding   It is especially difficult to acquire an empathic understanding of others whose strangeness is alien and threatening. Consequently, citizens in hitherto relatively homogeneous countries are likely to find it particularly difficult to sustain a sense of a common good, and even a concern for fundamental human and democratic rights, when they witness a dramatic increase in the number of people in their midst who are ethnically or racially distinct. This problem, which has been central to the political life of the United States for two centuries and more often than not has profoundly impaired its democratic potential, has now entered into political life in European democracies. Very likely, the severity of the problem will increase. Indeed, it may well become the central political issue in democratic politics in the coming century.

The question arises, therefore, as to whether and how it may be possible to promote a more widespread capacity for empathic understanding among citizens. In this task, clearly both the schools and the media—television in particular—can play crucial roles. Yet although it is easy to call attention to their importance, feasible solutions are harder to come by. If, as seems likely, highly divisive conflicts over ethnicity move to center stage in the older democracies as well as the newer ones, then few questions will be more urgently in need of research and appropriate action.

It is on this tentative note, then, that I wish to conclude. My suggestions are obviously not meant to be taken as full-scale designs; all require further investigation and experimentation. No doubt, too, there are many other possibilities, perhaps some even more feasible and effective than the ones I have briefly described here.

My aim, however, is not to set forth solutions to the problem of citizen competence, but rather to pose it as a question for bold inquiry and judicious experimentation.

NOTES

1. My reasons for thinking so can be found in *Democracy and Its Critics* (New Haven, Conn.: Yale University Press, 1989).
2. It would be possible to distinguish "interests" and "good," but I shall not attempt to do so here.
3. For one attempt to confront this problem, see my "Dilemmas of Pluralist Democracy: The Public Good of Which Public?" in Peter Koslowski, ed., *Individual Liberty and Democratic Decision-making* (Tübingen: J.C.B. Mohr, 1987).
4. I do not believe that an intellectually satisfactory solution to the problem of "aggregating" or "composing" diverse interests has yet been discovered. The conventional solution in democratic systems is majority rule. What a principle of "majority rule" requires is by no means clear; contradictory interpretations abound. Moreover, most democratic countries have modified the principle in practice, usually in favor of processes that are more consensual than straight majority rule.
5. The following is adapted from *Dilemmas of Pluralist Democracy: Autonomy vs. Control* (New Haven: Yale University Press, 1982), pp. 143–148.
6. A fuller discussion with citations to relevant works can be found in the book cited in note 1 above.
7. Or to the market. However, I assume for purposes of this discussion that the market is not an adequate solution.
8. See Jeffrey B. Abramson, F. Christopher Arterton, and Gary R. Orren, *The Electronic Commonwealth: The Impact of New Media Technologies on Democratic Politics* (New York: Basic Books, 1988).

CHAPTER 28

On Restoring the Moral Voice

AMITAI ETZIONI

Audiences who are quite enthusiastic about the communitarian message, which I carry these days to all who will listen, cringe when I turn to discuss the moral voice. One of my best friends took me aside and gently advised me to speak of "concern" rather than morality, warning that otherwise I would "sound like the Moral Majority." During most call-in radio shows in which I participate, sooner or later some caller exclaims that "nobody should tell us what to do." *Time* magazine, in an otherwise highly favorable cover story on communitarian thinking, warned against busybodies "humorlessly imposing on others arbitrary (meaning their own) standards of behavior, health and thought."[1] Studies of an American suburb by sociologist M. P. Baumgartner[2] found a disturbing unwillingness of people to make moral claims on one another. Most people did not feel it was their place to express their convictions when someone did something that was wrong.

At the same time, the overwhelming majority of Americans, public opinion polls show, recognize that our moral fabric has worn rather thin. As noted in Chapter 14, a typical finding is that, while schoolteachers in the 1940s listed as their top problems talking out of turn, making noise, cutting line, and littering, they now list drug abuse, alcohol abuse, pregnancy, and suicide. Wanton taking of life, often for a few bucks to buy a vial of crack or to gain a pair of sneakers, is much more common in the United States than it is in other civilized societies and than it used to be in America. Countless teenagers bring infants into the world to satisfy their ego needs, with little attention to the long-term consequences for the children, themselves, or society.

How can people recognize the enormous moral deficit we face and at the same time be so reluctant to lay moral claims on one another? One reason is that they see immorality not in their friends and neighborhoods but in practically every other place. (In the same vein that they find members of Congress in general to be corrupt but often reelect "their" representative because he or she is "okay," just as they complain frequently about physicians but find their doctor above reproach.) This phenomenon may be referred to as moral myopia, for which there seems to be no ready cure.

In addition, many Americans seem to have internalized the writings of Dale Carnegie on how to win friends and influence in society: you are supposed to work hard at flattering the other person and never chastise anyone. Otherwise, as generations of Americans have been told by their parents, you may lose a "friend" and set back your networking. A study found that when college students were asked whether or not they would tell their best friend if, in their eyes, the person the friend had chosen to wed was utterly unsuitable, most said they would refrain. They feared losing the friend. They would rather the friend go ahead and in effect be hurt rather than take the risk of endangering the friendship. This clearly indicates that they ranked their fear of losing a friend above the commitment to help that very friend. Also, Daniel Patrick Moynihan has argued convincingly in his recent article in *The American Scholar*,[3] "Defining Deviance Down," that people have been so bombarded with evidence of social ills that they have developed moral calluses, which make them relatively inured to immorality.

When Americans do turn to contemplate moral reform, many are rather a-sociological: they believe that our problem is primarily one of individual conscience. If youngsters would be taught again to tell right from wrong by their families and schools, if churches could reach them again, our moral/social order would be on the mend. They focus on what is only one, albeit important, component of the moral equation: the inner voice.

In the process, many Americans disregard the crucial role of the community in reinforcing the individual's moral commitments. To document the importance of the community, I must turn to the question: what constitutes a moral person?

I build here on the writings of Harry Frankfurt, Albert Hirschman, and others who argued that humans differ from animals in that, while both species experience impulses, humans have the capacity to pass judgments on their impulses. I choose my words carefully: it is not suggested that humans can "control" their impulses, but that they can defer responding to them long enough to evaluate the behavior toward which they feel inclined. Once this evaluation takes place, sometimes the judgments win, sometimes the impulses. If the judgments always took precedence, we would be saintly; if the impulses always won, we would be psychopaths or animals. The human fate is a constant struggle between the noble and the debased parts of human nature. While I reach this conclusion from social science findings and observations, I am often challenged by those who exclaim, "Why, this is what religion taught us!" or as one heckler cried out, "What about the rest of the catechism?" As I see it, although some may find it surprising that religions contain social truths, I see no reason to doubt that the distillation of centuries of human experience by those entrusted historically with moral education resulted in some empirically solid, sociologically valid observations.

It is to the struggle between judgments and impulses that the moral voice of the community speaks. The never-ending struggle within the human soul over which course to follow is not limited to intra-individual dialogues between impulses that tempt us to disregard our marital vows, be deceitful, and be selfish—and the values we previously internalized, which warn us against yielding to these temptations. In making our moral choices (to be precise, our choices between moral and immoral conduct rather than among moral claims), we are influenced by the approbations and censure of others, especially of those with whom we have close relations—family members, friends, neighbors, in short, our communities.

It may not flatter our view of ourselves, but human nature is such that if these community voices speak in unison and with clarity (without being shrill), we are much more likely to follow our inner judgments than if these voices are silent, conflicted, or speak too softly. Hence, the pivotal import of the voice of communities in raising the moral level of their members.

I need to respond to various challenges to this line of argumentation, beyond the general unarticulated uneasiness it seems to evoke in a generation that has largely lost its moral course and voice. Some argue that the reliance on community points to conformism, to "other-directed" individuals who seek merely to satisfy whatever pleases their community. This is not the vision evoked here. The community voice as depicted here is not the only voice that lays claims on individuals as to the course they ought to follow. Rather, it is a voice that speaks in addition to their inner one. When the community's voice and the inner voice are in harmony, this is not a case of conformism, of one "party" yielding to the other, but one of two tributaries flowing into the same channel. (For example, if I firmly believe that it is wrong to leave my children unattended and so do my neighbors, and I stay home, this is hardly an instance of conformism.) If these two voices conflict, I must pass judgment not only vis-à-vis my impulses (should I yield or should I follow the dictates of my conscience?) but also on whether or not I will heed my fellow community members or follow my own lead. In short, the very existence of a community moral voice does not necessarily spell conformism. This occurs only if and when one automatically or routinely sets aside personal judgments to grant supremacy to the community, which happens when personal voices are weak, but this is not a congenital condition of the existence of a community voice. To put it differently, whereas conformism is a danger, so is the absence of the reinforcing effects of the communal voice. Hence, the antidote to conformism is not to undermine the community's voice but to seek to ensure that the personal voice is also firmly instilled.

Above all, it must be noted that, although the moral voice urges and counsels us, it is congenitally unable to force us. Whatever friends, neighbors, ministers, or community leaders say, the ultimate judgment call is up to the acting person. . . .

Others argue that the community voice is largely lost because of American pluralism. Individuals are subject to the voices of numerous communities, each pulling in a different direction and thus neutralizing one another. Or the cacophony is so high, no clear voice can be heard. The notion that no community is right and all claims have equal standing, a view especially championed by multiculturalists, further diminishes the claim of the moral voice.

Although all this is true, there is no way to return to the days of simple, homogeneous communities. Those communities quite often were found to be rather oppressive. The contemporary solution, if not salvation, lies in seeking and developing an evolving framework of shared values, which all subcultures will be expected to endorse and support without losing their distinct identities and subcultures. Thus, Muslim-Americans can be free to follow the dictates of their religion, cherish their music and cuisine, and be proud of select parts of their history. (No group should be encouraged to embrace all of its history.) At the same time, they (and all other communities that make up the American society) need to accept the dignity of the individual, the basic value of liberty, the democratic form of government, and other such core values. On these matters we should expect and encourage all communities to speak in one voice.

Other critics argue that the essence of individual freedom is that every person follow his or her own course and that social institutions leave us alone. More technically, economists write about the primacy of our preferences and scoff at intellectuals and ideologues who want to impose their "tastes" on others. In honoring this pivotal value of free society, we must be careful not to confuse allusions to freedom from the state, its coercion and controls, with freedom from the moral urging of our fellow community members. We can be as opposed to state intervention and regulation as a diehard libertarian and still see a great deal of merit in people encouraging one another to do what is right. (Technically speaking, the reference here is not to frustrating people and preventing them from acting on their preferences, which is what the coercive state does, but rather to appealing to their better self to change or re-order their preferences.)

Indeed, a strong case can be made that it is precisely the bonding together of community members that enables us to remain independent of the state. The anchoring of individuals in viable families, webs of friendships, faith communities, and neighborhoods—in short, in communities—best sustains their ability to resist the pressure of the state. The absence of these social foundations opens isolated individuals to totalitarian pressures. (This, of course, is the point Tocqueville makes in *Democracy in America*.)

In my attempts to dialogue with students and others about the moral voice, I have borrowed a leaf from Joel Feinberg's seminal work *Offense to Others*.[4] In his book, Feinberg provides a list of activities others may engage in that he believes we will find increasingly offensive. He asks us to imagine we are riding on a full bus on which we cannot readily leave or change seats. He then presents a series of hypothetical scenes that would cause offense, ranging from the person(s) next to us playing loud music to scratching a metallic surface that makes a whining noise, handling what looks like a real grenade, exposing himself, engaging in oral sex, and so on.

I am interested not so much in the question of what members of the community find tolerable versus unbearable, but what will make them speak up. Hence, I asked students and colleagues to "imagine you are in a supermarket and a mother beats the daylights out of a three-year-old child—would you speak up?" (I say "mother" because I have learned that if I just say "someone," most of my respondents state that they would not react because they feared that the other person might clobber them.) Practically everyone I asked responded that they would not speak up. They would at most try to "distract" the mother, "find out what the child really did," and so on. However, when I asked them to "imagine you are resting on the shore of a pristine lake; a picnicking family, about to depart, leaves behind a trail of trash—would you suggest they clean up after themselves?" Here again, many demurred, but a fair number were willing to consider saying something.

Possibly, my informal sample is skewed. However, it seems to me that something else is at work here: American society has a consensus-building grand dialogue about the environment. Although sharp disagreements about numerous details (for instance, about the relative standing of spotted owls versus loggers) remain, there is a basic consensus that we must be mindful of the environment and cannot trash it. However, we have had neither a grand dialogue nor a new consensus about the way to treat children. This would suggest one more reason why our moral voice is so feeble and reluctant: too many of us, too often, are no longer sure what to state.

A return to a firm moral voice will require a major town hall meeting of sorts, the kind we have when Americans spend billions of hours in bowling alleys, next to water coolers, on call-in shows, to form a new consensus, the kind we had about the environment, civil rights, and excessive general regulation, and are now beginning to have about gay rights. This time we need to agree with one another that the common good requires that we speak up while we are also enunciating the values for which we speak. To reiterate, heeding such a consensus should never be automatic; we need to examine the values the community urges upon us to determine whether or not they square with our conscience, and the basic values we sense there is a compelling reason no person or community has a right to violate. However, here the focus is on the other side of the coin: it is not enough to individually be able to tell right from wrong, as crucial as this distinction is. We must also be willing to encourage others to attend to values that we as a community share and ought to seek actively to uphold.

NOTES

1. "Busybodies and Crybabies," *Time*, vol. 138, issue 6, August 12, 1991.
2. Baumgartner, M. P. *The Moral Order of a Suburb*, New York: Oxford University Press, 1988.
3. Moynihan, Patrick. "Defining Deviance Down," *The American Scholar*, Winter 1993.
4. Feinberg, Joel. *Offense to Others*, New York: Oxford University Press, 1988.

CHAPTER 29

Communitarian vs. Individualistic Capitalism

LESTER THUROW

In March 1990 the two biggest business groups in the world, Japan's Mitsubishi and Germany's Daimler-Benz-Deutsche Bank, held a secret meeting in Singapore to talk about a global alliance. Among other things, both were interested in discussing how to expand their market share in civilian aircraft production. From the U.S. perspective, everything about that Singapore meeting was highly illegal, violating both antitrust and banking laws. In the United States, banks cannot own industrial firms, and businesses cannot sit down behind closed doors to plan joint strategies. Those who do so get thrown into jail for extended periods of time. Yet today Americans cannot force the rest of the world to play the economic game as they think it should be played. The game will by played under international, not American, rules.

With economic competition between communism and capitalism over, this other competition—between two different forms of capitalism—has quickly taken over the economic playing field. Using a distinction first made by Harvard's George C. Lodge, the individualistic, Anglo-Saxon, British-American form of capitalism is going to face off against the communitarian German and Japanese variants of capitalism: The "I" of the United States or the United Kingdom versus "Das Volk" and "Japan Inc." The essential difference between the two is the relative stress placed on communitarian and individualistic values as the best route to economic success.

SHAREHOLDERS AND STAKEHOLDERS

The United States and Britain champion individualistic values: the brilliant entrepreneur, Nobel Prize winners, large wage differentials, individual responsibility for skills, easy-to-fire/easy-to-quit, profit maximization, hostile mergers and takeovers. Their hero is the Lone Ranger.

In contrast, Germany and Japan trumpet communitarian values: business groups, social responsibility for skills, teamwork, firm loyalty, growth-promoting industry, and government strategies. Anglo-Saxon firms are profit maximizers; Japanese and German business firms play a game best termed "strategic conquest." Americans believe in "consumer economics"; the Japanese believe in "producer economics."

In the Anglo-Saxon variant of capitalism, the individual is supposed to have a personal economic strategy for success, whereas the business firm is to have an economic strategy reflecting the wishes of its individual shareholders. Because shareholders want income to maximize their lifetime consumption, their firms must be profit maximizers. For the profit-maximizing firm, customer and employee relations are merely a means of achieving higher profits for the shareholders. Using this formula, we find that lower wages equal higher profits—and wages are to be beaten down where possible. When not needed, employees are to be laid off. For their part, workers in the Anglo-Saxon system are expected to change employers whenever opportunities exist to earn higher wages elsewhere.

Whereas in Anglo-Saxon firms the shareholder is the only stakeholder, in Japanese business firms employees are seen as the No. 1 stakeholder, customers are No. 2, and the shareholders are a distant No. 3 whose dividend payouts are low. Because employees are the prime stakeholders, higher employee wages are a central goal of the firm in Japan. The firm can be seen as a "value-added maximizer" rather than as a "profit maximizer." Profits will be sacrificed to maintain either wages or employment.

Workers in the communitarian system join a company team and are then considered successful as part of that team. The key decision in an individual's personal strategy is to join the "right" team.

In the United States or Great Britain, employee turnover rates are viewed positively. Firms are getting rid of unneeded labor when they fire workers, and individuals are moving to higher wage opportunities when they quit. Job switching, voluntary or involuntary, is almost a synonym for efficiency. In both Germany and Japan job switching is far less prevalent. In fact, many Japanese firms still refer to voluntary resignations as "treason."

COALESCING FOR SUCCESS

Beyond personal and firm strategies, communitarian capitalists believe in having strategies at two additional levels. Business groups such as Japan's Mitsui Group or Germany's Deutsche Bank Group are expected to have a collective strategy in which companies are financially interlocked and work together to strengthen each other's activities. At the top of the pyramid of Japanese business groups are the major *zaibatsu* (Mitsui group, twenty-three member firms; Mitsubishi group, twenty-eight member firms; Sumatomo group, twenty-one member firms; Fuji group, twenty-nine member firms; Sanwa group, thirty-nine member firms; and Dai-Ichi Kangyo group, forty-five member firms). The members of each group will own a controlling block of shares in each of the firms in the group. In addition, each member firm will in turn have a group of smaller customers and suppliers, the *keiretsu*, grouped around it. Hitachi has 688 firms in its family; Toyota has 175 primary members and 4,000 secondary members.

Similar patterns exist in Germany. The Deutsche Bank directly owns 10 percent or more of the shares in seventy companies: It owns 28 percent of Germany's largest company, Daimler-Benz; 10 percent of Europe's largest reinsurance company, Munich Rai; 25 percent of Europe's largest department store chain, Karstady; 30 percent of Germany's largest construction company, Philipp Holzmann; and 21 percent of Europe's largest sugar producer, Sudzucker. Through its trust department, Deutsche Bank indirectly controls many more shares that don't have to be publicly disclosed.

When the Arabs threatened to buy a controlling interest in Mercedes Benz a few years ago, the Deutsche Bank intervened on behalf of the German economy to buy a controlling interest. Now the bank protects the managers of Mercedes Benz from the raids of the financial Vikings: it frees the managers from the tyranny of the stock market, with its emphasis on quarterly profits, and it helps plan corporate strategies and raise the money to carry out these strategies. But it also fires the managers if Mercedes Benz slips in the auto market, and it prevents the managers from engaging in self-serving activities such as poison pills or golden parachutes, which do not enhance the company's long-term prospects.

GOVERNMENT'S ROLE IN ECONOMIC GROWTH

Both Europe and Japan believe that government has a role to play in economic growth. An example of this philosophy put into practice is the pan-European project called Airbus Industries, a civilian aircraft manufacturer owned by the British, French, German, and Spanish governments, designed to break the American monopoly and get Europe back into civilian aircraft manufacturing. Today it is a success, with 20 percent of the aircraft market and announced plans to double production and capture one-third of the worldwide market by the mid-1990s.

Airbus's penetration into the aircraft manufacturing industry has severely affected U.S. manufacturers. In 1990 Boeing's market share of new orders dropped to 45 percent—the first time in decades it had been below 50 percent.

McDonnell Douglas's market share has been reduced from 30 percent to 15 percent. In this particular industry, a greater European share can only mean a smaller market share for Boeing and the demise of McDonnell Douglas.

The Europeans now have a number of pan-European strategic efforts under-way to catch up with the United States and Japan. Each is designed to help European firms compete in some major industry. European governments spend from 5 ½ percent (Italy) to 1 ¾ percent (Britain) of the GNP [Gross National Product] aiding industry. If the United States had spent what Germany spends (2 ½ percent of GNP), $140 billion would have gone to help U.S. industries in 1991. In Spain, where the economy grew more rapidly than any other in Europe in the 1980s, government-owned firms produce at least half of the GNP. In France and Italy, the state sector accounts for one-third of the GNP.

SOCIAL MARKET VERSUS MARKET ECONOMY

Germany, the dominant European economic power, sees itself as having a "social market" economy and not just a "market" economy. State and federal governments in Germany own more shares in more industries—airlines, autos, steel, chemicals, electric power, transportation—than any noncommunist country on the face of the globe. Public investments such as Airbus Industries are not controversial political issues. Privatization is not sweeping Germany as it did Great Britain.

In Germany, government is believed to have an important role to play in ensuring that everyone has the skills necessary to participate in the market. Its socially financed apprenticeship system is the envy of the world. Social welfare policies are seen as a necessary part of a market economy. Unfettered capitalism is believed to generate levels of income inequality that are unacceptable.

The United States, by contrast, sees social welfare programs as a regrettable necessity brought about by people who will not provide for their own old age, unemployment, or ill health. Continual public discussions remind everyone that the higher taxes required to pay for social welfare systems reduce work incentives for those paying taxes and that social welfare benefits undercut work incentives for those who get them. In the ideal Anglo-Saxon market economy, social welfare policies would not be necessary.

ADMINISTRATIVE GUIDANCE

In Japan, industry representatives working with the Ministry of International Trade and Industry present "visions" as to where the economy should be going. In the past, these visions served as guides to the allocation of scarce foreign exchange or capital flows. Today what the Japanese know as "administrative guidance" is a way of life, and it is used to aim R&D [research and development] funding at key industries. An example can be found in the Japanese strategy on semiconductor chips, which was similar to Europe's Airbus plan in that it was lengthy, expensive, and eventually successful in breaking the dominance of U.S. firms. The government-financed, "very-large-integrated-circuit-chip" research project was just part of a much larger effort in which a combination of patience, large investments, and American mistakes (a reluctance to expand capacity during cyclical downturns) paid off in the end.

The idea of administrative guidance could not be more foreign to the minds of U.S. officials. According to the politically correct language of the Bush administration, the U.S. government had no role in investment funding and had a "legitimate" R&D role only in "precompetitive, generic, enabling technologies." These rules are sometimes violated in practice, but the principle is clear: Governments should protect private property rights, and then get out of the way and let individuals do their thing. Capitalism will spontaneously combust.

HISTORY AS DESTINY

These different conceptions of capitalism flow from very different histories. In the formative years of British capitalism during the nineteenth century, Great Britain did not have to play "catch up" with anyone. As the initiator of the industrial revolution, Great Britain was the most powerful country in the world. Similarly, the United States had a head start in its industrial revolution. Protected by two great oceans, the United States did not feel militarily threatened by Britain's early economic lead. In the last half of the nineteenth century, however, when it was moving faster than Great Britain, Americans could see that they were going to have to catch up without deliberate government efforts to throw more coal into the U.S. economic steam engines.

On the other hand, nineteenth-century Prussia had to catch up with Great Britain if it was not to be overrun in the wars of Europe. Their subjects expected the rulers of the German states to take an active part in fostering the economic growth of their territories. To have its rightful place at the European table, Prussia had to have a modern industrial economy. German capitalism needed help to catch up.

The Japanese system similarly did not occur by accident. Admiral Matthew Perry arrived in the mid-1800s and with a few cannon balls forced Japan to begin trading with the rest of the world. But the mid-nineteenth century was the height of colonialism. If Japan did not develop quickly, it would become a colony of the British, French, Dutch, Germans, or Americans. Economic development was part of national defense—perhaps a more impor-

282

tant part than the army itself, for a modern army could not be built without a modern economy.

In both Germany and Japan, economic strategies were important elements of military strategies for remaining independent and becoming powerful. Governments pushed actively to ensure that the economic combustion took place. They had to increase the intensity of that combustion so that the economic gaps, and hence military gaps, between themselves and their potential enemies could be cut in the shortest possible time. Under these circumstances, it was not surprising that firms were organized along military lines or that the line between public and private disappeared. Government and industry had to work together to design the national economic strategies necessary for national independence. In a very real sense, business firms became the front line of national defense.

U.S. history is very different. Government's first significant economic act—the Interstate Commerce Commission—was passed to prevent the railroads from using their monopoly power to set freight rates that would rip off everyone else. A few decades later, its second significant act—the antitrust laws—was passed to prevent John D. Rockefeller from using his control over the supply of lighting oil to extract everyone else's income. The third major source of government economic activity flowed from the collapse of capitalism in the 1930s, when government had to pick up the resultant mess.

As a result, adversarial relations and suspicions of each other's motives are deeply embedded in American history. Although very different histories have led to very different systems, today those very different systems face off in the same world economy. Let me suggest that the military metaphors that are now so widely used should be replaced with the language of football. Despite the desire to win, football has a cooperative as well as a competitive element. Everyone has to agree on the rules of the game, the referees, and how to split the proceeds. One can want to win and yet remain friends both during and after the game. But what the rest of the world knows as football is known as soccer in the United States. What Americans like about American football— frequent time-outs, lots of huddles, and unlimited substitutions—are not present in world football. It has no time-outs, no huddles, and very limited substitutions. It is a faster game.

CHAPTER 30

Beyond Left and Right:
A New Political Paradigm[1]

DAVID OSBORNE

During the 1980s, a fifty-year trend, in which political innovation tended to take place at the national level, reversed itself. In Washington, politics degenerated into an ideological stalemate between one set of ideas that dated from the 1960s and another that reached even further back for its origins. But out in the cities and states of America, there was a tremendous growth in innovation and experimentation.

The problem is that most political reporters are based in Washington, and they still interpret reality using the labels of the past. When a new initiative or idea is put forth, it is categorized as either liberal, that is, associated with the ideas of people like Hubert Humphrey, Walter Mondale, and Ted Kennedy, or conservative, that is, associated with the ideas of Ronald Reagan and George Bush. If it fits neither of these categories, then it must be moderate.

This process of filtering new ideas through old lenses has blinded us to much of what's going on in American politics. Consider just a few examples. During the 1980s, a governor of a large industrial state created perhaps the most aggressive and most intelligent industrial policy this nation has ever seen. He spent more than $30 million a year—which in a state is a great deal of money—investing in technological innovation. He even went so far as to target these investments to specific technologies in specific regions. In other words, he tried to pick winners. The governor described his approach as follows: "I think government has a role as a partner and a facilitator. Decisions made by private investors and employers are going to create economic growth, but government can be a catalytic agent that can provide the tip-over component in any particular decision. That's where the real interplay between business and government ought to be."

I would argue that most people cannot tell if that is a liberal or a conservative speaking, a Democrat or a Republican. In fact, it was Dick Thornburgh, the Republican governor of Pennsylvania. Most people in Washington call Dick Thornburgh a conservative, but he implemented the most extensive and most expensive industrial policy in the United States in the 1980s.

A second example has to do with education. In the mid-1970s, a group of very liberal, if not radical, educational reformers came up with a new approach to education, a fundamental reform. About ten years later, a liberal Democratic governor in perhaps the most liberal state in the country embraced the idea. It took him four years to get it through the legislature: he had to fight the teachers' unions, the superintendents, and the principals, but he got it through. The state was Minnesota, and the idea was public school choice. If you read the political press, public school choice has been labeled a conservative proposal. But the idea was pioneered by liberals.

A third story concerns welfare policy. In 1986 another governor of a major industrial state released a blue-ribbon report about welfare. It recommended that able-bodied people on welfare be granted a set amount of time—say, three years—to get off welfare voluntarily. If they had not found private-sector jobs, given the training, education, and child care that the report recommended, they would be offered publicly created jobs. And if they would not accept the public jobs, their welfare would simply be cut off.

The commission was created by Mario Cuomo, the governor of New York State. It harkened back to the New Deal, with its emphasis on public jobs rather than public welfare assistance. Yet when Bill Clinton makes virtually the same proposal, the media call it a conservative idea.

Welfare reform, public school choice, and economic policy are not exactly fringe issues, and yet the Washington media consistently mislabel new ideas in all three areas as either conservative or liberal, based not on the ideas but on who advocates them. If the idea is associated with Dick Thornburgh or Jack Kemp, it must be conservative. If it's associated with Mario Cuomo, it must be liberal. And if someone like Bill Clinton says it, well, they're not quite sure where Clinton stands, so it must be moderate.

Such confusion, I think, is one of the reasons why Americans believe Washington is divorced from reality. (I often give talks outside Washington, and I can always count on a big laugh when I describe the District of Columbia as "30 square miles bounded by reality.") Why the confusion? I think it is because there are two ideologies that dominate thinking in Washington, both of which have roots in the past and no longer respond to most of the problems we face. Nor do they capture most of the creative solutions that people around the country have evolved. The first, traditional liberalism—the liberalism that emerged in the 1960s—has one basic impulse. When liberals see a problem, they say, "That problem must have been created by the private sector, and we've got to use the public sector to solve it." So the solution is a public program with public employees using taxpayers' dollars.

Sometime in the 1970s, the American people decided that approach was not working too well, and they rejected it. When Ronald Reagan was elected in 1980, he turned the equation on its head. He said, "The basic problem is not the private sector. The basic problem is government, and the solution is the private sector. If we cut spending, kill programs, deregulate, and get government out of the way as much as possible, the marketplace will solve our problems."

In my view, Reagan's ideology was merely the flip side of traditional liberalism. It was not a new ideology designed to solve the problems of a postindustrial era; it was simply a rejection of liberalism. Everything that traditional liberals were for, Reagan was against, and vice versa. In articulating his politics, Reagan was essentially reaching back to a Jeffersonian vision of a free market economy and a laissez-faire state that dominated American politics in the nineteeth century, before we became an urbanized and industrial economy.

Neither of these ideologies has a whole lot to do with the problems we face today. We live in a global marketplace. Technologies change overnight, and entire industries can be decimated in a matter of years. Thirty years ago, 20 percent of the goods we produced in this country faced foreign competition; by 1980, 70 percent of them did.

When you are in a purely domestic economy, economic policy involves dealing with macroeconomic policy, with changing such quantitative factors as interest rates, fiscal policy, and tax rates. But when you are in a global economy and you are competing with Japan and Germany and the rest of the world, suddenly the qualitative factors become equally important. In global competition, it is not just a matter of how much is produced, it is how well it is produced. It is not just a matter of how much capital you have at what interest rates, it is what kind of capital: Do you have enough patient capital? Do you have enough risk capital? It is not just how many workers you have and what wages they earn: it is how well trained and well educated they are, and how well they work together. It is not just how much research you fund: it is how quickly you can commercialize the fruits of that research.

Issues such as these create all kinds of new challenges for government, challenges that traditional liberals and conservatives are not prepared to deal with. They are issues of microeconomic policy, and microeconomic policy is not on the old map.

Another change that has come with a global economy has been a decline in our standard of living. Our average standard of living—how much the average American makes in real, inflation-adjusted dollars per hour—has gone down since 1973. For wage earners, it has gone down 20 percent. This loss of real income has, in my view, fueled the incredible resistance to taxes that we've seen in this country since 1978. The heart of the tax revolt was not the affluent. The heart of the tax revolt was working- and middle-class wage earners who were feeling the economic squeeze. It is their strong aversion to higher taxes that has put pressure on government to produce more for less, to make government leaner and more effective.

But what do traditional liberals advocate? More government. Historically, the Democratic position has been, "If you want problems solved, if you want public services, it costs money. Big government is expensive, it's bureaucratic, and we have to live with that. If you want it, you have to pay for it." That's an offer the public has been glad to refuse.

In contrast, Reagan conservatives offered less government, less spending, and fewer services. Unfortunately, that did not solve the problem either because, as pollsters show, the tax revolt was not a demand for fewer services. If anything, people want more from government today; they just want it for less. They want services delivered more efficiently and effectively. They want more for less.

DIFFERENT GOVERNMENT

What we need today is not more or less government: we need different government. Outside Washington, beyond the Beltway, mayors and governors have begun to develop ways to deal with the new realities and to give people what they want. These state and local executives are creating a third way, which blends the activism of traditional Democratic politics with the aversion to big government of traditional conservatism.

When I called this third way "a new political paradigm" in *Laboratories of Democracy*, I never dreamed the phrase would become a kind of political slogan in Washington. A paradigm is really nothing more than a set of assumptions about how the world works; it's a worldview. And although there are many different ways to describe the kind of new worldview that our more innovative governors and mayors are beginning to articulate, they all seem to share a few common assumptions. Perhaps the best way to present these assumptions is to contrast the old paradigm with the new. In the old paradigm, government essentially tried to do most things itself. If there was a problem, then the solution must be a government program employing public employees. Today, government can't afford that approach, so governors and mayors often try to act as catalysts. They attempt to get others into motion—private companies, community organizations, neighborhood groups, families. That is why there is so much interest in public–private partnerships today. Government steers, but it allows others to do more of the rowing.

The second assumption is related. In the old paradigm, government used administrative approaches—programs. In fact, the words *government* and *program* are wedded to each other—like ham and eggs. But increasingly, our mayors and governors do not impose programs; they try to restructure markets. When there is a problem they try to solve it by changing the marketplace. They are "market-oriented."

Suppose that a person wanted to buy a house back in 1930. He or she would have had to put 50 percent down and pay off the mortgage in five years.

That is the way banks did business. During the New Deal, however, Franklin Roosevelt created the Federal Housing Administration, which pioneered thirty-year, 20-percent-down mortgages. Then the quasipublic corporations that the federal government created, such as Ginny Mae and Fannie Mae, created a secondary market so that banks could resell these thirty-year mortgages, and the banking industry converted. Now everyone takes 20-percent-down, thirty-year mortgages for granted. That is the kind of market restructuring governors and mayors are reaching for when they approach problems.

The third assumption: in the old paradigm, government was essentially bureaucratic. To get things done, leaders used top-down, centralized bureaucracies, most of which were monopolies. But in the new paradigm, they try to avoid bureaucracy and create a more entrepreneurial form of governance. They encourage competition between service providers. They try to curtail rules and red tape and focus on results. They treat people as customers rather than as clients. For example, new paradigm leaders often use vouchers, which put purchasing power in the hands of the customers, rather than simply saying, "Here's your service, take it or leave it."

The idea of choice is closely related to the fourth assumption. In the old paradigm, government operated essentially "for the people." That is, professionals and bureaucrats provided services to dependent clients. But what we are seeing now is government operating, as Lawton Chiles says, "by the people." Governments are empowering people and communities to solve their own problems.

Examples abound. Tenant management and ownership of public housing empower people to solve their own problems. Public school choice empowers parents to make the decision to leave one public school and go to another. In Chicago, parents are serving on boards of directors that run the schools; in other words, Chicago is empowering parents within the education system.

The fifth assumption: The old paradigm also dealt with most social issues by using entitlements, and those entitlements were offered without any demands for reciprocal behavior. The word *entitlement* means that one is entitled to a service or an income regardless of what one achieves. New paradigm leaders stress "opportunity" more than "entitlement"—and with opportunity comes responsibility.

Take, for example, welfare reform. The old welfare paradigm was to give people checks; the only debates were about how high the amount should be and how many people should be eligible. Today, the focus is on giving people opportunities: education, training, child care, even self-employment efforts, so that people can create their own jobs. In addition, governments are demanding responsibility on the part of welfare recipients—demanding, for example, that they work. Some states, such as Minnesota, are demanding that teenage mothers who have not graduated from high school go back to school. Others, such as Wisconsin, are demanding that if people on welfare have kids they must make sure the kids stay in school.

Finally, the most obvious assumption has to do with decentralization. The old paradigm was built around centralized government. If leaders wanted to solve an important problem, they did it in Washington. New paradigm leaders are pushing decisions and authority down to state and local governments. And within those governments, they are delegating more authority to the workers who actually do the work. Decentralization is the basis, for example, for school-based management in education, for participatory management, and for Total Quality Management (the management philosophy developed by W. Edwards Derning), all of which are on the rise in the public sector.

I suggest that these six assumptions provide a rough sketch of where American politics is heading. We are moving toward government that steers more than it rows, catalyzing others into action; that is market-oriented; that avoids bureaucracy and uses more entrepreneurial governance; that stresses empowerment rather than simply giving people services; that stresses opportunity and responsibility rather than entitlement; and that decentralizes authority.

DIFFERENCES WITHIN THE NEW PARADIGM

These assumptions define the overall shape of political discourse, the shared assumptions. Within this paradigm, however, there are still disagreements. There is still a left and a right and a center. But the debates tend to be about how much we should restructure the marketplace, what direction we should steer in, and so on rather than simply about how much we should spend and how much we should cut taxes.

This transition is even becoming apparent in Washington. Consider the front-burner issues Washington is debating right now, such as health care. From 1948 to 1976, the debate in this country was between liberals who basically wanted a public health service somewhat like the British model and conservatives who wanted government to leave health care to the marketplace.

Today, the debate is increasingly about how we can restructure the health care marketplace to obtain universal coverage and cost control. No one wants a British system. Some people prefer a Canadian-style program, which leaves health care in private hands (private doctors, private hospitals) but has a single payer. Some people like the German model, which uses a thousand different nonprofit insurance companies but has government enforce cost control on the entire system. Some people want to use the tax code (as the Heritage Foundation and [former] President Bush proposed) to expand coverage and encourage competition.

The point is: The debate is not about instituting a publicly produced, public employee-driven health care system. It is about restructuring the private health care marketplace.

The same is true for educational reform. In 1983 we decided we had an education crisis. We threw money at the problem for five years, increasing real spending on public education by 29 percent in the 1990s. Yet we gained rather little in the way of results. The dropout rate is higher today than it was in 1980, and test scores are just about the same.

Now our leaders are suggesting that the way to solve education's problems is not to spend more and more but to restructure the education marketplace. They are talking about choice for parents and children, competition among public schools, decentralization of authority through school-based management, and the empowerment of parents, as in Chicago. One could make the same argument about child care, about welfare policy, or about environmental policy. But the point is clear. Debate is beginning to emerge within a new set of assumptions—within a new paradigm.

I believe that the party that first embraces these new assumptions and this new approach to government will be the party that dominates the coming era. I do not know what we will call such leaders—whether we will talk of "New Democrats" or a "New Partnership" or "Progressive Republicans." (I don't think we will talk about a "new paradigm.") But I do believe it will happen. Until it does, the overwhelming frustration that Americans feel today with politics and government will continue to intensify. People want government to do something about the problems that concern them. They are worried about their jobs. They are worried about whether their company is going to be driven under by the Japanese. They are worried about their kids' schools. They are worried about whether they can afford college and whether they can afford health care. They are worried that one day the epidemic of drugs and street-corner shootings is going to reach out and hit one of their kids because he or she is in the wrong place at the wrong time.

Instinctively, people understand that we do not need more of the same— that we need government not only to do different things, but to do them differently. Yet they see traditional Democrats and Republicans clinging to the old ways. As Thomas Kuhn, who originated the notion of a paradigm, said, people never abandon an old paradigm until there's a new one they can jump to. Yet most old-line politicians are not clear where to jump, and so they do nothing.

In the absence of a new paradigm, we get negative campaigning. Politicians are afraid to say what they stand for because they know voters think it's irrelevant, so they attack their opponents. This tactic just increases public cynicism and frustration, encouraging such trends as the term-limitation movement.

It is almost as if our politicians are standing at the edge of a void wondering how to get across, and the voters are coming up behind them to give them a shove. What we need to get out of this period of frustration and impotence is a new vision, a new set of ideas, a new paradigm. Because if we do that, we will become a nation that is hurtling into the future instead of one with its eyes fixed firmly on the rearview mirror.

NOTE

1. This chapter is a transcript of a speech given at a conference cosponsored by the Democratic Leadership Conference and the Heritage Foundation, December, 1991.

About the Authors

Benjamin R. Barber is Professor of Political Science at Rutgers University.

Ronald Bayer is Professor at the Columbia University School of Public Health.

Lisa Belkin is a journalist. She wrote the article included in this collection for the *New York Times*.

Robert N. Bellah is Professor of Sociology at the University of California-Berkeley.

Roger Conner is Executive Director of the American Alliance for Rights and Responsibilities.

Robert Dahl is Professor Emeritus of Political Science at Yale University.

William Damon is Professor of Education at Brown University.

Amitai Etzioni is University Professor at George Washington University and editor of *The Responsive Community*, a communitarian quarterly.

Dennis Farney is a reporter at *The Wall Street Journal*.

Brian Forst is Associate Professor at American University's School of Public Affairs.

Mary Ellen Gale is Professor of Law at Whittier Law School.

William Galston is Deputy Assistant to the President, Domestic Policy Council. He was Professor in the School of Public Affairs at the University of Maryland at College Park when he wrote the article appearing in this volume.

John Gardner is Professor in Public Service at the Graduate School of Business at Stanford University.

Elizabeth Ginsburg is a journalist. She wrote the article included in this collection for the *New York Times*.

Mary Ann Glendon is Professor of Law at Harvard University.

Suzanne Goldsmith is the Director of the Community Service Project of the American Alliance for Rights and Responsibilities.

Robert E. Goodin is Professorial Fellow in Philosophy at the Australian National University.

Christopher Lasch was Professor of History at the University of Rochester until his death in 1994.

John Leo is a nationally syndicated columnist and writer for *U.S. News & World Report*.

Dallin H. Oaks is a retired Utah Supreme Court Justice and member of the
Quorum of the Twelve Apostles, serving a lifetime position in answer to
the call of the Church of Jesus Christ of Latter-day Saints.

David Osborne is a government consultant and writer.

Sharon J. Pressner is a graduate student at the John F. Kennedy School of
Government.

Diane Ravitch is Visiting Fellow at the Brookings Institution.

Donovan D. Rypkema is a real estate and economic development consultant in
Washington, D.C.

Isabel V. Sawhill is presently Associate Director for Human Resources at the
Office of Management and Budget. She was a Senior Fellow at The Urban
Institute when she wrote the article appearing in this volume.

Fred Siegel is Associate Professor of History at The Cooper Union in New
York.

Lester Thurow is Dean of the Sloan School of Management at the Massachusetts Institute of Technology.

Kathleen E. Toomey is the State Epidemiologist and Director of Epidemiology
and Prevention Branch of the Division of Public Health for the State of
Georgia.

Juan Williams is a columnist for the *Washington Post.*

Robert Wuthnow is Professor of Sociology at Princeton University.

Acknowledgments (continued from the copyright page.)

John Gardner. "Building a Responsive Community." Copyright © 1991 *The Independent Sector.* Reprinted with permission.

Dennis Farney. "Mosaic of Hope: Ethnic Identities Clash with Student Idealism at a College." Reprinted by permission of *The Wall Street Journal.* Copyright © 1992 Dow Jones & Company, Inc. All rights reserved worldwide.

Benjamin Barber. "A Mandate for Liberty: Requiring Education-Based Community Service." Copyright © 1991 Benjamin Barber. Reprinted by permission of author.

National Public Radio. "L.A. Gated Communities." Copyright © National Public Radio® 1993. The news report by Ina Jaffe was originally broadcast on National Public Radio's "All Things Considered" on August 11, 1992, and is used with the permission of National Public Radio. Any unauthorized duplication is strictly prohibited.

Elizabeth Ginsburg. "This Town Will Die without Our School"; *Lisa Belkin.* "Where Necessity Ends for Hospital Care." Copyrights © 1993 by The New York Times Company. Reprinted by permission.

Lester Thurow. "Communitarian vs. Individualistic Capitalism." Copyright © 1992 the *New Perspectives Quarterly.* Reprinted by permission.

John Leo. "Schools to Parents: Keep Out." Copyright 1992 *U.S. News and World Report.* Reprinted with permission.

David Osborne. "Beyond Left and Right: A New Political Paradigm." All rights reserved by the author. Reprinted by permission of International Creative Management, Inc.

"The Responsive Communitarian Platform: Rights and Responsibilities." Copyright 1992 by The Communitarian Network, 714-F Gelman Library, The George Washington University, Washington, D.C. 20052.

Earlier versions of the following pieces appeared in *The Responsive Community: Dallin H. Oaks,* "Rights and Responsibilities"; *Roger Conner,* "Checkpoint at Inkster: Reasonable or Unreasonable?"; *Sharon J. Pressner,* "Pornography: Free Speech versus Civil Rights?"; *Donovan D. Rypkema,* "The Misunderstandings of the 'Property Rights' Movement"; *Robert E. Goodin,* In Defense of the Nanny State"; *Isabel V. Sawhill,* "The New Paternalism: Earned Welfare"; *William Galston,* "A Liberal-Democratic Case for the Two-Parent Family"; *Benjamin Barber,* "A Mandate for Liberty: Requiring Education-Based Community Service"; *Suzanne Goldsmith,* "Crossing the Tracks: A Lesson in National Service"; *Fred Siegel,* "The Loss of Public Space"; *Brian Forst,* "Community Policing"; *Lester Thurow,* "Communitarian vs. Individualistic Capitalism"; *David Osborne,* "Beyond Left and Right: A New Political Paradigm."